THE SIGHTED SINGER

THE SIGHTED SINGER

Two Works on Poetry
for Readers and Writers

by Allen Grossman with Mark Halliday

THE JOHNS HOPKINS UNIVERSITY PRESS
BALTIMORE AND LONDON

Against Our Vanishing: Winter Conversations with Allen Grossman on the Theory and Practice of Poetry, Conducted and Edited by Mark Halliday, © Allen Grossman, 1981, was originally published by Rowan Tree Press. *Summa Lyrica: A Primer of the Commonplaces in Speculative Poetics*, Copyright © 1989, University of Utah, originally appeared as a special issue of *Western Humanities Review*, Spring 1990.

"The Runner," "Pat's Poem," "The Thrush Relinquished," from *The Woman on the Bridge over the Chicago River*, by Allen Grossman, and from *New Directions in Prose & Poetry 43* are reprinted with permission of New Directions Publishing Corporation. © 1977, 1978, 1979 by Allen Grossman. "The Runner" first appeared in *Poetry*. "A Little Sleep," by Allen Grossman, was published in *Canto* (vol. 3, no. 2). "Location," by Mark Halliday, first appeared in *Poetry*. "To a Poet" is reprinted from *The Dream of a Common Language, Poems 1974–1977*, by Adrienne Rich, with the permission of W. W. Norton and Company, Inc. Copyright © 1978 by W. W. Norton & Company, Inc.

The Johns Hopkins University Press, 701 West 40th Street
Baltimore, Maryland 21211-2190
The Johns Hopkins Press Ltd., London

Library of Congress Cataloging-in-Publication Data
Grossman, Allen R., 1932–
    The sighted singer : two works on poetry for readers and writers / by Allen Grossman with Mark Halliday. —Rev. and augmented ed.
        p.   cm.
    Rev. and expanded ed. of: Against our vanishing. © 1981.
    Includes index.
    ISBN 0-8018-4242-5.—ISBN 0-8018-4243-3 (pbk).
        1. Grossman, Allen R., 1932–   —Interviews. 2. Poets, American—20th century—Interviews. 3. Poetry.   I. Halliday, Mark, 1949– . II. Grossman, Allen R., 1932– Against our vanishing.
III. Title.
PS3557.R67Z474   1992
811'.5409—dc20   91-2944

Contents

Author's Note   *vii*

Preface   *ix*

I. AGAINST OUT VANISHING:
    CONVERSATIONS ON THE THEORY
    AND PRACTICE OF POETRY
    WITH MARK HALLIDAY   1

    The Winter Conversations (1981)   3

    The Summer Conversations (1990)   135

II. SUMMA LYRICA:
    A PRIMER OF THE COMMONPLACES
    IN SPECULATIVE POETICS   205

    The Primer   209

    Works Cited in *Summa Lyrica*   377

    Index to the Two Works   385

Author's Note

Part I of the following book is, as it appears to be, a fully collaborative work by Allen Grossman and Mark Halliday. It was first published in 1981 by Rowan Tree Press as *Against Our Vanishing: Winter Conversations with Allen Grossman on the Theory and Practice of Poetry.* It has now been greatly expanded by the addition of "Summer Conversations" (1990). The Preface and Part II, *Summa Lyrica: A Primer of the Commonplaces in Speculative Poetics,* are entirely the work of Allen Grossman. Part II, now appearing in revised form, was first published as a special issue of the *Western Humanities Review* (Spring 1990) and would not have seen the light of day without the intelligence and care of the editors, Barry Weller and Charles Berger.

Preface

Poetry is a principle of power invoked by all of us against our vanishing. The making of poems is a practice—a work human beings can do—in which civilization has invested some part of its love of itself and the world. The poem is a trace of the will of all persons to be known and to make known and, therefore, to be at all. Insofar as love wills the existence of what it loves, the principle of poetry is a collective and perpetually renewed act of love that brings the world to mind, and mind to mind, as the speech of a person—at the moment of the vanishing of world and persons which is every moment of conscious life. Poetry is one means by which human beings engage, as they can, in the maintenance of a human world in which they can meet one another, affirm one another, remember, see, and foresee one another.

In order to know itself, the mind requires a medium in which it can become present to itself. In poetry the mind becomes present to itself by becoming present to others in the medium of an art by which the general will to presence of the human world is made actual and particular. Reading, writing, thinking, and talking about poetry engage the mind with itself on the grounds of the work of love that wills the world in terms of concrete discourses of two kinds: Discourse, first, about facts which are the poems we always find already in the world beyond our imagining of them (this discourse is the purview of the *Summa Lyrica*); and discourse, second, about practices, the making of poems that is always going on (the purview of the *Conversations on the*

Theory and Practice of Poetry). Poems, the work of three millennia in the West, are always there before us, and are open to all; the making of poems, a practice or work with which everyone is somehow engaged, is also always going on, and is open to all. Poetry is the least solitary of enterprises. It pitches persons toward one another full of news. Its purpose is to realize the self; and its law is that this can only be done by bringing the other to light.

As an aid to this purpose and responsive to this law, the *Conversations*, the first of these two works on poetry, is designed to help the reader to the kind of thinking that the making of poetry gives rise to in our time and place. It consists of talk, as it happened, between two men, an elder and a younger poet, who are brought together because they both make poems—that is, because there is a principle called "poetry" given to them, as to everyone, by the world's love as a ground on which to meet, and because persons become present to themselves and one another in the social work of making that kind of love real. In the first set of conversations (*The Winter Conversations*), the younger poet sets himself the task of bringing the mind of the elder poet to light. Ten years later (1990), in a second set of conversations (*The Summer Conversations*), the same two men continue their talk on new ground, as history and the practice of the art as it unfolds in their lives demand.

The *Conversations* introduce the second of these two works, which is called *Summa Lyrica: A Primer of the Commonplaces in Speculative Poetics*. Because poems are traces of the love of the human world for itself, and because the will that drives such love intends the continuation of that world as a whole, the thought to which poems, always before us, gives rise is general, must be about the whole world, and intends to bring the whole of mind to light. But because there is no world that can be known by poetry except the world constituted of persons who speak, the thought to which poems give rise is also concrete and destined to the life of particular minds. All persons are, as readers of mind, poets; and all poets are, first and last, readers of the poems that come before and are obligated to them, as to themselves and to other persons in the interest of love, to make sense. The *Summa Lyrica* is designed to help the reader to this kind of sense making.

Both of these works take responsibility for thought; but neither of them, by the technique and intention of their construction, claims thought on its own behalf or on behalf of its authors. They both intend your thought, as poetry can be its occasion, which will be your making and destiny beyond my imagining.

I.   AGAINST OUR

VANISHING:

CONVERSATIONS

ON THE THEORY

AND PRACTICE

OF POETRY WITH

MARK HALLIDAY

The Winter Conversations
(1981)

Contents

1. What Is Poetry For?
   Discourse about poetry serves to refine language as a means of relationship, 5. Does poetry have a function today? 7. Poetry makes persons acknowledgeable, 9. Poetic structures have political implications, 10. Poetry as magnanimity toward the beloved, 12. John Keats' "When I have fears," 13. The activity of the reader of poetry, 17. Selves and persons, 19. Presence of persons, 20. The unfinished business of Modernism, 21. Mark Halliday's "Little Star," 25.

2. Where Are We Now in the History of Poetry?
   Situation of poetry in the fifties: Lowell, 28. Search for immanence: Roethke, Jarrell, Plath, 32. Discrediting of the national symbol, 35. Difficulty of starting out in the late sixties, 37. Reconstruction of the family as a poetic project of the fifties, 38. Our divergent responses to literary authority, 41. Contemporary masters: Ammons, Ashbery, Merrill, Bishop— disappearance of a common world, 43. Our different ways of deciding whether a poem is good, 46.

3. The Development of a Poet Who Started out
   in the Fifties

   Lineages and authority, 50. "A Poem for Statesmen" from A
   Harlot's Hire, *52. Freedom: poetic structures model social
   structures, 54. Postmodern search for structures adequate to
   experience, 55. Taking the Moderns' privilege but not their
   analysis, 56. Refusal to ironize desire, 59. Grossman's poetic
   motive: completion of his mother's speech, 60. "In My
   Observatory Withdrawn," 62. "The Runner" from* The Woman
   on the Bridge over the Chicago River, *64. Demonization, 66.
   Successful poetry exhausts the motive to poetry, 71. "The Thrush
   Relinquished," 73. Death as the space where self and other are no
   longer separate: the value of poetry, 74.*

4. Voice

   *Voice as portrait of a person, 79. The poetic speaker does not find
   his voice but is found by it, 80. The counternotion: poetic speech
   as social mediation, 81. Poetry serves as a common place where
   "I" and "you" can meet, 83. Poetic language is the language of a
   class, 85. Poems allude to the authentic speech they imitate, 87.
   Slowness of official culture to acknowledge oppressed classes, 89.
   All good poems are anonymous, 91. Urgency today of human
   dignity as a problem of poetic representation, 92. Adrienne Rich's
   "To a Poet," 94. The nightmare of the shattered face, 95.*

5. The Teaching of the Self

   *The motive to teaching and to poetry: completion by the self of its
   own nurture, 100. The motive to theory and to poetry in
   Postmodernism: fundamental ontological reconstruction, 102.
   An origin of difficulty in poetry, 104. "A Little Sleep"—a model
   of the teaching of the self, 106. Poetic impersonality as
   magnanimity, 109. Legitimacy of making claims upon readers,
   111. "Of the Great House"—the poet's reading of his poem,
   112. Culture does nothing for its participants, 120. The question
   of an audience, 121.*

6. "Of the Great House"

I . WHAT IS POETRY FOR?

H   Allen, we come at this conversation from what I feel to be drastically different kinds of experience—both as poets and as theorists about poetry. You've remarked that I stubbornly present myself as someone who just began thinking about poetry this morning; and you strike me as someone who has *always* been thinking about poetry. Since we're so different in age and in temperament, I've sometimes felt during my years at Brandeis that we couldn't make much sense to each other. Still, we have kept on talking.

G   We have poetry in common. I feel, Mark, when people are talking about poetry and its function, they are aware from the very beginning that their being with one another, the fact that they *are* talking together is a consequence of the poetic text between them.

H   You mean we wouldn't be here in this room now if it weren't for poetry.

G   Exactly. One of the functions of poetry is to bring people together, to pitch them toward one another with news about the poems which they both have read. Poetry functions, when people are together talking about it, as a principle of the relationship of persons one to the other. It is a special kind of relationship and should not be ignored.

H   Now, is that different from the way two people might come together to discuss photographs, or paintings, or the dance?

G   One difference is that when people speak to one another about poetry, they are employing language to talk about other language;

as a result, they are in a heightened state of consciousness with respect to language altogether. Therefore I think that discourse about poetry, language about language, is situated more decisively on the crisis of the elaboration of language *toward* relationship than discourse about other classes of art objects.

H   "The elaboration of language toward relationship . . ."

G   I use this expression because I am convinced that the greater function of poetry (if there *can* be a greater function than to bring people into discourse one with the other) is the keeping of the image of persons as precious in the world. Language is inherently a principle of relationship, and when language is about language there is required a refinement and searching of that principle—so that talk about poetry tends toward the perfection of the means of relationship.

I have always been attracted to those accounts of the function of poetry which specify the *keeping* of the image of the person in the world as its principal outcome. The most ancient poets are found making possible the recollection across time of the images of heroes. The most passionate advocacies for the art of poetry in sophisticated late periods, such as the period of Horace, turn upon the function of poetry as keeping alive, across the abysses of death and of the difference between persons, the human image. Horace says, for example, that there were many heroes who lived before the heroes whom Homer recorded, but since they lacked a poet, they are overcome in darkness—they cannot be remembered.

> Many heroes lived before Agamemnon
> but they are all unweepable, overwhelmed
> by the long night of oblivion
> because they lacked a sacred bard.

That assertion is not merely a poetic extravagance.

H   Horace is making a claim there for poetry as something more equipped to preserve images of persons than simply history. It's a claim whose demand could not be satisfied by a historian—it's not that those earlier heroes simply lacked someone to report the actions of their lives? Or would he have made that distinction between a historian and a poet?

G   Horace is recording a fact of his civilization and of our civilization: that Homer was the principle of the recovery of the image of Achilles and the other great persons of value who are the subject of his poems. One of the issues we have to be concerned with, in discussing the function of poetry, is the change across time which arises as a consequence of the increase in means for recollection by a civilization of its own past.

But Horace's assertion that the heroes before Homer were *inlacrimabiles*, incapable of being wept for, does carry with it an implication different from the mere suggestion that Homer was the principle of the transmission of a message. It suggests that there's something fuller, and more consistent with the whole nature of the person as precious, about the holding-in-mind by the poem of the picture of the person.

H   So you're speaking of Homer as having created images of heroes that made it possible to weep for them; and Horace is recognizing that achievement by Homer, something Homer did that was, as you're saying, "fuller," a larger achievement than simply recording the fact that these men lived and then died. And I've heard you speak many times in classes here about poetry being the work of preserving the images of persons. Now I want to ask you whether we who write poetry in this century are embarking on the same task that Homer was working on.

G   Yes, we are. We have begun by specifying two functions of poetry. One is the function of poetry that is exemplified by the very fact that we are discoursing together, that we have something to talk about as between us, something that brings to mind the question of persons and the conserving of their value across time. Secondly, we have observed that the most ancient cases of poetry seem situated on the business of preserving the images of persons. Homer is one example, and Horace is a second. Homer and Horace differ, for Horace, while speaking of Homer as one who makes the Homeric heroes weepable, capable of our compassion, administered that capacity on behalf of his own individual personhood, taking the great privilege of the hero, the privilege of continuity of image, and bestowing it upon himself, declaring that his poetry was a monument of his own selfhood.

H   Are you implying that what we do today changes the function of poetry as drastically as Horace changed what Homer did?

G   There are important things to say about poetry in this present, this winter, 1981, with the snow on the ground. Poetry is now an art which seems, to me as a practitioner, virtually dead. It is an art which has been driven into a corner, which requires justification; it is an art which has more practitioners than readers; an art the function of which is hard to discern. In ancient times poetry conserved enormous ranges of cultural fact—facts necessary for the survival of the community, kinds of information about the world which are now (and for a long time have been) conserved by other institutions of the civilization. Therefore, poetry cannot at the present time have the same centrality for a culture as it had for either the Greece of Hesiod or the Israel of the exile in Babylon.

Really, a question of great moment is the following: does poetry have a function left that is not usurped by other means of the transmission of images across time? We live in a world which is flooded with images, images which flow as it were through the hands of Thomas Alva Edison toward us from sources unanticipated by the great poetic makers, who felt that they held in *their* hands the privilege of conferring visibility, or withdrawing it even from the greatest heroes. I think no discussion of the function of poetry now should get farther than we have gotten without considering this usurpation of the function of transmitting images by other media.

H   I hadn't realized that we would run so immediately into the difference between our electronic age and the civilizations of the ancient poets when we tried to describe the function of poetry. You seem to be saying that it is now impossible to do with poetry the work that in its first conceptions poetry was meant to do, because the written word, really, has been pre-empted by electronic images. So I guess the question is, Is there something poetry can do that is not done more speedily and more abundantly by other kinds of communication?

G Yes. And this is a question different from your earlier question about whether talking about poetry leads to different kinds of discourse than talking about the other arts. The question of the function of poetry must be considered in the face of the recognition that the older purposes for which persons turned to poetry are no longer within the province of the poet. In the nineteenth century, the effort to recover centrality for poetry, by specifying poetry as Arnold did as a successor culture to other cultures which seemed to be withering, constituted an effort to justify the enormous prestige which poetry still claimed. It is important to observe that the idea of poetry carries with it the prestige of functions which it can no longer execute.

Now, I began by alluding to the use of poetry *for conserving the human image*—because I think *that* function constitutes the singular importance of poetry now and also specifies the particular dangers within the practice of poetry to which we are heir. When the poem ceased to conserve information about how to till the fields, about what flood-plains could be inhabited because they were free from cyclical dangers of inundation, when poetry ceased to be the principal instrument for conserving human laws (—it must be remembered that Solon wrote his laws in poetry, and that the Delphic oracle uttered its prophecies in poetic form, and that it was felt by most of Western civilization that the laws of Moses and the agonies of Job were embedded in poetic structures—) what was left for poetry was that fundamental function to which Horace refers: the function of making persons present to one another in that special sense in which they are *acknowledgeable* and therefore capable of love and mutual interest in one another's safety. It is the function of poetry as making persons present, as modeling the conditions under which persons *can* be present, that seems to me to survive to us and to justify the prestige of the poetic art.

In part, I believe also, the immense equivocalness of poetry at the present time is a consequence of the use of poetry as an instrument of private self-legitimation. It is as if poetry could function now only as fame, or as the rumor of the existence of other people; whereas in fact it can function only so well as people themselves can function in view of their passion for just that status of acknowledgeability. Poetry is situated upon the central question of our civilization—how do we know a *person* is present?—and suffers all of the strains which we feel when we contemplate the precariousness of our visibility to others in this Postmodern world.

H I've sometimes sat in classes you were teaching and thought from the point of view of an undergraduate who hears for the first time about how persons in our world are invisible to one another and wonders what sense this Professor Grossman is making. You're speaking metaphorically, and it may not be clear to others in what sense they are "invisible."

G That's a perfectly intelligible complaint.

When we first began talking this afternoon, I noted that it is winter and there is snow on the ground. This covering up of the ordinary marks, the sense of erasure of tracks, of the indications of direction in the world, which snow brings to my mind, is closely related to my sense of how things are in the world of persons.

I observed the beautiful function of poetry which is manifested by the fact that it has brought us together to talk, and to talk in the presence of others who might hear us talk and be pitched toward talk about our talk and thus give some outcome to our own effort to specify the function of poetry by enacting an aspect of that function in relation to others in turn, and so on endlessly. It is the case that most discourse about poetry in its concrete terms— terms that are embodied in such matters as prosody, and line— tends to be conducted in the language of political science. We find, for example, in our American tradition, that our greatest experimentalist, Whitman, made reference to his particular and magnanimous innovations in poetic structure in terms of the language of the American Constitution, which he regarded poetry to be a continuation of by other means. Milton, when he described his own innovations, at the beginning of *Paradise Lost*, spoke of rhyme as a form of bondage—thus also specifying the intimate features of poetry, its way of arranging sentences in lines, in terms fundamentally political. I think that wherever we turn there is a political, a legislative, and therefore a sociological implication about the structures of poetry, and this implication is a mirroring of its fundamental content, its deepest and most efficacious content altogether.

Now, it is my feeling that the great wars, the First and Second World Wars—which have been the occasion first of our High Modern poetry, the poetry that overshadows everything we do, and then of our Postmodern poetry—these wars were great erasures, great crises in the continuity of civilization, as Eliot in *The Waste Land* so clearly (and, in a way, simply) showed. The status of Postmodernism, the world since let us say Pound's *Pisan Cantos*, seems almost wholly determined first by the obliterations of the First World War, that were responded to by Eliot, and later by Yeats in "In Memory of Major Robert Gregory," and then by the erasures of the Second World War, to which *we* have not yet fully responded. Nuclear war threatens the obliteration of all persons whatsoever, and stands in the imagination as an obliteration even greater than Horace's "long night of oblivion." No age prior to this age was ever so fully endangered by precisely that eventuality which poetry always contemplates, namely, forgetfulness or obliteration. The crisis in which we find ourselves as poets is determined, first of all, by this enormous threat, and secondly, by the inadequacy of our means to respond. But poetry is the right means: poetry is the historical enemy of human forgetfulness, the historical agent of the name of man against the obliterative powers of the world—of Nature, as Horace suggested, but now also of man himself. Consequently, the disappearance of persons one to the other shadows all our presence to one another in this Postmodern world.

H   Now, as I listen to you talk about obliteration, with the great wars
    as instances, I have difficulty associating those threats of oblitera-
    tion with "the presence of persons to one another," of which I take
    your presence to me now and my presence to you now to be an
    instance, or the presence of any two people in one room at one
    time. When I think of poetry as the enemy of erasure of speakers,
    I most naturally think of the relationship between a poet and his
    future readers, between the poet and posterity to whom he appeals
    in case his contemporaries fail to appreciate his work, or even if
    they do appreciate it. I'm certainly aware of the familiar idea that
    the poet is struggling for immortality through his work, as Shake-
    speare talks about in his sonnets. But you are speaking of this con-
    test between obliteration and the preservation of persons in a more
    general way. . . . For example, you speak of "forgetfulness" and
    "obliteration" as if they were the same thing. Now, if we are wiped
    out in a nuclear war, I don't see that forgetfulness is an appropriate
    word to describe our problem—it won't be that we have been for-
    gotten, it will be that there's no one around to remember us.

G   Poetry has inside it the principle not merely of recollection in the
    personal sense you refer to, but indeed the profounder principle of
    the continuity of a whole human world, which requires for its con-
    servation not merely a speaker but the answerer as well.
        Now I think you make a generational error, Mark, characteris-
    tic of the eighteen years' difference between the two of us, by view-
    ing poetry as having as its function the continuity of the image of
    the poetic writer. Poetry traditionally, and in my view fundamen-
    tally, deals in the continuity of the image *not* of the poet but of
    the poet's *beloved*. Therefore poetry is an act which models the
    act of the civilization, when the civilization acts as a constellation
    of persons whose interest, whose stake is not expressed as the con-
    tinuity of their own image but as the continuity of the image of
    another. Poetry is a case of the magnanimity of the self toward the
    other—toward the beloved, or toward the hero (who is another
    form of the beloved), or toward the god (who is a still further form
    of the beloved)—magnanimity toward the beloved, which has as
    its *consequence* the continuity of the image of the image-maker,

but *not* as its substance, not as its primary obligation.

One of the difficulties in which we find ourselves as poets now is expressed by this tendency to regard poetry as having its beginning and its end in its author. Poetry is not a proper instrument for the mere self-characterization of speakers. Poetry's function is performed properly, is performed safely, only when it is conceived of as an act of respect for another—only when it is conceived of, therefore, as *interactive*. When a poem is truly present in the world, it is present in the form of an interaction which is as profound and extensive as the social order itself.

In the most primitive terms, the presence of a poem involves a complete triadic state of affairs, in which there is a self, and the beloved of that self which always has a transcendental character ascribed to it, and a third—the third being the audience, the ratifier, the witness, and the inheritor of the drama of loving relationship to which the poem gives access. Poetry is therefore a principle of the interaction of persons, which has inside it the very conditions for the continuity of the social order; not merely a speaker and a hearer, but a speaker who is in love, and a hearer who has a capacity for being in love which is enhanced by the spectacle of the speaking.

H I'm trying to think of where I got this idea that poets, as their main work, or as their main motivation, are trying to win immortality. I'm thinking of Keats, for example. Now, how does the sonnet "When I have fears that I may cease to be" fit with what you're saying about the poet expressing his love for the beloved, and ourselves as the audience learning to love his beloved better? What *is* the beloved in this case?

> When I have fears that I may cease to be
>   Before my pen has glean'd my teeming brain,
> Before high piled books, in charactry,
>   Hold like rich garners the full ripen'd grain;
> When I behold, upon the night's starred face,
>   Huge cloudy symbols of a high romance,
> And think that I may never live to trace

Their shadows, with the magic hand of chance;
And when I feel, fair creature of an hour,
    That I shall never look upon thee more,
Never have relish in the fairy power
    Of unreflecting love;—then on the shore
Of the wide world I stand alone, and think
    Till love and fame to nothingness do sink.

G The beloved in Keats' poem is the most complex, and at the same time the most precious of the possessions of a speaker; namely, the principle of the continuity of that speaker who in his terror contemplates his own disappearance. Keats expresses anxiety about the impossibility of writing out the nature of the world; Keats obtains for us all a sense of the enormous obligation which poetry sponsors to specify an object of love—for it is the object of love (his "fair creature of an hour") which is the cause of his fear. The object of love calls attention to the stake of the speaker in the world, and the stake of the speaker in the world is recuperated by the act of writing, so that, out of the anxiety which the beloved by her perishing beauty and by her dependence on the lover for her being arouses, there comes this record which stands as a modeling of the courtesy to which love calls us: the courtesy of song, of magnanimous acknowledgment.

H Looking now at Keats' poem, I do see that in line 9 he turns to someone who is apparently a beloved woman—and that begins to *seem* as if the poem fits into the analysis you were making about poems celebrating and trying to preserve a beloved other; yet, as I look at those three and a half lines that refer to a relationship to another person, they don't seem enough to me to make the poem centrally about his hope that *she* will somehow survive. That is, it seems to me different from the gesture that Shakespeare claims to be making in many of his love sonnets, which is a gesture of preserving the love and, in some sense, the beloved person. *This* poem seems more centrally about what it's about at the beginning: his own fear for himself. So if I were asked to specify a beloved object for this person, I would say, without intending any invidious criticism of Keats as a human being, that the beloved object is his own "teeming brain."

G   The contrast with Shakespeare which you bring to mind is entirely relevant. The predicament which I am elaborating, and which I am calling "our" predicament, yours and mine, is a predicament which is fully present in the period of Keats. In fact, we are, as poets in 1981, writing as if the High Moderns (Yeats, Eliot, Pound, and Stevens) did not exist. Consequently, it is entirely reasonable to look hard at Keats' sonnet, for to do so is to work much more directly with the situation in which we find ourselves than we would be doing if we were to look at one of Eliot's early poems.

Now, it is perfectly correct that in Shakespeare there is a firm sense of something *not* the self of the speaker which requires to be conserved, and for which the instruments of record are adequate: the "black ink," in which Shakespeare's beloved *will* "shine bright," is capable, so long as eyes see and men breathe, of doing the business of remembering; it is in effect an inerasable inscription.

For Keats, however, the predicament of the self and the predicament of the other have tended to converge, so that the instability of the objectivity of the other, the virtual imperceptibility of *her*— that "fair creature of an hour"—suggests why the poem is situated upon fear at all. Keats is contemplating the immortality of Fame and the immortality of Love as if they were the *same* immortality. The incapacity of obtaining a record of the contents of his speaker's mind is directly equivalated with his sense of his incapacity of obtaining relationship with the beloved. Consummated love would constitute for him a perpetualization of his sentiment—its actualization as truth. The manner in which this poem ends with contemplation of "nothingness" is a precise indication of the terror of image-loss of which I am speaking. The solitude which he specifies—"on the shore / Of the wide world I stand alone"—is a solitude greater than any contemplated in Shakespeare's sonnets, a solitude more fiercely realized (though not different in kind) than that which is expressed over and over in our Postmodern poetry. Keats' poem, by its great and pathetic excellence, calls attention to the rigor with which he has conceived the task of the keeping of the self, and to the crisis involved in the new psychological realism under the auspices of which his enterprise was undertaken. *But,* it is the presence not of a mere dyad, but of that triad of powers—the self, and the beloved, mediated by the principle of representation toward an audience which would constitute a future for the beloved—that makes up the whole of this poem.

H   Allen, I got you into talking about this Keats poem as an effort to understand what you mean when you speak of "the presence of persons," and I believe this is a difficult theoretical idea, one that I expect we will have to come back to. It's certainly clear that Keats is trying to use language in this form to confront the prospect of his death, his death from a disease that he fears he has. And the work of preserving an image of the self, *or* of the beloved, is a problem in the face of death.

I think in our conversations we will agree, although using different language to express it, that poetry is intimately involved with the expectation of death, the awareness that death will come to the speaker, and to the people he's talking to—and, you will say (and I may find myself agreeing), that death *will* come to the person whom the poet is talking about.

G   What I will additionally say, which I think will seem bewildering to you, is that the existence of poetry requires the existence of something which is deathless. I will, throughout our conversations, draw relationships between the capacity of the mind of a person to conceive of something which does not die, and the capacity of that same person to produce and make sense out of—and that means making use of—poems.

For Keats, Love and Fame are inextricably and bewilderingly bound up one inside the other: eternity in love, eternity in poetic representation, are in effect the same eternity. I am trying to make plain that where these two eternities become confused, then indeed we are, as the speaker in Keats' poem was, afraid; and that that confusion, that state of fear, characterizes our sense of things at the present time.

H   The fear arises when people confuse the desire for immortality of an image with the desire for immortality of oneself, the actual person.

G   Yes, that's correct—

H   Immortality of love, that is, the transcendent survival of this woman Keats addresses, or of himself, is confused with the possible survival of this representation of the two of them.

G   That's correct. When the singer dies, the music must be regarded as living on. After all, we live in recent memory of the deaths of the central poets of our culture, at least here in the northeastern United States: Elizabeth Bishop and Robert Lowell are recently dead. And in the larger world of singing, we have just experienced the murder of John Lennon. We are compelled to think together of this question of the transcendental difference between the poem and its lineages, on the one hand, and the poet and his mortality on the other.

H   When we talk about survival, or immortality, or "preservation" of an image by a poem, do we mean simply and literally that the poem will be read by people whose lives are yet to come, and therefore as a vital object the poem lives? Or is there some more transcendent, more religious sense that you mean?

G   The poem, in my view, is a principle of access: a portal, a gate, a way into the relationship between the speaker and the means he has for making himself visible to others. Since these means are always transcendental—as the community is larger than and beyond the individual, or as the god of the community is larger than and beyond both the individual and the community, or as Nature is prior to and posterior to any self, or as the stars, insofar as they are eyes, and not mere stones, constitute the promise of acknowledgment beyond the acknowledgment of persons in any generation—the poem is a principle of access to transcendent reality, and reading is the recovery of the transcendental affiliation which the poet has, in the making of his poem, obtained. In other words, the reading of a poem is an entrance into a world of privilege, which the poet has made accessible by his achievement of it. That is why I think the reading of poetry is not merely active upon the reader, more so than other kinds of reading, but is more fundamentally efficacious, more purposive.

Does it seem to you odd that I regard poetry as having a function at all, as being an instrument for doing work, or does that seem to you a familiar notion?

H   That is an idea that I like; and I want to believe that my poems do have a purpose for me and a value to listeners. I'm against the theorizing about poetry that one hears sometimes, about poetry existing in a neutral and isolated space away from the intentions and desires of the poet, away from the obvious needs of the audience. No, I like the idea that a poem has a purpose, that it is written with a purpose, and that people read it for a reason, out of a need.

G   I think you come to that liking more immediately than I do; because when I was educated, in the fifties, the ruling conception of the poem was a Symbolist conception, which bereaved the poem of any specifiable function. The poem existed as an object complete in itself, which was the privileged possession, for unspecified purposes, of the class which had the leisure and the education to contemplate it. I do, however, think that when I speak of the function of poetry, and you agree that it has a function, we are not thinking about the same thing. The conception of personal presence which I have laid before you still, I'm sure, seems bewildering; and yet in that conception of presence, the *keeping* of that image, the whole burden of what I am today saying to you lies.

H   Well, I guess I've already expressed some trouble with this language you have for the purpose of poetry. You've spoken of two things really: one is in some sense making persons present to one another; and you've also spoken of modeling the conditions under which persons *can* be present to one another. To the extent that I understand either one of those as what poetry does, I understand the second one better. I think I can speak of my own efforts in writing poems in terms of showing conditions under which one person can make a lot of sense to another person, and helping the reader understand, and imagine being in a relationship with, the speaker. But I do sometimes feel bewildered when I hear you speak of poetry as a presence-making art—because I keep feeling there is a "mumbo-jumbo" aspect to that language, as if the writing of a poem was equivalent to setting up a séance.

G Right. And you remind me that part of my function in the world, Mark Halliday, is to be a source of bewilderment to you. Let me say something that may seem even more troublesome. I believe that prior to any other image which we derive from a poem, prior to any *sense* which a poem makes for its reader, there is a more fundamental transmission, something more profound (the word does not terrify me)—and that is *the image of the person* that is encoded in the very language-matter of the poem itself. In other words, I think that the first announcement that a poem makes is the announcement not of a world or a meaning, but of the credible fact of a speaking voice which, because of that first general and primitive sense, has inside it the assurance of a particular personal presence. Poetry is peculiar to and indeed confined to the kind of utterance that makes the person present (what is commonly called writing with "style") and *then* situates that person in a world about which it is possible to make specific, "sense-making" sentences.

Now, I am making a distinction which I think is alien from the way you think about things: a distinction between *selves* and *persons*. I believe that poetry is fundamentally antipsychological, and I would summon as my witnesses the High Modern poets with their advocacy of impersonality, which led them all, each in his own way, to reject the analysis of the "real" self that we find in Freud. I am in effect saying to you that poetry has a destiny not in selves, but in persons; and that, whereas selves are found or discovered, persons and personhood is an artifact, something that is *made*, an inscription upon the ontological snowfields of a world that is not in itself human. I view the world, and I think poetry by its very structures calls attention to the world, as not human; and in the presence of that world not human, the world that lies in the white spaces upon which our words are inscribed—on that world poetry writes the name of the person. And the distinction between person and self is that the *person* is value-bearing: the person is that fact in the world which we are not permitted to extinguish, which has rights. It is for this reason that I take very seriously, as I have already suggested, the relation between poetic structures and social structures, particularly political versions of social structures—for I think the poet is by his or her peculiar instrument of discourse the custodian of the value of the person, however that value may have been initially derived, whether from the politics of the community or its religion. When I speak of *keeping* the human image, I am speaking of keeping, not selves, but the value of selves.

What I mean by "presence" is the person-making power of evoking the disposition to honor selves which is expressed in, but not identical with, love. The disposition to honor selves, awakened by poetry, must be responded to if poetry can be said to be truly read. This is what differentiates the kind of presence I'm talking about from mere *being with* in the world.

H   Yes. There are two crucial words in what you're saying: one is "presence" and the other is "person." You have begun to clarify for me what you mean by a person by distinguishing it from a self. One feeling I have while hearing you talk about that is a pity for selves, who are left out of the work that you see poetry doing. I guess what you mean is that a self, as distinct from a person, is not available for preservation in art—a self is that which is reflected by our physical presence to each other now, and it is not something that we can hope poetry will do anything for in the face of death. A person is an artifact; it is the construction that we make as we try to deal with another person's self.

G   That's certainly true. The world that you describe, a world of selves shut out from the privilege of personhood, is indeed a feeling and accurate description of the sense of the self in this Postmodern moment. My feeling is that the poet is summoned, rather like

Horace's rescuer, to bring selves into the bright circle of acknowledgment. The poet has always found himself in a world of selves who have a destiny as persons; and the poet administers that destiny with what means he has.

In the world in which we live, we see enormous evolution of the capacity to make images: in television, in photography, in the large images of the poster world, in the images of the film screen. Internal to these images is the search for another form of visibility. The subject matter of representation today is the search for an acknowledgment such as I have attempted to specify, in an abbreviated way, as personhood; and the vastness of this common culture of imaging confesses to its incapacity to bestow true presence. If the poet has any function at the present time, it is to lay hold of this anxiety about true presence, which is his inherited obligation, and to try to mediate a profounder, more gratifying, more magnanimous, more joyous sense of being toward persons in the world. The poet has a role—because, from the time of Homer, it has been *his or her* business to make images meaningful. The word *person* does not specify a static or isolated state of affairs, but a profound interaction, a drama always going on, of acknowledgment and presence.

H   Well, I am relieved to hear you say that a "person" is not something static or isolated; because, again reacting more emotionally than intellectually to what you're saying, I do have this feeling that although it might be nice to be preserved as a person, it would be much better if one could be preserved as a *self*—and that does not seem to be offered by the art that you propose.

G   The bitterness of poetry, as it is expressed by the great masters from Virgil to Yeats, is precisely the felt pain of the paradox which you indicate. When Yeats came to contemplate the relationship between the obligation of the poet to establish personhood, and the inevitability for the poet of his being a self, he found that personhood and selfhood were indeed in irreconcilable conflict. The problem that poetry presents us with now is the reconciliation of the strange and desolating complexities of personhood with the intimacies and gratifications of the psychological self. The High Modern period continuously expressed and reexpressed the necessity of establishing the value of the person, and the bitterness of the gap between the means by which the self was to be rescued and the very life of the self. Culture turned against culture is what we find everywhere in our world. The capacity of man to administer force has turned against the life of man; and it was what one might call the testamentary inscription of the Modern poets that the reconciliation of the business of civilization with the business of selfhood remained the unfinished task which they, in their large way, set their successors. The immediate monumental poetic culture which we receive is still the culture of Yeats, Eliot, Pound, and Stevens, and that culture solved the problem of personhood without solving the problem of the relationship between the person and the self.

Now, the poetry which you write is situated in the self, and attempts to recover the self from the vast overshadowing of the poetic process. Indeed, the principal response to our predecessor masters has been to retrench upon that very region of the world to which they did not make effective reference—namely the perishing individuality which we all perceive ourselves to be primarily; and our Postmodern culture set itself the task in the fifties of recovering that selfhood, and must now, it seems to me, if it is to do the business of the art, set itself the next-on task, the task which is residual from the great accomplishment of the masters: to reconcile the self with the person.

We live in a world in which poetry is produced under the auspices of communities seeking selfhood—such as the feminist community, which may be the greatest and most original contributor to poetry today. These communities face the bitter problem of establishing the personhood of their members by means which are discovered to be at odds with and maybe in fundamental competition with the ends which the community seeks.

H   Wait, I don't follow that—the feminist movement is an example of a conflict between the ends which are sought, and what?

G   I believe that the pursuit of self-establishment through poetry, by
    any group which attempts to use poetry as a way of obtaining ac-
    knowledgment for previously unacknowledged selves—as the fem-
    inist movement does, and should—has come to the point where
    the group must contemplate the conflict between naming them-
    selves as mortal persons and the very means of that naming which
    is poetry; for poetry demands an impersonality which is precisely
    the state of affairs against which such movements are struggling.
    The effort to be *human* and the effort to be a *person* (in my sense)
    may not be harmoniously reconcilable today. At any rate, I do not
    think the issue is spoken to by an attempt to establish a literature
    merely of the self alone.
        We began by talking about the function of poetry. Have we got-
    ten anywhere?

H   Well, your distinction between a self and a person is a step in being
    able to talk about what you and I are trying to do in poetry.
        A moment ago I was imagining a cinematographer who would
    claim that his art, or her art, in presenting vivid and moving im-
    ages of people, has the best chance of capturing the value of
    ephemeral selves, and that that is, in a universe without a god,
    the work that most needs doing and all the work that *can* be done,
    in our confrontation with death. And that cinematographer would
    argue that this business he or she sees us engaged in, of trying to
    create "deathless," comparatively static artifacts (—a poem as held
    against a film, which has to be seen through time again and again
    but which is not in front of us in its entirety at any moment—)
    that we are engaged really in a deathly business, preserving sort of
    mummies rather than capturing the essence of people's *lives*.

G   I would like to avoid setting one art against another in our conver-
    sations. But I admit that poetry is immensely conservative; and it
    does appear at present, despite various modifications in the mode
    of presenting it in public, to be static, death-laden, just as it is so
    often death-referenced.

H   When I first heard you lecture at Brandeis, and began to under-
    stand your sense of poetry involving knowledge of death and also
    in a strange way being a deathly activity—because it removes
    things from the stream, what you regard as the obliterative stream
    of life and meaningless event—at that time I sort of sat in the
    classroom and thought, Why does he keep talking about death?
    And why does he keep saying these nasty things about poetry? I
    was more inclined to think of the writing and reading of poetry as
    entertainment, and as celebration. Lately I think of poems, and
    specifically my own poems, more consciously as responses to the
    knowledge that I will die and the people I love will die.

G   It is part of the perennial wisdom about poetry and poetic struc-
    tures that poetry is not different from the central facts of the hu-
    man world, of which death is one. Poetry is in truth the point at
    which those central facts come to light and can be scrutinized.
    Insofar as the announcement of the poem is always first and fore-
    most the announcement of the presence of the person—

H   —an announcement of the presence of the poet?

G   No, of the *person!* The business of poetry is not to announce the
    presence of the poet. The poet, in my mind, has no privileges; he
    stands in for the person—

H   —the person who *could* speak these words?

G   The person who could speak these words, who is most specifically
    and most severely *not* the privileged or segregated artisan who
    makes poems. Just as Horace spoke of the poet *serving* the heroes,
    so I in my way imagine the poet as serving the person. You, Mark,
    are just such a poet. In your poem called "Little Star" you reach
    out and confer upon us all the duty to rescue from oblivion, fol-
    lowing the trace of a song's memory, the name of a singer, not
    yourself.

H   I decided to write this poem when I realized that an artist whose
    name I didn't know had created a work which really touched me,
    really connected with and brought to light a nuance of emotion
    deep in my spirit. The relative triviality of this work of art I speak
    of in my poem—it is, after all, a minor work even in the limited
    genre of early rock music—gave a special poignancy to the ano-
    nymity of the singer.

G   You take the privilege of Homer, and practice it in a world he
    could not imagine, to rescue the unknown singer, *not yourself*, not
    as an "artist" which is only a piece of a person, but as a soul worthy
    of love, as a star.

Little Star

"Stop here, or gently pass!"
    —Wordsworth

                    I

"Little Star" by the Elegants (1958)
is one of those perfect early rock/pop songs
that radiate confidence in a few
orderly truths. Above all,
if you have the right girl as your girlfriend—
you know, the one who walks that way
and tosses her hair, the one who dances
just a little between cheers at the football game—
if you've got her, you're golden,
there's nothing else you could wish for.
Oh, God, do you remember the golden liquidity
of the lead singer's voice
as he expresses this shapely truth—
he could get it across without needing to rely
on the mere meanings of words—
he could do everything with golden syllables!

Who was he?
Can anybody tell me the name
of the lead singer for the Elegants?
In view of that grand confidence
it would seem a name worth preserving.
Really—if you can give me his name
I'll give you six dollars.
(I thought of offering ten, but that seems
more than I can afford, especially since
his name may be fairly easy to discover;
five dollars nowadays seems paltry,
so I'm offering six.)

II

This is not the first time I've tried to
get a rock-&-roll song into a poem and it won't be
the last; it is my need to call out
This counts too!
I don't deny Homer, or Virgil, or Dante
I'll take your word for it about Bach and Beethoven
I don't question the importance of the Bible
though it never lived in my life,
I love Shakespeare and admire Milton as much
as you do, but our lives go on
in these years, 1958, 1959, 1960,
"the Sixties," and still on in these years like
1977 and still on now, as I write this
in September 1980 with the sun bright
almost as if new—and we are small,
we are postmodern and small, but not therefore worthless;
so it is for our sake
that I try to insist upon the wafer-thin golden value
of a certain addition to the long, long,
overtalented symphony of culture.
Of course it's no match for some hundreds
or even thousands

of novels, poems, operas etc. we could name,
nor for fifty rock songs I could name;
but I want to say
"This, also, was not nothing."

III

Where is he now?
The Elegants would be in their forties now.
Is he a vice-president of Arista Records?
Is he a wise quiet junkie on the Lower East Side?
Is he dead—killed by something that golden syllables
can't fix? Or maybe
at this moment he sits with another Elegant
in a Pizza Hut in L.A.,
planning the impossible comeback!

If you can let me know where he is
I'll send him a fan letter—
the unforeseeability of this gesture would make me feel,
at least for a day, that a million debts were paid.
However, the six dollars will be yours
for no information more than his name—
his name. The point
is just to make it true
that someone twenty-two years after a small
fact of art can unexpectedly pause and say,

This man sang lead on "Little Star."

2. WHERE ARE WE NOW IN THE HISTORY OF POETRY?

H   We were talking yesterday about death, and you focused that by mentioning the deaths in the last four years of Robert Lowell and Elizabeth Bishop. We also mentioned the very recent death of John Lennon in connection with ideas about music dying when the creator of that music dies.

G   It was one of the headlines announcing his death: "The Day the Music Died."

H   Now, particularly since the deaths of Bishop and Lowell, we look around at a landscape of American poets in which there are no giant sequoias; there are no hero poets. At least, speaking for myself, it is true that there is no living poet (setting aside friends of mine) whom I regard as—certainly no one whom I regard as great and no one whom I constantly regard as potentially great. There are only poets whose failures in my eyes or whose disabilities interest me almost as much, if not more, than their achievements.

G   I'm very struck by the fact that you have, in effect, no contemporaries of stature, no contemporaries who persuade you as the High Moderns persuaded me. You were born about 1950—

H   1949.

G   You were born in 1949, and we are almost twenty years separate in age. I think one of the reasons for the absence of a sentiment of vital contemporaneity among persons of your generation lies in the willed disavowal of majority by the productive poets who were dominant during the time when you were educated. It seems as if Yeats and Eliot, Pound and Stevens used up the idea of greatness or implicated that idea in complex ways with aspects of the civilization—

H —that produced the Second World War.

G That produced the Second World War. The spectacle of Lowell seems to be particularly instructive in this matter. Lowell was the dominant poet in the world in which I was educated; that is to say, the dominant poet in the Northeast United States during the fifties. The major act by which Lowell's development is characterized in my mind, and the minds of virtually all his readers as I think, is an effort in his third major volume, *Life Studies* (1959), to effect a disencumbrance of mediations, to obtain a direct relationship to the life of his own consciousness unmediated by the vast structural interpositions of the greatest predecessors, of whom Yeats is the example that most often comes to my mind.

H I notice that your observation of Lowell's disavowal of central majority, or of what you call "greatness" when we talk about the High Moderns, is associated with a rejection of, or inability to any more use, structures, what you're calling mediations. In other words, in your mind, those mediations go with greatness; they come together.

G I think that the sentiment which surrounded Lowell's massive and persevering effort to obtain a poetry which was more fully immanent to the world of his consciousness, and less fundamentally characterized by the self-reference of poetry to its own history, represents a response to that predicament which I was speaking of in our first conversation. It represents an effort to obtain a poetry which is in harmony with the life of sentiment; that is to say, the life of human immediacy rather than, as in Yeats, a poetry which demanded of what he called "the intellect of man" that it choose between a perfection of the life, for which he had little talent, and that perfection of the art for which he was so massively gifted.

But I think, as you suggest, that the whole history of Lowell's writing, down to his last work, the work published in the year of his death, called *Day by Day*, is an experiment to discover whether there is some power of writing which can situate itself at the point of intersection between the life lived and the transcendental ex-actions of art. This search did indeed constitute a disavowal of greatness, a disavowal of universal stature. Lowell's discovery, I think, was that poetry written at that zero point of coincidence between world and mind really has no meaning and no end, really confers no consolation, yields no story but the account of its own production as story. This discovery of Lowell's was by no means a failure of enterprise; but it did delegate to those around him the obligation to construct the poetry which he sought the possibility of, a possibility which he kept alive by the patience of his labors but the actuality of which he did not, in fact, achieve. Lowell's poetry, therefore, is not situated upon its achievement but upon its process, and constitutes a testament toward a posterity whose safety in the world consists in discovering what he was in search of rather than repeating what he accomplished.

H   As you know, I'm not an intense admirer of Lowell's poetry, but we both have friends who are. I feel now I should try to speak for or represent such admirers. You speak of Lowell's work having failed of a kind of achievement. You say that the only story he found he could tell in that style was essentially the story of the production of the words, the obsessively inward-turning story of a man's strug-gling to write in a new way. That is, you say that it is the image of the process he undertook in those last books, rather than what was actually gotten onto the page, that is deserving of respect and wins our interest; whereas I should think that Lowell said things that needed to be said and that the ideas *are* achieved on the page. I'm thinking, for example, of the fierce and persuasive indictment of bourgeois America in "For the Union Dead."

G   Lowell was a great agonist. By agonist I mean a great struggler. It does not in my mind diminish the magnificence and terror of that

struggle to declare that he did not finish the work which he undertook. The admiration for Lowell, which passes into a profitable
imitation of a certain kind, directs itself toward his specification of
an unalterable world of fact, primarily social fact, which indeed he
did bring into the horizon of the poetic eye with a savage vigor, a
relentless and almost barbaric insistence, more fully than anyone
before him, unless the great predecessor is John Donne.

H   You speak of *Life Studies* having been a crucial turning point in
    the poetry of the 1950s. It appeared in 1959, when I was ten years
    old. I didn't read it when it came out. What process did Lowell
    move through from the time of his *Lord Weary's Castle* which was
    mainly an effort in that mode of central greatness, speech for the
    culture as a whole? What process did Lowell move through to get
    to *Life Studies,* and was that happening in the work of other poets
    in the 1950s?

G   I think it is of considerable importance for you to bring to mind
    that history which in effect assembled the world in which you
    yourself began writing. When did you begin seriously writing
    verse?

H   1968.

G   In 1968. Who were the poets that were initially the models for
    you? What was the earliest poem that was of importance to you?

H   I was most conscious of Anne Sexton and W. S. Merwin.

G   When you became conscious of Anne Sexton and W. S. Merwin,
    what poets from the deeper past had become significant to you?
    After all, somewhere along the line there must have been a poem
    that put the idea of poetry as a thing to do in your mind.

H   Well, for models of greatness, I was then most conscious of Keats,
    every one of whose poems seemed magical. I sat in the library one
    day and discovered someone named William Butler Yeats and read

his early romantic poems, which also seemed to have a magical power. I did not begin *writing* in that way, but still, that was what struck me as evidence that it would be good to write poetry.

G   There are no American poets among these ancestral originary poetic experiences?

H   I remember taking a course in which Theodore Roethke and Howard Nemerov were both taught. There was one poem by Roethke, called "Dolor," which struck me as a very good thing to have written. But no, they did not figure for me as giants or as models.

G   You are a writer without a deep past. That is a matter of very great interest. The situation of poetry to which Lowell addressed himself in the self-revising action which is represented in *Life Studies* is therefore, in some sense, unintelligible to you. Lowell in the mid-fifties became not so much the beginner as the inheritor of a new style which was coming to mind all around him, particularly in the work of W. D. Snodgrass and, I think also, of Sylvia Plath and Anne Sexton. These poets were attempting to recover poetry for precisely that self for which you were speaking in our last conversation. It was as if poetry had up until that time been not the friend but the enemy of the person who aspired to acknowledgment—not the friend but the enemy of the world in which it was necessary to make hard choices, the world of which it was necessary to make sense in order to understand the pain everyone felt but could give no name to, or within the aspiration for naming could give no dignity to.

H   You're saying there was a sense that poetry was not helping us learn how to live.

G   Poetry was not helping us learn how to live because the High Moderns did, as I have said, set poetry against life. They seemed to have established the outcome of poetic enterprise outside of life in unreachable transcendentalisms which no longer made any sense at all. The immediate response to the High Moderns was first to conserve them academically and therefore neutralize them, and then to retrench upon the world not of transcendental reality but of what, loosely speaking, can be called an immanent counter-reality. The poets who mediated the Moderns for the world of the late forties and early fifties were poets such as you encountered in your earliest education in poetry: Theodore Roethke, who strangely and with extraordinary originality modeled poetry not upon personal growth, toward maturity and transcendence in the above, but upon regression and the turn toward earth, the re-rooting of cuttings—the descent into a nurturant world where language was not the father language of the high culture, but a language which promised great novelty: the new language of an as yet undiscovered mother culture, the culture of the world below. This generated in Roethke's case an experimental region for poetry, represented by his lost son, the male child without origins, and began in him (he did not complete the task) to generate a new language.

Roethke's incompleteness as a writer was in some sense repeated by other writers of his generation; for example, by Randall Jarrell, whose effort to obtain not immediacy in the epistemological sense but immanence, to construct a new family of earth-referenced persons, was also incomplete, leaving behind the trace of a great enterprise, but in fact a set of brilliant and, on the whole, evasive fragments. In general, the response to the Moderns—which included, first of all, as I have said, their institutionalization and then the effort to recuperate a human world from that greatness of theirs so profoundly implicated, as a violent thing out of scale, with the experience of the Second World War—pointed the way toward the kind of redemption of the self which Lowell's *Life Studies* sought.

But the case of Plath is relevant at this point as an instance of the internally conflicted character of the effort to obtain the representation of the self upon new grounds. Plath lived for a time in one of the houses near Bloomsbury Square where Yeats himself had lived and thereby avowed a continuity between her enterprise and Yeats'. Her most passionate poems represent the effort to solve the new problem of the reconciliation of art and immanence in the old way. Poems which everyone knows, such as "Ariel," are poems destructively situated upon the passion of transcendence, riding into that sun, the eye of acknowledgment. And a male eye at that. In that way it was like the poetry of Hart Crane, for whom the immense passion to complete the promises of desire came into catastrophic conflict with the requirements of representation; that is to say, with the abstractness and unyielding resistance of the medium of poetry itself.

H   So Plath then, in this analysis, sounds like an exception to the pattern that you are describing: the movement toward the earth and toward real life as lived that you observed in the work of Roethke and Jarrell and Lowell.

G   She is an exception only in the sense that she conceived the bitter task of art in a clear-sighted and severe way. An exception only in the sense that the intensity of her passion for actualization as acknowledged person was profounder and more focused than the others. Only in that sense was she an exception, for wherever the effort was undertaken to obtain what Altieri calls a new poetry of immanence, that enterprise encountered the conflict between the terms of art and the goal set for art which is the modeling of the completion of the self, the modeling through speaking of a credible person.
    Poetry must always reconcile all of its terms at the point of speech. Its one unchanging obligation is to give a credible account of the human voice. All of the powers that converge in poetry are checked and reconciled at the point of the image of the person which the human voice constitutes.

H   When you speak of the search for a poetry of immanence, I'm not sure I understand how you're using that word "immanence."

G   It is initially a theological word, and it means indwelling; and that inness always implies an internality to the human world, to the world of earth—a world that it is easier to see when it is not so cold as it was yesterday.

H   So in a poetry of immanence we would be able to find value in the
    present reality that we see and that we share.

G   That is the perpetually renewed hope. It was upon this hope that
    Wordsworth and Coleridge founded the novelty of their experi-
    ment as recorded in the fourteenth chapter of the *Biographia Lit-
    eraria*. I'm inclined to think the enterprise of regrounding the
    business of being human in the immanent pole of the immanent-
    transcendental dichotomy is the perennial strategy toward novelty
    and hope of the poetic inheritor. The difficulty with this intention
    lies in the fact that the idea of immanence is not independent of
    transcendence, and consequently the intending of immanence
    does not constitute a changing of the terms of art.
        For example, Ginsberg, in *Howl*, undertook "to recreate the
    syntax and measure of poor human prose" on the basis of immedi-
    ate relationship between persons. The enormous opening sentence
    of *Howl* constitutes an effort to extricate a single relationship from
    the predation of transcendence upon the fragile scene of human
    love. In Ginsberg's poem, the whole world of drugs is indistin-
    guishable from the central culture of decadence, and the angelic
    transcendence of a prior metaphysicalism embedded in the Beat
    jargon which he practiced, hardly distinguishable from the Mo-
    loch which he calls contemporary society.
        It is also of great importance to note that the forties and fifties
    inherited a world in which the national symbol, always a resource
    for the grounding of poetic authority, was discredited. The discred-
    iting of the national symbol—"America" for the American poet—
    continued relentlessly through the sixties and early seventies (the
    Vietnam period) and disempowered one great basis for immanent
    legitimation of the self—the nation. When you started writing,
    there were fewer means for speaking immortal language than, it
    seems to me, at virtually any time in the tradition. Transcendence
    had been disqualified. The great muse of the Moderns had passed
    into the Teeth-mother, as Bly calls her in a powerful poem of the
    late sixties. So when you began to write, the instruments that
    came to your hand were indeed very fragile. Why, when you began

writing poetry, did you think poetry was a good thing to do? What
was there in it for you?

H   In the latter part of my freshman year at college, I wanted to write
     love poems for my girlfriend, because I knew she would approve
     and be impressed, and it wouldn't cost much money. She had a
     kind of admiration for Rupert Brooke, and I thought I could write
     poems that romantic and perhaps more witty. I did write some that
     rhymed, but rather quickly I decided that I couldn't do something
     I liked with rhyme. I also had a good friend my freshman year who
     published at Brown, where we were in school, poems that got an
     amazing amount of his real life onto the page in what seemed a
     lasting way. They used skillfully, I think, the technique of half-
     rhyming. Yet they sounded something like the way he talked in
     syntax and diction; they partook of our lives as students. I envied
     not only the prestige he won by publishing those poems but some-
     thing about the permanence that he seemed to be winning for his
     life. I thought that I had excitement, and interesting kinds of
     learning and humor in my life, but that they were vanishing every
     day. I wanted to be able to seize some of that value, make it last.
     He showed me Yeats' poem "Lapis Lazuli" and cited it as proof,
     especially the first stanza of that poem, that language could sound
     natural and yet also be beautiful and be saying more than it would
     be saying if it were prose.

G   So you began writing poetry for the purpose of obtaining a rela-
     tionship, the relationship to your girlfriend. What year was that?

H   1968.

G   You continued writing poetry to give some permanence, which
     must mean to give both *manifest* life—that is, public, dignified
     life—and to give some kind of *lasting* life to the sentiments and
     experiences which you had. That's one of the subjects of "Little
     Star." One sees these two poles at the beginning of your writing:
     the desire for the facilitation of relationship, and the desire for
     permanence.

H   Let me say also, in the effort to be honest about this—

G   We must always be honest.

H   (It's worth a try)—that there was very soon a clear competitive dimension to my writing poetry. I felt competitive with this friend of mine I spoke about, although for years I felt his achievement was beyond anything I could reach. I began reading poetry magazines a lot when I should have been reading the classics (that you would have forced me to read if you had known me). I developed a sense, which I could have articulated as early as 1969 or 1970, that most people who were publishing poetry did not really know what they were doing or did not achieve something that was terribly impressive or terribly deep. I saw gestures, that I thought were imitative, derivative, and I sensed that I could play that game. Then, for at least five years, I wrote a lot of poems, and I'm only partly ashamed to say that this competitive motivation was involved in a lot of that writing. I wanted to show that what was being done and praised and published could be done rather easily and at a somewhat deeper level. I sensed that I could do something more interesting.

G   In the context of the history of our present state of affairs, I think that your sense of competitiveness had, from the point of view of poetic culture, a rather special meaning. The poetry which was prestigious when you began writing was a poetry as fully identified with the social presence in the world of persons as poetry has ever been. Sexton and Plath, the Snodgrass of *Heart's Needle*, and other writers had made possible the validation of the common middle-class life which you were leading. At the same time, they had constructed a poetry that had inside it its own seeds of disintegration, its own futurelessness. For at the very point in the culture where the construction of a common enterprise should have been the principal motive of creative struggle, they had placed a social self which was necessarily subject to that scarcity of fame which all persons must feel in a social world. In other words, the effort to fulfill one of the promises of poetry, namely, to assign a name and a significance to every person whatsoever, had come in conflict with the fundamental finitude which inheres in merely social presence.

I began writing in a serious way also in college. My work was to find a lineage, an ancestry or family other than my human and personal family: an affiliation in which I could find some outcome of desire different from that promised me in the social world. In a clear way, I began as a creature of the Yeatsean kind and have continued to develop the implications of that beginning to this day.

H   Am I right in thinking then that when you were twenty years old in 1952 the poets that you refer to as the High Moderns, especially Yeats, Eliot, and Crane, were living presences, not merely classroom texts the way they were in my mind in 1968?

G   That's certainly true. The great poets whom I went to hear were in fact Eliot, and Stevens whom I heard read in Chicago in 1950. They included Cummings and Thomas, very much in evidence at that time. Thomas' death had something of the same effect upon my group that the death of Lennon has had upon yours. Certain Moderns were, indeed, still alive in fact, and others unavoidable in mind. The poets who challenged me more immediately were Lowell, whom I saw and heard so many times during my years at Harvard, and Richard Wilbur, who was regarded, I must remind you, not as a poet of Augustan decorum then but as a poet who had discovered something new about the wilderness of life. Like yourself, I could not find my place among these writers, but for a different reason from the reason which makes it difficult for you to affirm contemporaries. My affinities were in some ways atavistic. The conception of a lineage which came to my mind required that I acknowledge not the immediate contemporaries whom I encountered as my competitors in the world, but the great masters—Virgil and Milton—access to whom it was my whole project to obtain on my own grounds.

But I wish to return to this matter of the family. I think that your sense that the goodness of poetry lay first in the facilitation

of relationship and then in the validation of your own lived experiences corresponds to my effort to reconstruct a family of significance from the ruins of a family which bewildered rather than
fulfilled my sentiment. Lowell, in *Land of Unlikeness,* and then
subsequently in *Lord Weary's Castle,* was continuously engaged in
the business of constructing a family, which he first of all did not
conceive of as a human family (that was his Catholic period) and
later struggled to make a human family through a succession of
marriages and the birth of first a girl child, who was his counter-
player in the world and his hope, and then a male child, who was
his repetition calling attention to the recursive or receding aspect
of his work in later life. The confessional poets, so-called (the
term is poor and derives, I think, from the early Catholic obsession
of Lowell), were also concerned with validating the family, always
broken and always in trouble, as in Snodgrass' *Heart's Needle* or in
the early and gorgeous manic poetry of Sexton's *To Bedlam and
Part Way Back.*

   The poets of passion in my youth were all one way or another
insane children, driven wild by the inability to complete the family which would, in turn, complete by acknowledgment the self.

H   Now let's define what we mean by family here, or what you mean.
   A family in the sense that it can be created in art and not just
   created with one's spouse is what? It is a set of interlocked lives
   that love, recognize one another.

G   That love one another, that recognize one another, and enact the
   invention, the validation—not merely the physical nurturance but
   the profound and moral legitimacy—of the self. And you are perfectly right. There are two kinds of families. There is the mortal
   family and the immortal family. The immanent confessional poets,
   who announced the world in which you began writing, turn from
   the transcendental family to the mortal family, attempt to construct a poetry internal to that mortal family, a poetry founded in
   the notion that the language adequate to produce the picture of
   the person as precious is consistent with the language of ordinary
   life.

But more specifically, I am inclined to regard the family as the very scene of reading, as I began to say in our last conversation. The family is the scene in which the self becomes real, and reading is a repetition of the scene in which the self becomes real—when reading is the reading of poetry in that extensive, veracious inter-active way I have spoken of.

But tell me, Mark, do you find the business of doing poetry gratifying? Is it, now that you have become good at it, a fulfillment of the motive which continuously leads you to write?

H Often the answer is yes. But there may be more than one thing that we're talking about. I often do feel, in the act of writing a poem, that I am doing what I wanted to do. That's not to say that the words I actually set down feel as if they are precisely the poem that got me to sit down in the first place. Often I have the feeling that I think many poets have expressed, as Strand put it once: "the poem that drew these words from me is not this poem." But in the last three years, I have felt that I was doing what I set out to do, and the anticipation of sympathetic reading by friends and the hope of eventual publication has made the whole thing satisfying. I don't feel that there is an anguish filling the work.

G This capacity to be satisfied with the work is something I am not gifted with.

H Well, I think it means that I don't have a kind of vast hope for the work that you have, which I guess means that in some sense the work is not central to my hope, as it is for you.

G I think that this is a very, very important difference between us, and a difference which is consistent with the difference that we are trying to define between our moments of entrance into the busi-ness of doing poetry. I am in some unchangeable way a transcen-dentalist. I was ten years old in 1942. The most persuasive public experience that I can bring to mind from that time is the experi-ence of helpless spectatorship of an historical drama of mutilation and the extinction of persons. The "I" of my poetry derives from a sense of the self as obliterated, surviving only by accident. My most fundamental impulses are toward recovery, the securing once again of selfhood in something that lies invulnerably beyond history, something which promises enormous, inhuman felicity.

My incapacity to be satisfied with the human family, which seems to me perpetually and centrally threatened, must constitute the difference between the manner in which you and I practice our verse. I have admired over and over again the capacity of your language to be in repose at the point of ordinary experience. I think you have been as irritated as you will allow yourself to be at my unwillingness to allow language to rest in the ordinary experience which you regard as so precious. I am, in a way, a child of the same impulses which were so profoundly in conflict in the work of Sylvia Plath. You are a child of a later and different time.

H   There's something in the history of you as a person of the twentieth century that I would like to bring out here. In your summary of the reactions of the poet-inheritors in the 1950s to history—the Second World War, the Holocaust—and to the great progenitors—the Moderns, whom the inheritors associated with that war in some way, with the civilization that led to or allowed totalitarianism—you point out that those inheritors—Lowell, Jarrell, Roethke, Snodgrass, others—turned away from transcendental hypotheses toward natural life. Roethke turned toward the earth. Other poets that we've spoken of turned toward the human relationships in the actual physical family. You, twenty years old in 1952, conscious of the Holocaust as a helpless spectator—

G   Bewilderingly conscious.

H   —you nevertheless did not follow them in their turn away from the High Modern claim to central and gigantic utterance. You somehow wanted to do what those father figures had done.

G   Indeed, and you have exactly specified the conflict inside poetry as I received it. I did not respond to Lowell's reinvention of the world of actual consciousness in *Life Studies*. I did not respond to the

Augustan reduction of wilderness in the poetry of Wilbur. Like yourself, but in a different way, I did not respond to my contemporaries or to my contemporary world. Ginsberg seemed to me to solicit an unconscious life without form. And the search for alternative families—that is to say, alternative paths of access toward the earth such as were and are still being pursued with integrity by Gary Snyder, for example—did not seem open to me as a Jew and as a frightened man. I did indeed return to the great masters. My entrance into poetry was as much by way of Virgil or, on the American side, the Miltonic imitations of William Cullen Bryant as it was through the poetry that was written around me. By contrast, the present in which you live is more alien from the past than the present in which I began writing or than any other present in relationship to its past that I can think of.

What has happened in your mind to the notion of authority? It is, after all, by *authority* that literary culture normally administers questions of value and focuses enterprise upon models, makes literary work a common work, makes of a poetic life a life not solely the struggle of an individual for self-validation.

H   Well, I do feel that something has happened. It's confused in my mind with certain limitations of my own personality that I'm aware of; I have, as you have observed, a deep tendency to dabble, which I think you don't have. I suspect that when you were an undergraduate (or younger than that, I don't know) and you decided that you were interested in Yeats, you read all of Yeats and became deeply aware of his stature and of the shape of his whole career; whereas I read a few Yeats poems and savored their flavor and did not feel threatened by his stature. I did not feel challenged by his stature—

G   Or obligated.

H   —nor by the stature of Eliot or Stevens, both of whom I dabbled in. When I took poetry courses I had a sense of multiple options: many people writing in many different ways. I thought of Eliot as only vaguely more important and more frightening than certain living poets, such as Lowell or even Anne Sexton, who seemed to me manifestly vulnerable. I know I'm speaking in a kind of an athletic or military vocabulary, but that was the way my thoughts were running. I'm repeating myself, but I had a sense that there were no great standard bearers in the culture around me; rather that the culture of poetry was a maze of different paths which made claims for themselves, but none of the claims had great authority.

G The absence of a world that is organized by authority seems to me, from the point of view of my generational difference, to be enormously disabling, and yet at the same time, enabling in a fashion so open it lacks the magnanimity of direction.

Let's look around us a little and see if we can identify the poets now writing who have an importance for us as constituting that large set of directions of which you speak. I myself see the world in which we live as immensely heterogeneous. On the one hand, there are indeed master poets, such as Ammons and Ashbery—whose genius and productivity seem to me beyond question, yet who seem to be writing in virtually autistic isolation, one from the other. Ammons, on the one hand, situates his poetry on the fundamentally romantic problem of epistemology, the problem which focuses the business of personhood upon the question as to how the way in which we know the world affects the way in which the world is experienced. Ammons' world, spherical, without determinate coordinates of up and down, is organized to defeat precisely that metaphysical structuration which I so passionately advocate. His enterprise is an enterprise without end, specifically designed to have no center: a world evacuated of divinity and sternly situated upon the advocacy of minority, which is also the advocacy of that separate or unsponsored humanity which you so articulately desire.

H Why is Ammons not a hero to me? The first thing I think of, when you ask me that, is his thoroughgoing informed interest in the natural world and the scientific facts that he knows about the natural world—as contrasted with my rather blithe (and, I know you think, distressing) ignorance of trees, bushes, rocks, birds, and rivers and what they do all day. But there is also a kind of lack of moral ambition in Ammons, to the extent that I know his work, which puts me off, which is not something I want to emulate, because I want to have effects on how people live with each other. Maybe that's the main problem I have with Ammons: that he does not have much to say about social life, which is all I have anything to say about.

G   Your mind is poised upon the ethical issue, and your sense of humanity is more urgent than the sense of humanity that is accommodated in Ammons' eloquent and elaborate unfolding of the implications of a universe that escapes tragedy by escaping terminal structure. In that perhaps limited sense, there is an insufficient moral integrity in Ammons.

The other immensely productive writer whom I admire and whom I know you have considered is, of course, John Ashbery—a poet whose creative power, particularly whose capacity to conceive of ways of entering into discourse inconceivable to me until he showed the way, excites the highest admiration in me. As Ammons makes a transit of the world without allowing it to obtain a structure, so Ashbery seems to search the resources of discourse without ever allowing them to complete themselves. He is a poet who disencumbers himself of the terrors of history, not by reinventing the world in a new way but by allowing no argument of the past to complete its tragic implications. The world of Ammons, with its rocks and stone and trees and rivers busy all day, is as alien to you as, let us say, Virgil or Hesiod or Sappho is; and the fate of rocks and stones and rivers is the same as the fate, for you, of the authoritative antiquity with which my mind was from an early age filled. In the case of Ashbery, I should think, it is the sentimentality of his relationship to the past that he undertakes to conserve in a structure which has, as he says, the shape, or antishape, of falling snow, but which is still a world characterized by snow and by rain and by sentiment: is still a landscape with the seeds of tragedy inside it, seeds which he does not allow to germinate, but from the promise of which he derives his significance as a writer. Ashbery I suppose would be alien to you in part because he is fundamentally a manager of traditional resources.

H   A manager of traditional resources in that one feels, when reading an Ashbery poem, that there is a melting together of many syntactical fragments that could have been quite at home in a poem from an earlier age. It is true that Ashbery is one more of these poets who interest me but do not attract me profoundly. Whether or not that is the reason, I'm not sure. In fact, one of the things that *has* attracted me to Ashbery is humor, what I have felt to be really an ongoing parodic humor in his poetry: making fun of pomposities in literary language. However, I'm aware that larger claims are made for Ashbery as an epistemological philosopher. I seldom give those claims much credence. I have often found passages in an Ashbery poem that I enjoyed very much for their image of the movement of the mind from one way of thinking to another—one perception to another, but also one way of thinking and formalizing one's thoughts to another in, I think, a realistically smooth transition, the way our minds often move. That is something that I would like to get into my own poetry sometimes, but I could not see that as the central ambition of an important poem.

G   I think that one of the things our world has done is to drive all of us into a private transaction with the reality that we separately perceive. Ashbery is an epistemological genius whose world has arrayed itself around him as a world in which it's possible for a man to live on condition that he reserve his passion for totality, as it were for another life. His world is a separate world in which it is impossible to meet another soul.

I think this fragmentation, this shattering, in Yeats' phrase, of the mirror is characteristic of the whole literary system into which you were born. Ashbery is not so much an epistemological writer as a writer about ontological orientation. The world that he perceives exacts of him strategies for survival, and his strategies for survival take the form of the construction of matrices, of brilliant, evasive subsystems, each characterized by a point of entry which is also a point of exit: a way in which is, at the same time, and triumphantly, a way out. All of the poets by whom we are surrounded, whatever their abilities, are engaged, as I have said, in making a separate peace with a reality that is at present so profoundly fragmented that it is difficult to accept the poetry of another as authoritative for the peace of the self. Another case in point is the enormous new poem by James Merrill, a parody of Dante's *Divine Comedy* situated on the notion of comedy as the survival and triumph of the self. The accomplishment of Merrill's three volumes is to provide occasions for simple, affectionate relationship through the hypothecation of a forgiving universe, a universe that is responsive to the human desire to remain with the other beyond death. The disability inherent in this pouring forth of genius by Merrill lies in his unwillingness to define the resistances to being—his self-sponsored liberation toward affection, a liberation that, in my view, can be admired but cannot be shared.

The same sense of constructing a separate, as it were, a unilateral peace with the world, I feel in the poetry of Elizabeth Bishop, whose concern is neither a concern about how we know nor is it a concern about what there is, but is a concern about the management of perception in the absence of decisions about these two great matters. It excites admiration at the point where it expresses the consequences for sentiment of the relentless focus which she everywhere practices. But it is a poetry, once again, that is self-limiting in its consolatory powers, except to a class that prides itself in the perfection of a particular kind of literacy.

I can deeply understand your sense of a poetic world without authority. Do you feel that there is any evaluative center in the world in which you live to which you can give respect? How do you go about judging whether a poem by you or by me or by another is good? Are there procedures that you feel to be agreed upon?

H   I am aware only of a set of questions that I ask myself about a poem and that I can ask more effectively the more distance I have from the poem. That is, if I ask them immediately after having written it, I often answer the questions incorrectly. So I don't think those deserve the name of procedures, which is what you're asking about. The other thing I do is simply to show a poem, whether it be one of my own or someone else's poem, to certain friends (one of whom is you, another of whom is Frank Bidart) and see what they think; so that I have in my life now, in the last four years, these sort of local authorities. But I don't think that is the answer you were looking for.

G   It is exactly the answer which is consistent with the account of the poetic world you have presented in this hour of talk. It bears out my sense of a centerless poetic world in which we re-interpret poetic value in terms of the human judgments which lie immediately around us. It is characteristic of literary communities to assimilate social relationships and literary relationships, one to the other, but the extreme fragmentation of poetic judgment in our Boston world reflects, I believe, the larger predicament of a literary universe of enormously gifted people whose sense of the goodness of their work is to be validated only by those who share the space of the universe in which they themselves live.

H   Whereas, what other procedures could be followed? Are you contrasting the present situation with the situation you found in the fifties?

G   The impulse of the High Moderns was to draw their standards from a remote past. I believe my impulse was similar to the impulse of the Moderns. Since the world at hand was a world in which it was impossible to imagine structures equivalent to experience, and since the future is not an inheritance that any writer can use, the effort was to establish a family—that is to say, a significant scene of reading and therefore of personal being—which had its origins outside of history, in a past remote in time and, from the point of view of the psychological analogy, in a self remote from consciousness; which past and which remote self would be administered to rescue or render innocent the present and, by implication, the future.

H   My question though is: when you were a student, if you wanted to know whether or not a poem had succeeded, how did you know? What was available to you then that's not available to us now?

G   There is a mystery about this issue of availability. I think the question of what constitutes the goodness of poems—every poem is made as an offering toward the goodness which one hopes to find in poetry—I think that this question of the goodness of poetry has to be answered by both of us through some inquiry into what we ourselves have undertaken to do as poets.

    By the way, it is a good deal warmer today. I think our conversation today has turned on subjects somewhat less external to the human world than yesterday's conversation. When it is very cold, I feel the pressure of the world which is not the self so overwhelming—

H   That you need abstractions.

G   That I need abstractions, for abstractions are a dream even deeper than a dream that I can make human. They keep me warm.

3 · THE DEVELOPMENT OF A POET WHO STARTED OUT IN THE FIFTIES

H   Allen, let me begin our conversation today by wishing you a happy birthday, which I neglected to do when I saw you earlier today. You are now forty-nine years old.

G   Thank you. Yes.

H   And I know that you've been thinking these things that you've been saying to me about the purpose of poetry for a long time. It would be good to talk now about the ways in which those ideas have resulted in poetry by you, the ways you have found to write poems that live up to or live out your ideas about what poetry should and could do for humanity.

G   I think that's a useful thing to do, Mark. So far as I can distinguish poets from other kinds of persons, I see poets obligated to make sense out of what they think in a particularly constraining way, in fact, in the most constraining terms imaginable to me: that is to say, the terms that are set by the representational constraints on speech when speech is vivid and like the language of a person.

I started writing somewhat younger than you did, as I see from our last conversation. My first book, A Harlot's Hire, published in 1961, collected poems that were written as early as my teens. The meanings of that book and, indeed, even its tonalities are entirely recognizable as the speech of the man who has been talking to you in the last two conversations.

H   We observed yesterday, I remember, that in the early 1950s when
    you were a student, a young man, you did not accept the turn
    toward the earthly and toward the finite and the private that was
    being undertaken or accepted by the older and published poets
    around you. Instead, you wanted to insist on a kind of high speech
    and what might be called an upward-directed mode of expression.

G   Yes, I am certainly a high-style poetic writer. I was then and I am
    now. Whatever the merits of the low and referential style of poetry
    which was dominant in the fifties when I began writing, I have not
    been able to obtain those merits.

H   Instead, even at that young age (at the age of twenty-three, say,
    when I know some of the poems in A Harlot's Hire were written),
    you were determined to ask of yourself as a poet, and of anyone
    who wanted to be a poet in our culture, what the great Modern
    poets demanded of themselves: a kind of centrality, a determina-
    tion to speak for the culture as a whole. You wanted to believe in
    the potential power of the poet to redeem human selves, (to use
    the language of our first conversation) to redeem human selves by
    making them present through art.

G   That's certainly true, and this motive was intersected by another
    motive, and that was the motive to affirm a lineage; in my case, a
    lineage that was defined by my Jewishness. One of the strongest
    and, to my mind, the most magnanimous (as it is also one of the
    most imperfectly fulfilled) ambitions of the poets of the fifties was
    to place themselves in a lineage that was both poetic and cultural
    in the intimate mythic sense of culture in which it is possible to
    say that one is, let us say, a Jew. The idea of lineage has always
    been very important to me. A lineage is an account of the self
    which connects the present of the self not merely to the past but
    to the origins of all things; by its nature, a lineage has authority
    because it constitutes a story about how the self in the present has
    its origins in the same events in which the universe has its ori-
    gins—as the man who views himself as a descendant of a biblical
    lineage views himself as beginning very close to the beginning of

the world altogether. Not only, therefore, did I begin writing in the high style mediated by the Moderns as I acknowledged them, most particularly Yeats, but I began also as a poet seeking a poetic lineage intersected by a cultural lineage which was, in this period, the lineage of the destroyed, of the erased, a lineage which was at the point of extinction in 1945.

H Because of the Nazis' genocide against the Jews.

G That's correct. Many poets of my age (Sylvia Plath is an example) tended to associate themselves as abused and unacknowledged persons with the Jews, even when they had no ethnic right to call themselves Jews. All of the dead are Jews, as has been said. Certainly at that moment for me, all the dead were Jews.

H In that statement I sense an intersection between the desire to speak for humanity in its struggle against death and the desire to speak as a Jew, a person with a family lineage, a person with a specific ethnic background. That is, you've just said now that you felt in some sense all the dead were Jews, which means that as a Jew you were specifically entitled to speak for the dead, to speak for humanity in its response to death.

G That's correct; not only entitled, but obligated. And obligated in two ways: Obligated in the way a man is obligated to others and obligated also in the way a man is obligated to himself. It is my feeling that the enterprise of this way establishing a poetic lineage—that is to say, at the intersection of the ethnic and the cultural—is a failed enterprise. At the same time, much of the thinness and arbitrariness of poetry in the present time arises from the deliberate separation of these two elements.

H When you say it's a failed enterprise, are you referring to your own work or to the work of poets in the last thirty-five years?

G I'm referring to my own work to begin with, but I'm also ascribing that same failure to other poets of my generation. In retrospect one can see that even Yeats' effort to be, on the one hand, Irish and, at the same time, a poet in the European tradition led to a division of self which was never (and most particularly at the point of his "greatness") healed.

H   Allen, I'm looking now at your poem in *A Harlot's Hire*, "A Poem for Statesmen," and I see that the poem begins with a sense of that failure, or at least a sense of the failure of poets to win recognition as having achieved that kind of centrally satisfying statement.

G   In this passage, that sense of failure is anticipatory, for the opening stanza of "A Poem for Statesmen" begins by referring to the discredited state of the power which the poet administers, at the moment, as it were, *before* my undertaking of the work.

H   Let me read the first part of the poem we're talking about:

A Poem for Statesmen

I

Although discredited among you
And among the people, having been silent
Through so long an agony of ignorance
And the dying of so many thousand deaths
When no voice rose to call them beautiful,
And though I come in unfamiliar garments
Looking so like a man you do not know me,
Yet I am still a poet
With power to make you beautiful and free.

My voice is hoarse with such long silence,
And I am guilty of much suffering
Among the middle classes. Although they bred
A thousand poets to remember them
And each one ached, as I do, to make them beautiful
No child could think of them with wonder,
Not even their own children,

Until they have new names and deaths and dreams.
I come to teach their children love and wonder.

I can remember men who never were
They were so mighty. They care
For those who love them. They remember the place
Of abandoned graves, and the name of the unknown soldier
No matter what ignoble peace or war
He died in. Hear me and I shall open
The ghetto of ghosts
And give back to the nation the beauty of her dead
And they will walk beside the living, and make them free.

G   How does that strike you?

H   It strikes me as a rather bold way to talk to statesmen.

G   It was indeed not such a bold way to talk to statesmen, for states-men were not listening. It strikes me as an arrogant way to define human enterprise. It was, however, an effort, which I still affirm, to take into my hands as a man the particular powers which the poet administers and to use those powers for the ends of poetry; that is to say, to make others both beautiful and also (what is from the point of view of this poem the same thing) free in a specific way.

H   It seems to me a characteristically naked way of declaring ambi-tion, characteristic of your work. It is to be seen also, for example, in the first section of "Of the Great House," which we will look at in a later conversation. Those last two lines of the stanza that I read, "Yet I am still a poet / With power to make you beautiful and free"—I think it's clear that the poet writing those lines knows that there's an arrogance about them, but he is willing to risk not being taken seriously by some people because he is convinced that that is the power that the poet doing his job has to offer. This idea of freedom, however (let me at least note in passing), is one that I don't think we've talked about, and it's not clear to me yet.

G I have been astonished, throughout my life, at the poverty of the
   utterance of those persons who call themselves poets, their unwillingness, in the language of Yeats, to open their throats, to speak
   both directly and with a full sense of the privilege of the art that
   they practice. I believe at the present time there is an unaccountable self-restriction practiced by poets so that the spectacle of the
   poet as he speaks from the platform seems to me the spectacle of a
   person who speaks with only part of the privilege that, by reason
   of the authority of poetry, a poet does have. And much of my
   concern is to discover those sayings, those un-uttered words which
   belong to the power of poetry but which are not yet brought into
   voice. It was my intention then and is my intention now.
       The idea of freedom, you should remember, was implicit in
   some of the first sentences that we exchanged in these conversations, for at that time, I was attempting to make clear the sense in
   which I feel that the very structures of the poem are models for,
   embed within them, definitions of relationships among persons.
   You may recall that I suggested that the most appropriate language
   for discussing poetic structures was the language of the relationship
   of persons in states; that is to say, in whole societies. I made allusion to Whitman, who spoke of himself as writing a democratic
   verse, and Milton, who spoke of himself as liberating persons,
   through a new kind of verse, from a bondage which he specifically
   identified with the Catholic church and with other forms of false
   governance. Therefore, both from a practical and theoretical point
   of view, it should at least not seem alien that I would, when describing my work as a poet, include the notion of freedom and
   particularly freedom toward relationship. I have described reading,
   not as an act of recovering meaning from words, but as a practice
   of relationships.

H All right. Now, speaking about the end of the first stanza of "A
   Poem for Statesmen" a couple of minutes ago, you said that for the
   purpose of this poem the beauty and the freedom to be achieved
   through poetry's power are the same thing.

G   Beauty is always a state of affairs to be interpreted. It is, in that
    sense, like death. It has no meaning until one assigns it meaning.
    When this poem speaks of beauty, it speaks not of a pleasing state
    of the body or mind but of a larger felicity, such as Dante would
    have understood: a felicity which includes in it all the safety and
    gratification, and of course, also, all the magnanimity and obliga-
    tion, of persons in relationship; for both beauty and freedom in
    my verse mean the safety and certitude of persons in relationship,
    what Whitman calls "the certainty of others."

H   This "Poem for Statesmen" is deeply conscious of the danger to
    persons most gigantically epitomized by the Holocaust, to which
    the poem refers. The poem is spoken by a man speculating on
    what poetry can achieve in a world filled with doubt about whether
    that kind of felicity really can be achieved. I wonder if you could
    say something now about that ambition of the poem and how it
    shaped the poem.

G   One could put these matters much more simply, Mark. My poetry
    is a frightened poetry from beginning to end. The structure of this
    poem (a version of the greater ode) is large, as the style is high, in
    proportion to the fear, in a sense, of disintegration, which as a
    poetic speaker I experience in the world around me. I experienced
    that as a sentiment about history when I was younger. I now ex-
    perience it as a sentiment about my mind and body as I grow older.
    The ambition in this poem is clearly expressed in the third stanza
    of the first part: "Hear me and I shall open / The ghetto of ghosts /
    And give back to the nation the beauty of her dead / And they
    will walk beside the living, and make them free." The poem then
    proceeds to declare what Yeats had declared in "Lapis Lazuli": that
    the system of representation available to mind in Western civili-
    zation has become inadequate to the representation of the major
    fact of history, of which the Holocaust is now the sign.
        The poem declares that the oldest and most prestigious monu-
    ments of agony are broken by the facts of historical experience and
    that sorrow has entered into stone like an iron root and has shat-
    tered that stone. The poem then declares that the muse has be-

come a mourner, and it is the business of the poet, in some sense, to console the muse, to find a structure *adequate* to experience in order to recuperate that experience and to provide it with a future unlike its past. My sense of failure, which I will confer (perhaps not magnanimously) upon my contemporaries as well, centered around my inability to find a structure adequate for taking in the range of experience which it has been our historical destiny to contemplate. This poem, like all my poems, tells the story of a man who knows more than he can take into account. This poem, like all my poems, gives the very image of a man seeking a structure which will permit him to take into account, that is to say, to make intelligible, what has happened to him.

H Yes, it seems to me as I look at this poem that however great the fear and the despair may be, the hope in the poem is still stronger, and still is the controlling influence on the shape of the poem. I say that thinking about this poem as one written after Eliot's *The Waste Land*, and yet a poem which ignores *The Waste Land*. That is, the speaker who says "the oldest monuments of agony are broken" is an Eliotic speaker locating himself in the Waste Land, but he speaks as someone who is not confined to the assemblage of fragments and is not to be consoled only by some kind of leap into an alien culture, an Eastern culture. Rather, this poem, it seems to me, hopefully experiments with ways that the old, explicitly Yeatsean, "high style" can still be used to imagine a consolation. That consolation, or the figure who could offer such a consolation, is represented by an imaginary prophet-like figure in part three of this poem.

G Yes. The relationship to the High Moderns which you've described is rich. It was my effort as a Jew and a new writer not to imitate the accomplishment of the High Moderns, which seemed to me to involve (especially in the case of Eliot's *The Waste Land*) the description of a world which was not my world, but to take upon myself a privilege equivalent to the privilege which the High Moderns had taken upon themselves—and indeed, kept alive as a poetic possibility—and by administering that privilege in another way, to construct a new poetry to lay beside the High Modernist description of our state of affairs.

The rule was to write as if the Moderns had never written, to take back from them the privilege which they had practiced, to take the privilege but not their utterance which flowed from that privilege. It was one of the most difficult things for men of my generation to do: to separate my sense of the world from the sense of the world in *The Waste Land*. A great part of the ambition of *A Harlot's Hire* consisted in describing for myself the kind of evil which I felt to be abroad in the world, taking back, as it were, my pain; resisting or putting off what seemed to me a false description of the particular terror from which I suffered. It was *very* hard for me to separate the world I experienced from the world which had been described by *The Waste Land*.

H In what way was that description false to your experience?

G Eliot's *The Waste Land*—which really described history in terms of the failure of erotic potentiality, and the redemption of history in terms of the recovery of the earliest state of the authenticity of the Indo-European—the Sanskrit state, the "Shantih" state—seemed to me then as it seems to me now, first of all, a false account of the nature of our pain and a false account of the path toward our recovery of the world in view of that pain. Consequently, a large part of the language in my early poems reflects an effort to place in sentences the older, romantic terms of hope as if that language had never been disqualified by the Modernist revision of Victorianism. A sentence, a line and a half that I meditated on for years when I was young, runs as follows: "I had forgotten / To desire what I could no longer believe that I loved." Now you have pointed me to the third part of "A Poem for Statesmen," which begins:

Who is the man among you that is wise,
The old man not ignorant of night,
Content to set his plow to the desert
And live in desolate places with strange birds?
He alone can say that God is love

>   Or speak of liberty and set me free
>   By speaking of it, being himself free,
>   And draw tears down from speechless multitudes
>   Who have not wept since the last poet died.

H I'm struck with a sense that I would never have written this stanza,
   Allen. My feeling about that is not just a matter of diction or
   theme but a matter of the strategy the poem chooses now. The
   poem is aware of historical forces that make it very unlikely that a
   poet at this time in history can do these things for people, for the
   race. Yet the poem refuses to collapse into or be resigned to that
   defeat. Instead, the poem, as I'm understanding it, in this third
   section adopts a strategy of creating an imaginary person who
   could do it if he existed. The stanza that you've just read begins
   with this rhetorical question to which there may be more than one
   answer: "Who is the man among you that is wise?" That rings in
   my ears as a challenge to the audience being addressed, as if they
   better be able to come up with an answer. I guess the answer may
   be: it is the poet if only he were sufficiently recognized by us.

G The answer is more simple than that and perhaps also somewhat
   more difficult to see. The effort is to write straight through the
   problem and, having done so, to construct a negation—that is to
   say, a state of affairs alternative to and redemptive of the state of
   affairs of history as we find it—and to construct that negation or
   alternative state of affairs as some function of human possibility.
   The challenge is both to the audience and to the poet. One of my
   beliefs that I want to make plain to you is that I do not distinguish
   between poets and moral persons. When in my poetry the poet is
   spoken of, the personhood then spoken of is a personhood not
   only possible to all of us but obligatory upon all of us. The poet is,
   in my mind, the person who has realized his inheritance of possible
   integrations; so that when the speaker summons the new poet he
   is in effect summoning the new man, and that man is particularly
   beautiful and wise because he can take into account the largest
   possible range of what he knows. He is not ignorant of night. That
   is to say, he can as a person speak from a point of view which has

access both to his mind, his unconscious, and to history as terror. He is content in the desert to sow seed. In desolate places, he is not dismayed by the strangeness of the apparitions.

H This man is elaborately described despite the fact that he is imaginary; he does not yet exist. I think that the speaker of this poem, you, does not yet believe that he has become this man. We're agreeing that this is a speculative gesture. You spoke of it as the construction of a negation, and I see in this the belief, the faith, that if such a negation can be constructed, if it can be imagined fully enough, that in itself is evidence of its possibility in the world.

G Yes, there is confidence in this verse, a confidence which I can still affirm, that what can be imagined can also come to pass. It is a poetry which sees no reason to have forgotten what the mind most intensely loves. If my poetry summons persons to anything, it is to that confidence that what they love is, by reason of desire itself, real.

H The desire itself makes the object of desire real?

G The function of this poetry that I write is not to ironize the relationship of persons to the objects of their desire but to de-ironize that relationship; that is to say, to remind persons that the very fact of desire under the auspices of skepticism is evidence, compelling evidence, of the reality of the object.

H What do you mean by "under the auspices of skepticism"?

G My poetry is throughout a skeptical poetry. It is a poetry that assigns a structure to hope but no structure to the universe. It is, however, a *rigorously* (or intended to be a rigorously) skeptical poetry, which discovers that what the mind does not know is true may or may not be true. From skepticism it is possible to draw two conclusions: one, the pessimistic conclusion, that what one does not know to be is not; the other, the optimistic conclusion, that what one does not know to be may well be. The business of poetry in my hand is to fill that space of unknown possibility with the highest hypotheses of desire. It is this motive that leads me to write in a high style, for the high style is the style of high hope. It is this motive which I describe as the motive toward the de-ironization of discourse, rather than its distancing or bewilderment. From this vantage point, one can see both the attraction to my mind of Ashbery, of whom we spoke in the last conversation, and also the limits of my acceptance of his world.

H   Isn't it true that this belief in the hypothesizing of the objects of desire has led you in your poetry sometimes to, at least in passages of poems, *declare* the existence of objects of desire which exist in a transcendental realm? That is, isn't it true that at times your poetry, at least as a strategy, has affirmed as if confidently the existence of such validations or consolations? I'm thinking, Allen, of the first three lines of another poem in this volume, the poem "In My Observatory Withdrawn."

G   Yes, that is entirely true. In addition, the co-presence of an imagined world with a real world has led me to describe a bitterness attendant upon the very practice of hope, a competition between the beloved who is at hand and that golden Beloved, conceived virtually in the terms of Sir Philip Sidney's golden world, who not only consoles by the possibility of her graciousness the bitter enterprise of desire, but also interferes by her pre-emptive magnificence and strangeness between the historical and ironic self and its possible relationships and loves. I am, as you have not yet had the boldness to remark, to some degree an invented man. My sense of myself is similar to other men's sense of an artifact. The conception that both the self and indeed the world are invented states of affairs is extremely intimate to my mind and to my history.

H   What made you begin to invent yourself as a poet in the first place?

G   I thought you'd never ask. My poetry is a direct consequence of a motive as intimate and necessary to me as life itself, to construct a world consistent with the desire of a world which I encountered in the heart and soul of my mother. It is a commonplace that persons write poetry for their mothers. My poetry is, in the most literal sense, the speech of my mother, or rather, the completion of the speech of my mother.

My mother is a strange, dreaming person, and she is at this very day in Sri Lanka seeking a place where dreams are real. The sense in which my poetry is organized to justify hope goes deep back into a personal history of intimacy, of a mother who was restlessly and in some sense destructively dissatisfied with the world around her. The prolongation and, as it were, consummation of her will toward a golden world is as veracious an account as I can give of my motive to art. It went way back into my early childhood, when I wrote poems in the most uninstructed way.

H   That seems to me a strange, deep motivation, next to which some of the motivations I spoke about in reference to my own early twenties are blatantly trivial. You're saying (and I've heard you say another time) that your poetry is an attempt to write the speech of your mother, and you once refused to accept my rephrasing of that when I asked you if you meant that this was to be the poetry that your mother would speak if she could.

G   Yes, I have insisted, indeed, this very day, on the notion that it is *precisely* her speech. My unwillingness to de-realize the immediacy of her acting within me or acting through me is really a restatement of much of the stuff we were talking about in earlier conversations. I feel about poetry that it is a demonized activity, that it is not, as poetry so manifestly is in your own work, the speech of a mortal or merely singular person. Poetry in my view has its power because it is the speech not of an individual but of another who is more than and different from the individual. When I speak of it as the speech of my mother, I am speaking of it as if inside the word "mother," as one can see punningly, there is the word "other"—the speech not of the self, but of the other as mother, as maternal source, source of the world, the deep source of art, the point of intersection between nothing and something;

both for myself as an individual, as the mother is, and myself as the member of a cosmos which did itself have a beginning.

Perhaps if we turn back to "In My Observatory Withdrawn," we can make these matters a little plainer. I'll hear it better if you read it to me.

In My Observatory Withdrawn

To whatever face
Real or passionately imagined I turn up my eyes,
It is the Beloved who hears among her stars.

When I lay at my mother's breast
And took delight and gave delight
It was the Beloved who nourished and upheld.

When I took off my shoes, and with the forgotten stealth
Of the hunter searched the tops of the mountains
Where only night and the storm cloud darken the stone
It was She who put on the mask of sternness
And the tongue of steel and turned toward me the tremendous
    mystery.

And when I lay face upon the face of all my yearning
And body in the womb joyful, She stood close behind the veil,
Never until then so close.

Now in my observatory withdrawn
I am given up to the sky, and strain my eyes across the spaces
    between;
On cloudy nights I sit in a lower room dreaming,
And listening to the tick of the heart, until the wind rises
And the clouds turn and turn and depart, and I climb
To the unroofed upper room once more, and adjust my
    instrument
Praising the wind.

G   When I hear you reading my poem to me, I feel something of the
    force of demonization, the sense in which it is not the self that

speaks, but another that speaks through and to the self. This poem makes vivid the complex relationship between the beloved who is at hand and the Beloved, the transcendental Beloved, who, on the one hand, authorizes, and on the other hand, interferes between the speaker and his mortal woman. Perhaps the element from this very early work most fully retained in my later poetry is the sense of the self as an observer of the sky, the picture of the self as practicing observation with a lens. One of the analogies for the poetic instrument that occurs over and over again in my poetry is the lens. I feel that, like the lens of the telescope, the poetic instrument is a means of seeing: of seeing the above and of seeing the far and of mediating between the above and the far, on the one hand, and the mortal person, on the other.

We talked at the beginning of our conversations about the function of poetry. Within the functions that I have named there lies the sense of the poem and its constituent elements (which are, of course, more perpetual, more everlasting, and more general than the poem itself) as a machine, an instrument, or at very least, a technique, like a lens or a telescope, for seeing. What that telescope can see will, of course, be the Other, finally, and what the telescope makes possible is the certainty of the Other as the telescopes which see the stars provide certain evidence for the existence of worlds other than our own. The speaker of this poem "in his observatory withdrawn" climbs up after the dark cloudiness of night to once again sit down to his instrument which sees selves as poetry sees selves.

H   When you speak of the telescope that poetry is, ultimately bringing into focus the other, I wonder how that can be achieved if the telescope is pointed toward the sky.

G   The subject matter of poetry, whatever its means may be, however vast a net it throws over the world of objects, is always, in my view, the person. For poetry there is no sky which is different from the unknown inwardness of other selves, the knowledge of which will construct selves as persons. I see for poetry no possibility and, indeed, no need consistent with its nature or its purpose in the world to make any offering whatsoever toward a world which is not the person. The idea of Objectivist verse seems to me simply a premature conclusion about the function or nature of a particular kind of poetry, which addresses the self without giving it its proper name—in effect, an evasion. The most remote thing that can come to mind is the inwardness and very being of another, and it is only that that the telescope properly focused can see. Poetry is the lens by which that thing is seen and in this age may be the only such lens.

H   I wonder if we could turn now to a poem in your recent book, *The Woman on the Bridge over the Chicago River*, because it is explicitly about the relationship between a man and his mother, which might help me understand what you were saying before about your wish to speak your mother's words: "The Runner."

G   The poem called "The Runner" is a poem characteristic of the work I have just recently finished doing. It is a simpler poem than the earlier poems we have been looking at. It is a poem in which an action occurs—the moon rises—and the confidence that I've been speaking about, namely, the possibility of what is desired, is affirmed with the same inevitability with which the rising of the moon affirms the constancy of the universe. Let me read you this poem:

The Runner

The man was thinking about his mother
And about the moon.

               It was a mild night.
He was running under the stars. The moon
Had not risen,

               but he did not doubt it would
Rise as he ran.

               Small things crossed the road
Or turned uneasily on it. His mother

Was far away, like a cloud on a mountain
With rainy breasts. The man was not a runner
But he ran with strength.

                      After a while, the moon
Did rise among the undiminished stars,
And he read as he ran the stone night-scripture
Of the moon by its own light.

                          Then his mother
Came and ran beside him, smelling of rain;
And they ran on all night, together,
Like a man and his shadow.

In this poem, as the conclusion makes plain, no assertion is made about the real existence of that mother. She is as intimate to this runner, this man in the world, as a shadow and as much an absence as a shadow is. Nonetheless, the poem as I read it makes me feel once again a hope that is undiminished by the sense of fact. In this I would like to express to you, both my consistent—as I feel—skepticism in the realm of what is; and, at the same time, the sense that I have in me (not so much a personal, as a demonic sense) of confidence in the continuity of things, a confidence that is here expressed as my hope in the everlasting and never-ending relationship between this man and his mother, the man and the authenticity of his nature as that authenticity is expressed by the family in which a man becomes a person—in which he reads and is read.

H   Yes. The ambivalence is caught in and turns on the word "like" in the last line, "Like a man and his shadow"—that last line can be read as the concession to skepticism, as if the poem were admitting that all that's really happening is the man is running alone with his shadow and imagining something. But it can also be read the other way: if it is read in a kind of straightforward way, it says that a real thing is happening. A thing is happening, and it is like this other thing that happens in the world when a man runs alone with his shadow.

G   That's true.

H   That ambivalence I think is rather deftly caught by the use of the simile.

G   The intention, the meaning which I as a reader derive from this poem which is given me, is to put a different emphasis upon the implication of ambiguity—not to accept the ironic or deficit implication of ambiguity, but rather to affirm that ambiguity has inside it, beyond the implication of deficit, also an implication of abundance. I think that abundance is part of such public presence as I have as a poet, a portion deeply and unconsciously given of the vocality, the kind of vocal sound which I am able to give to the poems that I read. But this poem is a good and simple example of what I mean by the freedom that arises in the presence of beauty, a more lucid and stylistically mature statement of the same meanings that we were viewing when we looked at the beginning of my very early poem called "A Poem for Statesmen."

H   Two questions occur to me to ask now. One is about what you just said: in what way do you see this poem as more stylistically mature? Another larger question is in regard to this idea of writing the language of your mother, being demonized by the spirit of your mother who writes through you. Would that apply to this poem? It strikes me that this poem is something else, is outside that, and is *about* the relation between you and your mother, rather than being an example of this demonized writing.

G   Let me take up these two questions one at a time, because they are both quite rich and useful to us: I believe the language of this poem is no longer suspended between the language of irony and the language of romantic affirmation, bearing in mind that the idea of romantic affirmation is a positive and undiminished idea in my mind. The early poetry was seeking to repeat the language of affirmation by imitating the traditional cultural languages in which affirmation had last been heard. The sense of the natural speaker and the sense of the man of cultural ambition had not yet been integrated.

Insofar as there is an achievement registered in "The Runner," it is the finding of the actual language of the wise man; that is to say, the man who is fully *made* and in command of his experience. You will observe about this poem a homogeneity of terms and the elucidation of an action. In the earlier poetry, the action was prospective and at best purely rhetorical. In this poem, the language gives access to an action that is simultaneous with speaking. That simultaneity of speaking and praxis or action redeems poetry from the disabilities of rhetoric and tends, to my sensibility, to secure the reality of hope far more firmly than the inherently speculative and culturally divided language of my early writing.

H   But the success of the poem depends on the reader's sense that the poem really has achieved what it says it has achieved.

G   Certainly it depends upon that, and my assessment of that is not an authoritative assessment. Poems are for readers.

Let's turn to the second question which you introduced a moment ago. This word "demonize" is strange, and I'm surprised you haven't been more insistently questioning about its meaning.

Here I am invoking the oldest descriptions I know of the commissioning of the poetic person. Hesiod, for example, first meets his own voice in the persons of a chorus of young women descending toward him from the top of a mountain, at the base of which he was born. This demonization which leads the poet to address the muse in order to have her speak through him can be seen virtually everywhere in the Modern culture. There is no more vivid dramatization of demonization than the rock singer who breathes flame and enacts the ancient and traditional gestures of ecstasy by shaking and otherwise indicating that he is somehow moved by forces more violent than his own individual nature could generate. The traditional conception of poetry implies the replacement of the personal voice by another, impersonal voice, which permits mortal and dying speakers to utter words which are immortal and undying; that is to say, which are unlike themselves. Much of the terror of being a person, which is to say much of the terror of being a poet, for Yeats and the nineteenth-century French poets lies in the incompatibility of the immortal voice and the personal one. The demonic voice is, indeed, the voice not of the self but of that transcendental artifice that I have formally called "personhood."

The culture of representation turns against the culture of ordinary life because of the incompatability of selfhood, on the one hand, which you have described as your principal recognition in the human world, and that other, colder thing which speaks through the self and at the same time consoles the self but which is, at the very least, a bitter problem for the self as well—a problem which, as I say, I do not believe to be the problem merely of people who write poems but a problem of all people aspiring to be persons who have a stake in the continuity of things.

But it is very likely, Mark, that I fail to hear the voice of my mother in myself, and that indeed my poetry does not partake of the deep realm which I aspire to, or does not yet. In *talking about* poetry, one casts ahead of oneself or to one side. It is possible to hope vastly more riches with respect to utterance than one possesses, than one can as yet enact. I trust that you will not take what I say about poetry, when I imagine it in its most successful theoretical case, to be a statement of what I think to be true about my poems themselves. The most beneficial outcome of demonization is, of course, the integration or lostness of the voice of the Other *in* the voice of the self: an intimacy which makes the two voices indistinguishable and mutually sustaining. If I ever wrote a good poem in a successful style, it would be a poem in which the two voices were so fully hospitable to one another, so as it were profoundly and harmlessly in love, that they would be indistinguishable.

I have, in fact, written a poem about a Muse, that is to say, about a teacher:

Pat's Poem

Semper dum vivam tui meminero
    —Erasmus, *De Copia Verborum*

This is a poem for my old nurse Pat—
Who had something wrong with her heart.

                          Pat had
An old mother with a tongue like a cow,
With whom I slept.
And she had a father, out of sight, named John
Who died slowly in a back bedroom
Like an abandoned wagon rotting in
A low wet pasture.

              Pat had a boyfriend
Whose best song was, "The Trail of the Lonesome Pine"
And a brother, Vince, who went to the war
Leaving a chained hound in the barn that howled
Four years straight night and day.

Most things Pat taught me were not true. What she
Did have a knack for,
Like skipping stones far out on the Lagoon,
I never could pick up. I don't know
What became of her . . .

                 Pat, failed nurse
With a too small heart, with all-consuming
Shadowy love I loved whatever
Behind that constant uniform of official
Imposture your freckled body was.

                 First teacher,
Out in Denver or wherever marriage
Or the grave has swarmed over your hiding,
I'll tell the world that I remember
Every nuance of your plain brown hair
In Summer light.

                    Because of you I cannot
Tie good knots,
Because of you, I weep at marching bands
Because of you, I cannot depart
From any shallow friend, tell truth, keep measure
Or make an end . . .

                    So I talk on to you—
And on and on—all through the sleepless
Afternoon, as a child might to a stain
Upon a shade.
When will you come to wake me, Pat. Oh, when?
The long room darkens, and your poem's made.

                 ·   ·   ·

Out of the disturbed house, always below,
Robed as in summer curtains, sheer and white—
The dog's howl stopped, the confounded knot tight—
Comes up the stair dark, silence, and the years.
Semper dum vivam tui meminero.
All my life long I will remember you.

H I think this is widely a favorite among your readers for some obvious reasons, because it places before us a visible human being,
   another person, who is being honored and for whom your love is
   felt through the poem. This is one of your poems about which I
   can feel what I often do feel when I admire a poem, namely, I can
   imagine myself wanting to write that. It's a poem I could aspire, in
   some sense, to have written. That goes with saying that it's a poem
   I understand more readily than other poems of yours.
      You spoke in an earlier conversation about the intention of po-
   etry being the making of persons present to one another. I see this
   poem clearly as achieving a presence for this Pat in the mind of
   the reader. I see that as an ambition fulfilled. As I've said to you,
   however, this conception of demonization is not one I'm comfortable with. It's not a way of thinking natural to me. I would not
   describe "Pat's Poem" as a demonized poem, though it is about a
   teacher in your life. Now I'm asking you: what connections would

you make between the admiration I and others have expressed for this poem and your sense of the value of a poem that is achieved by way of demonization?

G   "Pat's Poem" is about the beginning of a life involuntarily devoted to the making of poems.

There is a paradox about the kind of poetry I have described myself aspiring to; and we are now directly upon the painfulness of that paradox: a poem which achieves what I wish to achieve would put an end to poetic enterprise altogether. My poetry is a peculiar kind of poetry, which seeks in effect to rid itself of its very status as poetry, of its very estate as text—utterance separated from the self; for it is clear that the integrated self does not speak poetry. Poetry is the perpetual evidence, the sadly perpetual evidence, of the incompleteness of the motive which gives rise to it.

H   Poetry is speech by someone who has a problem.

G   Poetry is speech by someone who is in trouble, and poetry takes as its subject matter precisely that trouble with the intention of solving the problem. That is why I talk so much in my poetry about a poetry which extinguishes itself, a poetry which does finally come to an end.

H   As in "The Thrush Relinquished."

G   As in "The Thrush Relinquished," which is the one among my poems which most fully expresses my sense of a good poetic outcome. It is, as would be consistent with what I've just said, a short poem.

H   And it comes out in a picture of the silence of wholeness.

G   Yes. Now, I think "Pat's Poem" is liked precisely because it describes a failure of nurturance, precisely because it gives an account of a relationship which should have, indeed, ended in and given rise to a whole life of silence, but instead gives rise to a whole life of struggle toward speech. Now, I am making an accusation here which I would like to repeat. There is a culture in which poetry is admired *for itself,* and the charms of poetry are regarded as somehow charms which are bound up not with the goals of poetry but with its literary on-going. In this poem, the pain of the on-going of utterance arises from the failure of the nurturance of this nurse, and the speaker is pitched toward poetry: "So I talk on to you— / And on and on—all through the sleepless / Afternoon, as a child might to a stain / Upon a shade"—pitched into the endless effort to heal a distance by utterance which itself endlessly makes more and more distance.

H   But what you're saying does not at all embarrass me about my liking for the poem. It seems to me that you are describing the way in which the poem is about the human condition, in which our desires are frustrated, and I don't think I have to be pushed into apologizing for a liking of literary works that give us images of our frustrated condition, images which also encourage and nourish sympathy for one another. That I see the poem doing; and yet you seem to be worried about the popularity of the poem in that it reflects a corrupt acceptance of frustration.

G   Well, I had hoped to embarrass you. There is about my poetry and about my motive to poetry an ugly seriousness, ugly in that it is not inherently sympathetic to the mere (how terrifying that qualification) facilitation of social relationship. This is a terror that I feel about myself: an inability to allow my work to rest in the space that lies open to us in the world of ordinary gratifications.

H   We are, in this language that we're using now, close to the difference between you and me. In the phrase, "the mere facilitation of social relationships," it is exactly true that your inclination to use the adjective "mere" separates you from me, because it is true of me that I feel there is nothing mere about social relationships, since I see a world in which that is all we have.

G   Let me read you "The Thrush Relinquished":

The Thrush Relinquished

One night there was no moon, and never had been.
In the space where the moon was

                              the weather
Stopped, everything happened for
The first time.

                I cannot imagine space
As it then was, the cradle unrocking
In the tideless air.
The man stopped, the shadow vanished,
There was nothing to read.

In their yellow groves the midnight villas
Went dark, as if the timid sleepers put
Out the fear lights, the dark being no more
"The dark." Patience in me ceased to betray
Itself by tears.

The poet is dead, and from his stare released
The stars weary of dance divest themselves
Of countenance.

                No poetry tonight. Death tonight.
The thrush relinquished, my hand is in the open.
I can see every way.

In the process of this poem, the world that takes its character from
our naming of it is released from the violence of our naming of it,
and tears, which are so pervasively the subject of *The Woman on
the Bridge over the Chicago River*, are finally brought to an end.
They are brought to an end at the point at which the poet dies;
and that sky (which we have seen in the very early poem called
"In My Observatory Withdrawn") becomes something so intimate
that it no longer has the nature of a person other from myself. It
is divested of countenance and loses its traditional mythology of
the dance of the heavens. This is my conception of what occurs
when poetry comes to an end: when the unhealing lesion between

the self and the other has been at last healed and we can declare "no poetry tonight."

The only word for that state of affairs is death, and death announces the relinquishing of the traditional demon of poetry— the thrush—which relinquishing leaves the hand formerly occupied with its servile task of inscription open, and the eye now turned away from the page free to be the beautiful eye of recognition and to be beautiful in the eye of the recognition of another— to see every way, meaning every way it can.

H   My problem with that ending for the poem is that it seems to me the poem two lines earlier has already, with remarkable explicitness, acknowledged that this is only an illusory state: "Death tonight." It is only as a solicitation of oblivion that I can understand the outcome of poetry that you hypothesize in this poem. Perhaps it's not hypothetical. I have thought sometimes reading this poem that this is an account of a moment in your life when you felt that you had reached this outcome.

G   At this point, I believe my poetry is really engaged with your incredulity, and functions for us as an instructive poetry. What I wish not to give up is the stern identification of the end of poetry, not with discourse itself and not with social life as you are urging me to understand it and to respect it, but with something much more terrifying to contemplate, something that has in it the profoundest kind of hope, which I in this poem called by the one name that it knows: death. I have, however, felt in the last month particularly, and I believe I feel today (it being my birthday) much too much in love with death. . . .

But there was something more that you had to say.

H   I can only confess to bewilderment at your attempt to describe what you mean by death in that line. In any case, I am troubled by the account you gave of the meaning of the end of the poem a few minutes ago. I'm attracted by it, but troubled because I'm not convinced by it.

G   Mostly troubled.

H   "I can see every way." Now, you said that that refers to a condition
    in which the mind is not dead. The mind has escaped the need for
    poetry, and the mind now has possibilities open to it that were not
    open before—possibilities of wholeness and, by implication,
    through wholeness of full encounter with another person. That
    sounds to me like a good idea, an attractive idea, but it doesn't
    seem to me as if the other, another person, is anywhere in this
    poem. I have read it as a lonely poem leading toward a kind of
    happy solipsism.

G   I am now insisting, Mark, upon a conception of relationship that
    perhaps because it is indistinguishable from unbornness does not
    involve the interactive distances which are implied by the relation-
    ship between the I and the you. The "mother of beauty," the
    beauty of the mother, is, as Stevens reminded us in an early poem,
    death. Stevens is repeating from Whitman "death's outlet song"—
    the song which extinguishes its status as text by letting, as it were,
    death out into the world. I'm summoning these conceptions of
    death, which are much older, obviously, than the Gospel concep-
    tion of death and the Socratic conception of death—I'm summon-
    ing these traditional implications of death as they have always
    been summoned as a challenge or, even more specifically, as an
    affront to your conceptions of sociability. For I believe that inside
    this sense of death lies the whole capacity for value I myself pos-
    sess.
        We have touched often upon the question of value, and since it
    is, in my view, both the hardest and the most important question
    that we can discuss (I've already said I regard poetry as a human
    value science, having no other weight or justification in the cul-
    ture), what then is the value for humanity that attends a poem?
    The term that in this poem I offer is the term "death," both empty
    and very full, the point at which the other disappears as the self
    disappears. The value of the person arises in the space of that
    disappearance, unqualified by the contingencies of reference, or
    even of hope as it is constrained by possibility.

There is, I think, for you a maniacal quality about this. And when you talk about something being un-understandable, I think you feel you are speaking about something that is wrong.

H I am willing to acknowledge the existence of poems that I don't understand that are doing good things, trying to do good things. However, this does seem to me the trace of your philosophy either going wrong or becoming incomprehensible in a way that would be very dangerous if interpreted wrongly. As I said, I have only taken this in as a reflection of love for death. It seems to me that this conception of the outcome of good art is suicidal. I'm re-minded—maybe this will help me to say what I'm trying to say— I'm reminded of an essay I once read on Shakespeare's *The Tempest* by a man named Harold Goddard. I was enjoying the essay until I found that he judged Prospero's throwing away of his book at the end to be an enactment of Shakespeare's belief that we all must get beyond art. I was very troubled by that, because it didn't sound like Shakespeare to me. It doesn't sound to me like the way we should live. I feel that we live *by* art and *through* art, and that that can only be and will always be an on-going process in *this* world, that it happens for better or worse each day, and that there is not something more to be hoped for.

G When I said at the beginning of this day's conversation that I felt it was necessary to *say more* under the auspices of poetry, I meant precisely that risk of transgression of the canons of ordinary hope, which we are now contemplating. I feel in your outrage at this idea of death—which you call suicidal and which I call actualiz-ing—I feel at the point of this outrage precisely that pressure to-ward risk and the opening up of a throat to let out what finally is an outlet song for death itself, the sort of poetic ambition I am beginning more and more to be possessed by.

H You feel pressed toward that ambition by the outrage that I'm ex-pressing?

G Yes, indeed. Or rather, I become more and more conscious of that ambition. In recent months, I have become increasingly con-cerned with writers whose business it is to utter outrage. I have spent much of the last month or two working through Nietzsche, for example. I must begin to learn more fully what my human voice wishes to say if only I could attend to it, if only my throat were not so constricted. I have to confess to you (in the face of your convincing reservations) that it is in this direction, the enter-ing of the forbidden space of death itself, that I find myself mov-ing. One of the things that we have to be attentive to is whether there is any authorization for this concern in the tradition, or whether this is not what you might rightly speculate upon as a neurotic disposition on my part.

Indeed, the book called *The Woman on the Bridge over the Chi-cago River* seems to me lacking in the credible presence of other people. The poems I value most are the poems which conserve the names and to some extent the words of lost friends, poems such as "The Department."

H Allen, I am puzzled by that because it sounds like what I would have said. Your worry that too many of the poems have failed to give credible pictures of other persons sounds like what Halliday might have written if he were reviewing this book for some peri-odical and praising "The Department" and "Pat's Poem" and criti-cizing as weird and solipsistic some of the other poems. I'm think-ing now of a shorter poem in the volume that I like very much, which I have thought of as one of my special favorites, namely, "The Holdout." It's a poem about a sad little girl troubled by what I know you have called the scarcity of fame, the way in which the presence of other people makes it difficult, if not impossible, for the individual to be special, to be specially recognized. Anyway, my liking for that poem depends on my feeling of the presence of that girl, your daughter, in the poem. I feel there is a picture of her. The poem becomes magical for me through the conjunction of that credible image with the language of her last line in the poem, which doesn't sound like a natural little girl. I know actually you've told me that your daughter really did say that phrase—"I won't come back," she says, "until the eagles shall / Forsake their hill and speech comes to the rook." Now, in the way the poem enables this angry and sad little girl to say those high-style poetic phrases, I feel an achieved magic in which this real person is linked with a kind of grand speech out of the long tradition of grand speech. But as I say, for me the human power of the poem depends on the picture of a feeling person. The point is not that it's not the speaker. It could have been the speaker for me to love the poem. The point is that this is an image of a person in our life, our life as I have perceived it and as I know it. It seems to me that the person who comes out at the end of "The Thrush Relinquished" is not a person who could describe this little girl.

G   Mark, the person whose hopes are uttered at the end of "The Thrush Relinquished" is the person sitting here before you. "The Holdout" is a poem for which I do not have great admiration. Your criticism of my book is a criticism which I feel and which I can acknowledge as credible and just. But in the course of our conversation this afternoon, you have driven me into the corner where I live—death's corner. I have tried to make death's case. I am not sure I have, but the consciousness of my meanings which you have drawn from me is a good gift from you. I take it as your birthday gift.

4. VOICE

H   We've said that today we'll talk about voice. I'll be interested to learn from you what requirements you feel are imposed on the speaking voice by the view of poetry that you have advanced in our conversations so far.

G   I have often spoken to you about the abstract pattern called line. But today we must do the harder thing and think of the line not theoretically as the unmanifest principle of poetic manifestation but as the lineament—the manifestation itself. When one speaks poetry, one takes the unmanifest abstract metrical principle into one's voice and implicates that principle with all the strange and precious constraints that the human image places upon the incarnation of any spirit. I am very interested in the problem of voice, because my own voice has been a troubling feature of my life. Voice is the invisible but truth-bearing portrait of a person, yet I have been always somewhat puzzled by the question, what person is portrayed by the voice which I speak, particularly the voice which I speak when I utter poetry?

H   I've heard you read poetry in public on several occasions. I've thought that there was never a more perfect example of what the word "oracular" means, in reference to the reading of poetry out loud. You read differently from any other poet that I have heard. To be concrete about that, you read more loudly than any poet I have heard, and you read with numerous long pauses between individual words. You read often with your eyes on the ceiling rather than on the audience. These facts and others do tend to give a sense that the voice we're hearing is not yours; it's certainly not your social voice.

G I'm very conscious of these characteristics. The idea of an oracular source, which your experience of my reading out poems brings to mind, seems consistent with the general description I've given of poetic speaking altogether; for the oracular speaker speaks not his own words but the words of the god which move demonically through his lips and use him (and often use him up) in the process of becoming manifest to a world to which that spirit could not be manifest without that voice.

H You have used the word "god" and the word "spirit." In an earlier conversation, you spoke of your relation with your mother and your belief that the work of your poetry is to speak the words of your mother. I expressed bafflement at that idea. I was inclined to understand that idea as your desire to speak *for* your mother, in the more common sense; that is, to speak words that your mother would say if she could or words that your mother would like to have spoken. That is not the conception you have in mind. You have in mind a more, in my terms, magical conception of direct speech through your lips by someone else.

G Yes. I have a sense not of being a poet who has found his voice, but rather a sense of being a person whom a poetic voice has found. Or in another, more biographical way of speaking, my development seems an effort to find in me the speech appropriate to the voice with which I have been gifted by powers that are not entirely the same as my own will.

H So then, Allen, when you read aloud, do you truly have a sense that that voice is speaking through you, or do you have a sense that you are trying to live up to the demands of that voice? That is, are you conscious of an effort to approximate what you produce to an imaginary voice you hear in your head? Or is it, in fact, the more involuntary and demonized experience that your theory proposes?

G In the process of composition, I seem to be seeking the words which would make plain the implications of the voice in which I *must* inevitably speak my poems. I am, however, profoundly uncertain about the relationship between my voice as a poet and my social voice. The voice that I utter as a reader of poetry frightens me, because it reminds me that I do not know what the appropriateness of these tonalities might be to this particular audience or to any audience.

In a general way, poetry is a picture of speech, not speech itself, and the speech which a poem depicts need not always be social speech. I think, for example, that the picture of speaking that we have in Whitman's poetry is really the picture not of vocalized utterance but of sub-vocal utterance, an utterance which implies a relationship to its audience that is more intimate than a social relationship; so that when Whitman says "what I assume, you shall assume," he really means that "I am facilitating your hearing of a voice that is always going on within us as a communal immanence, a voice that not only need not but cannot be mediated across the spaces which lie between social persons." By contrast, a voice such as I am compelled to employ seems to imply the mediation by me of a transcendental presence which is referenced to us as a whole, but not precisely to us as social persons.

The third possibility is the possibility that I think you and many of your generation are commissioned to practice: the possibility that poetry can be uttered in a social tone and can be devised in the language, or some clear function of the language, of persons in social situations.

H   Yes. My practice and my ambitions are drastically different from yours in this way. When I write and when I read aloud, I am trying to be, and really yearning to be, explicitly conscious of the social reality and the particular social identities of my listeners. And as I think I said in an earlier conversation, I aspire to bring into conjunction myself as a poet and myself as a social person. I want to retain what I call powers of poetry, while approaching sociability, through poetry, with those people. Let me give one concrete illustration of what I mean: When I read in Cambridge at the Blacksmith House (as I have done once, but as I imagine doing again), I am conscious that many of the people in that room are a particular kind of person. They are upper-middle-class, educated, North-eastern types, like you and me, and I suspect that, with very few exceptions, the people in that room are poets, who would like to be more famous. Some of them are closet poets; others are poets who have published books with small or large presses. Anyway, I would like to write poems and speak aloud poems that explicitly acknowledge the relations implied by those aspirations shared by them and me, rather than pretending that the social occasion of my appearing before them, or for that matter, one of them appearing before an audience that includes me, is somehow more time-less, more unreferenced to Cambridge, Massachusetts, in 1981.

G   Your effort then, when you put your poems in voice before an audience, is to specify the concrete social reality of that audience, and to make it plain and a conscious possession of that audience, and perhaps also to criticize it.

H   Yes, those are some of my intentions. I don't want to say that those are my only intentions, because I know that I want to write poems that are about my private experience, my internal life; but I want to deliver accounts of that experience in ways that acknowledge my reality as a social person and my awareness that I am writing to and being listened to by certain kinds of people, with whom I have other kinds of relationships.

G   I think that your way of interpreting poetic voice and my way represent different conceptions of what constitutes the nature of persons in relationships, and where the bounds and validities that secure those relationships derive from. There are, in the English poetic tradition, really two styles of poetic production which bear upon this matter of voice. There is, first of all, a demonic-mythographic tradition, represented monumentally by Milton, which hypothesizes that the humanity of persons is secured only by reference to a transcendental source, which it is the business of the poet to mediate. Such poets receive a voice not initially in human scale, the nature of which is very fully accorded with its source, the same as the source of reality itself. The gift of that voice to the community is a gift in the region of authenticity. That voice makes accessible to the community its own beauty in the scale of that beauty as God sees it. Such a voice secures the proper wealth of humanity from a space outside of the human world.

The other tradition in English—of which the great seventeenth-century example is George Herbert; a Romantic example, Coleridge, in his conversation poems; and perhaps the modern example is Stevens—might be called a eucharistic-mimetic tradition, in which the voice is distinctly gathered from the human scale of language and takes pride in its capacity to give an account of itself in the scale of social humanity. It is a voice driven back upon the actualities of the human world and deriving its pride from its capacity to give a veracious account of mortality, and to give that account, as it were, back to the community or even, if there is a god, back to the god.

You and I come together with these two traditions of diverse authority behind us. Both are legitimate.

H   I'm troubled by the word "authenticity" in your usage. I'm familiar with the adjective "authentic" as one that people use in a vague way interchangeably with words like "real," "genuine," and even "sincere." When I think of authenticity in human relations, I want to appropriate that word for my own meanings involving social reality. When you use the word "authenticity," Allen, or another word like "validity," which I've also heard you use often, it has an opaque quality to me. I feel unable to fill that word with meaning. I don't know what it is for the human community to gain authenticity in the sight of God.

G   We must examine here, Mark (leaving God to one side, for God is not the issue between us), what the sufficient conditions are of the human relationships which we both aspire to enter into and, as poets, to facilitate. The demonic-mythographic tradition, to which I have assigned myself as a member for the purposes of providing a history to this conversation, supposes that the "I" and the "you" in the mortal transaction cannot, merely as a set of two, obtain the relationship which both desire. I think that poetry attests, wherever it is found, to the disruption of the relationship of the "I" and the "you" along the merely mortal and merely time-bound path. You yourself speak to your audiences not in ordinary language but in poetry, and I would like to account in my terms for the reason why you appear *as a poet*.

A principle which governs *my* practice is that the "I" and the "you" do not have access to each other, because of the difference between persons and because of the re-statement of that difference by death, and that there is required something which has a status that we might call intersubjective, or we might call collective, or divine, or in the most attenuated case, literary. In other words, the "I" and the "you" need a "common place," upon which both can stand, different from the place of the mortal world. To obtain that common place, both you and I speak to others in poetry.

The specific mark which differentiates both your poetic utterance and mine from our ordinary language is that abstract principle we call line—for we both write in lines. It is upon that abstract principle as a common place that we summon those who hear us to join us in discourse. In fact, poetry is merely the provision of the sufficient conditions for an "I" and a "you" to come together in the common space provided by our art, and be with one another in discourse. I therefore think that though such notions as authenticity are, by their overuse and their casual use, discredited, nonetheless, it is somewhat disingenuous of you to suppose that when speaking to persons in public by means of poetry you are merely addressing them as social persons. If you were, there would be no need for the art that you practice, nor would there be any reason for the specific structures with which you invest your language when you make the poetry that you speak.

H   Yes, that is true; I accept that. I am aware that if I take on the role of speaking as a poet on a platform in front of other people, I am speaking across a gap, a gap that I have chosen. But I persist in thinking of this process, this artificial construction of a kind of relationship, which I admit is not a social relationship such as might go on in the Coffee Connection in Harvard Square—that I use this construction as a way of saying things that need to get said to facilitate healthier social relations between people, but which I am not able to bring out in the Coffee Connection, for various reasons: partly because it is so noisy there—there are competing voices—but more deeply because of embarrassments which clog the voice in social relations, because social relations are corrupted by competing versions of the self that we try to lay upon other people's perceptions.

G Yes. You attest, it seems to me, very eloquently to much that we have agreed to be true about the function of poetic structure, insofar as by closure it keeps out noise, and insofar as it becomes an occasion for seriousness in proportion as its structures are alien to ordinary life. At the same time, it strikes me, you have not as yet accounted for the motive of speaking in verse; and I think that this requires some further exploration of the difference between the voice in poetry and the voice in ordinary life, even though it is part of your ambition to make these two voices accord.

Let me try another way of approaching this matter: When poets, across time, speak of the language of their art, they do not speak of it as the language of an individual, what we might call, technically, an idiolect, the language of a separated particle of humanity. Rather, they speak of it as a dialect, or the language of a class: W. C. Williams speaks not his own speech but "the American idiom"; Wordsworth aspires to speak in the language of the middle and the lower classes, as we learn from his "Preface"; Yeats undertook to speak in the language of the archetypes—the dead, the heroes on the wind, the historical aristocracy, both divine and human; Shakespeare spoke in the language of his social betters, the language of the aristocracy of his time. Each poet chooses not the language of an individual but the language of a class—for reasons. Among these reasons are that the language of an individual has about it the mortality of an individual and the limited horizon of reference of an individual; whereas the language of a class has the immortality of a community and the extended horizon of reference of a community, and also, what is even more important, inside it the sanctions and authenticity of a community derived from the same sources that make the world possible, for it is in a community that reality, as a whole, is produced—the up and the down as well as the local arrangements by which persons govern their lives. Now, the dialect which you speak (for example, in "Little Star") seems to me a deliberately chosen dialect, as the dialect that I speak is a deliberately chosen dialect. That they are two different kinds of speech does not make each of them less the speech of a class.

H I would have thought that it was impossible not to speak in the speech of a class. I would have thought that that was more a given than a deliberate choice.

G It is certainly true that we do not make our language; therefore we are all demonized by language. Language, whether it is encoded in our genetic substance or whether it is acquired through acculturation, comes to us from outside us. Consequently, there is no individually constructed, voluntarily produced speaking. This, I think, is one of the perennial meanings which is expressed when the poet is represented as receiving his speech from outside himself. Nonetheless, we distinguish between language and talk—*langue* and *parole*, in the terminology of Saussure. The poet, I believe, is the man who speaks from consciousness that there is a difference between the language of the individual and the language of the collectivity. It is his business to find the point of intersection, and in effect, to model it paradigmatically. That is what I think is meant when we speak of poetic languages.

Now, a way of approaching this that will help us enter into both your work and mine, and re-express both our senses of voice, is the rather simple and obvious fact that much poetry seems to be language of one kind about language of another kind. I have often spoken to you about such poems as Wordsworth's "Solitary Reaper," where the poet represents himself as a mortal wanderer who hears someone else singing, and singing in a way which is unintelligible to him, and yet heartening, magnanimous, healing, and wise. Wordsworth's wanderer hears a solitary girl singing in a language which he does not understand and which, because he does not understand it, is not intercepted by his mortal bewilderment. It passes from the world external to himself to the world internal to himself in such a way as to make him more than the unconscious social man which he was before. What I am trying to say is that almost all poetry has inside it the authentic language which it models itself upon. Your poetry, for example, often makes reference to rock music, and that rock music, one of the most impersonal languages ever devised, has the status of the authenticity which your poetry is devised to mediate.

Authenticity means: proceeding from the reputed source. What is authentic is what proceeds from the source claimed for it, as an authentic painting proceeded from the hand which is claimed to have signed it. Authentic speech is speech that proceeds from the reputed source, and the reputed source of speech is always *general humanity;* and the reputed source of general humanity, upon which this authenticity is based, is not the individual—whether we consider language or the physical reality of the body or the vast artifact of the social world, Nature, or whatever.

H I'm confused now about the relation between that model of what a poet does and the model you've given of yourself speaking for your mother. What collectivity do you speak for, or do you want to speak for? You have been conscious in your poetry of being a Jewish poet, yet you don't seem to be centering your work around that identity—I don't feel that your poetry is an attempt to speak for all Jews, the collectivity of Jews. Nor do you seem to be centrally concerned with America, American idiom and American identity. So the question is: what collectivity do you want to represent?

G It is true that when I was young (and we've seen some of those poems) I thought that the problem might well be solved by associating myself with the Jewish source; but I find, for many reasons, that that is impossible. The Moderns, my masters, did all identify the collectivity which authenticated them and on behalf of which they spoke, enabled by and enabling the community in history: Yeats, his Ireland; Eliot, his strange, half-imagined England; William Carlos Williams, his America, which gives him the American idiom that he claims as his voice; Hart Crane, the spiritual America imagined by Whitman; and so on. The task I set myself in my most recent poetry is, indeed, somehow to make contact with my people, and to ask them the name by which they name themselves. When I explore the voice not entirely my own with which I speak poetry, and call it my mother's voice, and not *like* my mother's voice, I undertake to explore the affinities of my nature. From the mother comes the body. In my poetry, persons are related to the earth and to the stars as well as to the social constructions that we call other persons. My effort is to journey back into and through my mother, and through her into and through all the mothers until I arrive at the great mother who is identical with the beginning and the end of all things. That I do not do so as a journey toward father calls attention to the postponed business of my mind.

H   I don't see the connection between speaking for a collectivity, or the desire to find a collectivity to speak for, and this, it seems to me, more isolated, more individual desire to speak the language of your mother.

G   It is because my mother is the remnant, the last person who, if she would speak, could know the name of that people whom I over and over again in poetry invite to name themselves, so that I will know my own name.

H   Allen, those are strange ideas to me. They do seem, in some way, to jibe with the strange way that you speak poems in public. I see you, when you give a poetry reading, as a person soliciting or seeking with great effort a voice that is meant to come from somewhere else. I know that you are often, indeed habitually, disappointed in the way other poets speak their poems in public. This is probably centrally because you feel they are not seeking that other voice, that higher voice, in an energetic enough way.

G   My common response to the readings I attend can be summarized in the question, Why do not these speakers, since they have taken

upon themselves the privilege of poetry, speak in such a way as to
disclose more of their humanity, not merely more of their pain and
pleasure, though they speak with very little conviction of that, but
also more of the antiquity, indeed, the profundity, of their minds
and art? I feel that in poetry today there has arisen a criterion,
even among the reputed wild men of civilization, of gentility; and
I detest that gentility.

H What are the physical, vocal reflections of that gentility?

G I feel it as a sense of internalized constraint. Gentility manifests
itself as a set of rules defining what can and what cannot be said;
and I believe these rules are internalized by the poets of our generation. They speak neither very loud nor very soft, nor very passionately nor with great sadness. This gentility has overtaken in
particular the young. Though I do not entirely wish to account for
it, I would like to tell you what I am listening for.

So far, I have proposed that it is among the obligations and
privileges of the poetic speaker to speak the words which avow his
affiliation not merely to the mortal community but to the community of the dead, and beyond the dead, to the source of all
persons. I hear nothing of that antiquity, which even you cannot
deny pertains to every moment of both physical and cultural life.

At the same time, and this is another matter, I feel that the
subjects of poetry have not changed with sufficient ingenuity and
courage in accord with our changing sense of what constitutes
truth about the social world. Historically, political enfranchisement proceeds more rapidly than mimetic enfranchisement. I
mean that people are able to get the vote in a state long before
they are privileged to become the subject matter of the high art of
that culture. In the history of the last two hundred years, the In-
dustrial Revolution and the progressive enfranchisement of the
members of the political community have produced the mimetic
eligibility of many classes of persons previously not admitted to the
privileges of citizenship; and yet our art has been barbarically slow
to confer what I believe to be the essential dignity of representation upon these persons.

H   And women constitute one of the largest examples of such a class.

G   Yes. In the scholarly community, we find in the last fifteen years a
    brilliant flowering of theory with respect to the predicament of
    women historically and in our culture. But our poetry *labors* to
    find not only the voice of the woman but the image of the woman
    freed from the disabling servitude of her objecthood, a case of
    which we have obliquely viewed in that "fair creature of an hour"
    in the sonnet by Keats.

H   Allen, I imagine poets reading these exchanges between us and
    feeling challenged, perhaps, by your criticism of the constricted
    way you hear people delivering poems.

G   It is not a question of loud or soft, oracular or social ways of speak-
    ing. Poets these days do not find poems the occasion for the am-
    plification of consciousness with respect to language. They speak
    from a more restricted aspect of their being when they speak their
    poems than they do when they speak in social situations.

H   So it is not that you can be accused of wanting all poets to sound
    like Allen Grossman, but it is that you feel poets are concealing
    aspects of their reality in the limited way they speak out loud.

G   I do think that. When a poet speaks his poem, he is, in fact, its
    reader; for the speaking of poetry constitutes merely one case of
    the reading of it, and our poets are bad or limited readers of their
    own poems. To speak a poem is to manifest the state of humanity
    which that poem implies, and the disposition to speak poems in
    dream-burdened, narcissistic, and in fact, in every way *partial*
    voices really constitutes a judgment on the possibility of any read-
    ing, just at the point where reading should be most manifestly
    evidence of the vitality of the poetic culture.

H   Now, I'm in some sympathy with you on this point in that I want
    the reading of poems to be more intense than it usually is. My
    description of a successful reading might be different from yours,

but I accept your judgment that many poets read in a constricted way. However, let me say, imagining the defense that might be made by poets who read in such a way, that I think there's a notion of allowing the poem to speak for itself, a notion of choosing not to preempt the poem by a dramatic portrayal of the speaker speaking, which might fail to do justice to the complexity of language.

G When a poem is produced for the purpose of effecting a relationship between the poet and other members of his social community, then indeed anxiety about the poet's private appropriation of the poem is justified; but from my point of view, all poems that are meritorious are inherently anonymous. The poet is the servant of the voice that speaks through him. I have a feeling that the poetic readers who offer us what I think is improperly called *their* poems are afraid that, if they were to allow the poem to utter itself, it would shatter their countenance altogether. It would shatter their countenance because they have not made peace with the unconscious processes which are invoked when poetry is entered into. They have not constructed a principle of access toward the powers of the medium which they practice. Their countenance would be shattered; and for that reason, the poem, in effect, remains unuttered. The solution to this problem is a more extensive understanding of the nature of the poetic enterprise altogether. Only the unexperienced magician is destroyed by the demons he summons. He is destroyed by them because he has not learned how to manage them, and he cannot make their powers useful, either for himself or for the world.

H There's a paradox in your description of successful poems being, in a sense, anonymous, because at least on a superficial level, someone hearing Allen Grossman read is more conscious that it is Allen Grossman and no one else than would be the case with many other poets around, who share a kind of level intonation and a kind of neutral and distanced tone, which might have been the tone one would have identified as most anonymous.

G   It is because they make a mistake about who is speaking when the poem is spoken.

But I am interested in the relation between the question of who speaks in poems and the question, what is spoken about, because in the same way that I have solicited a more extensive sense of the nature of the poetic voice, so also I have, in a sense, solicited a more extensive subject matter for poetic speaking. In fact, I have suggested that poetry has not responded to the experience of persons claiming privileges of representation in the world in which we are living. I was, of course, brought up in a world in which it was clear that, as I've said before, there was vastly more experience than could be taken into account, and I have suggested that good poetry, *original* poetry today, would be devised in such a manner as to take into account larger and larger aspects of the experience which is thrust upon us.

H   I remember your speaking about Whitman's poem "The City Dead-House" in class as an example of a poem achieving that inclusion of new human subject matter within the precincts of poetry, that being a poem in which Whitman confronts and attempts to honor the body of a dead prostitute.

G   The topics of poetry expand and contract across time. Horace knew more subject matters for poetry than did his predecessors. Donne also, in his time, extended the subject matters of poetry. In the eighteenth century, they contracted once again, to expand in the Romantic period, and to contract again in the Victorian. I believe that at the present moment we are burdened with a weighty obligation to extend the subject matters of poetry toward history and toward society as never before. The likelihood is that the central determinants of our experience—nuclearism, for example; revolution, for example—are such as to be disharmonious with the very grids and matrices by which poetry admits experience into manifestation. This lays upon us, as I have said, a burden which cannot be avoided. It is a part of the problem of voice and the searching of voice.

H   You feel that in the nuclear age it is more urgently necessary than ever before to bring more aspects of our human reality into lasting representation, so that they can gain the dignity of such representation. Among your new poems that I have seen, the clearest example of that, I think, is your poem "A Little Sleep," which involves an insistently detailed, intimate description of a man in relation to his own body and his own sexuality.

G   In "A Little Sleep," in the poem called "Bow Spirit," in the poem called "Of the Great House," in the poem called "The Surgical Ward," and other poems which will form part of my next book, I have tried to press the horizons of my discourse back until they include at least something like my whole body, since if I cannot assign the dignity of representation to the body which is mine, I am very unlikely to be able to assign it to the body or soul of another.

  It is very important to note that this is the area of poetic theory which compels us to see poetry and politics as the same subject, for the privilege of representation which poetry confers is almost inextricable from social privilege altogether. If we knew ourselves as dignified in a way as profound as my sense of voice, in my mind, implies, then I think we would be more insistent about the cleansing of our world. We would be more conscious of the inappropriateness of our impending destruction.

H   We would refuse to be taxed by people who want to make nuclear weapons.

G   Indeed, and in addition, we would be better able to perceive the oppression which we inflict upon others. We would have a self-interest other than a material self-interest. We would understand security in a way which distinguishes it from exploitation. The man who does not understand his security as a function of the image of his honor is a man who seeks for his selfhood violently in the bodies and worlds of others. Poetry is not at the center of any political world; but the capacity of the poet to honor the person is the measure of the capacity of the culture to do that honor.

H   I think now of Adrienne Rich as a contemporary example of a poet straining to honor persons whom she feels have never been honored in their reality, in their true identities, by the literary tradition.

G   Yes. Adrienne Rich strikes me as a noble example of a person of my generation who has perceived this truth. The severity and the success of her effort to confer the privileges inherent in the art which she practices upon the world of persons with whom she has discovered her fellowship is, in my mind, admirable and exemplary. Let's read a poem by Adrienne Rich, "To a Poet":

To a Poet

Ice splits   under the metal
shovel   another day
hazed light off fogged panes
cruelty of winter   landlocked   your life
wrapped round you   in your twenties
an old bathrobe   dragged down
with milkstains   tearstains   dust

Scraping eggcrust from the child's
dried dish   skimming the skin
from cooled milk   wringing diapers
Language floats at the vanishing-point
incarnate   breathes the fluorescent bulb
primary   states the scarred grain of the floor
and on the ceiling in torn plaster laughs   *imago*

   and I have fears that you will cease to be
   before your pen has glean'd your teeming brain

for you are not a suicide
but no-one calls this murder
Small mouths, needy, suck you: *This is love*

I write this   not for you
who fight to write your own
words   fighting up the falls
but for another woman   dumb
with loneliness   dust   seeping plastic bags
with children   in a house
where language floats and spins
abortion   in
the bowl

1974

H   This poem from her most recent volume is addressed to a young
woman who is a poet but whose condition as a mother of small
children tends to prevent her from creating her art, uttering the
language that you would say could give her a fuller presence in the
world. She is a person cut off by her socialization, in Rich's view,
from full personhood. Her social role encloses her like the stained
bathrobe, and Rich writes to her, honoring her struggle to preserve
the true self inside that stained bathrobe who will be able to write
poems. Rich acknowledges the existence of a silent woman, a representative silent woman, other than the poet Rich is addressing
here, who cannot write, who is fully cut off by her socialization
from self-expression; and Rich says that although she addresses the
poem to this young woman whom she knows, who does write, still
the poem is dedicated to this other, silent woman, who is as yet
unreachable.

G   Yes. Adrienne Rich perceives that poetic line underlies human
lineament, and lineament is the mark of a countenance, and a
countenance is the manifest presence of the person. Adrienne
Rich takes the lines from Keats, which we have studied, and makes
them transitive. Keats' poem was reflexive: "When I have fears
that *I* may cease to be." Rich's poem is transitive: "When I have
fears that *you* may cease to be." This I believe to be an administra-
tion of the powers of poetry on behalf of another that is fully con-

scious of the predicament of the person. This is a poetry which is conscious of, first of all, the enormous significance of the manifestation which poetic procedures make possible, and secondly, of the enormously exigent moment in history in which those powers now must be practiced.

H   By quoting and changing those two lines from Keats, Rich shows that, as a radical feminist, she knows it is not possible to forget, totally turn away from and obliterate, the achievement of the poetic tradition which she sees as essentially a male tradition. She struggles to take from that tradition what can be used for the purpose of new representation of people.

G   As Keats took Shakespeare as his access to authenticity, Rich takes Keats. Keats changed Shakespeare, undertaking in the sonnet the portrait of the self, and Rich takes the powers of both Keats and Shakespeare and attempts to confer upon another, under the auspices of those powers, the image-making privileges of the tradition. In doing so, she expands voice's subject matter by criticizing social languages, placing poetic utterance adjacent to utterances of other sorts, and indeed, naming the unconscious parts of our social world: the abortion of that universe which has not been permitted to be born as a consequence of the inherent gentility, that is to say, the tyrannic limitations of the poetic tradition.

H   This poem by Adrienne Rich is not a poem that I love. I have come to value it more as a result of talking about it with you. It is a poem that I honor in its intentions: it seems to me an ethically admirable poem and one achieved with unmistakable skill. Nevertheless, I feel it is under strain—in the attempt to speak for an entire class of persons. In its effort to be a consciously political poem, I feel there is something pushing it away from the satisfactions that I have found in poems that I have loved.

G   Voice is a manifestation of the nature of the human world in terms of what a man or woman *can* say. Perhaps what can be said, and what of necessity is seen to be, are not in harmony. When I spoke a moment ago about my imagination of the countenance being shattered by the burden of manifesting what was inconsistent with its nature, I was revealing a nightmare to which I am subject. Is it possible that, when the demon of the world truly speaks through the voice of any person, that voice will become, first unintelligible, and then too loud or too soft or too subtle to be acquired by any human ear? It is the great virtue and goodness in poetry that it is the point at which the world not human, underlying the human world, is manifested in human form. It is the terror inside poetry that the human form may not be consistent with the most urgent facts of human circumstance.

H   The image of the shattered face that you cited as your central nightmare is, indeed, a frightening image. Do you see that shattering of the face, due to the effort to say too much, as having been the fate of certain poets?

G   We see it, of course, most catastrophically in the suicidal poet; but more explicitly, we see it in what we call the obscure poet. The young Yeats, who grew close to the unconscious, prayed that he not learn a tongue men do not know. Hart Crane is our native example of a man who spoke not as the viewer and interpreter of a central truth more than human, but as its attempted utterer himself. Wherever we find the potent obscurity which produces poetry that can, in some sense, not be spoken at all—and there is a large class of such poems—then indeed we encounter a version of that shattered or exploded countenance. The ugliness of those who have looked upon reality—the ugliness of Socrates, the torn eyes of Oedipus—are other images of this.

   The effort to obtain an intelligible account of central reality is the effort that informs my dreams for poetry. I aspire not to be an obscure writer, nor to be, as it were, the blinded son, but in fact, to find some congruence between the profoundest implications of voice, on the one hand, and mortal clarity, on the other. Often the truth, when looked upon directly, has silenced the singer, has blinded the eye, has shattered the countenance. The highest form which poetic ambition, in my mind, can take is to join together oracular profundity with the whole, intact, harmonious, and socially-addressed countenance. That is to say, to be a clear announcer to the long dim human avenue of precisely such momentous truths as pertain to our safety. These truths will be in the form of a reality taken and conferred.

5. THE TEACHING OF THE SELF

G   Do you think, Mark, these eclogues which we are having on very cold winter days would have been substantially different if they had been held in August?

H   If this were August, I'd be thinking more about playing tennis. In August I might be more apt to think that you were being unnecessarily lugubrious in your view of life and the work that needs to be done by art.

G   I'm glad you got around to saying that. I do think that these conversations are different from any essay that either I or you might write. There is a substantial truth in discussing the business of poetry in a form so intimate to poetry as conversation, since poetry is a particular kind of discourse, referenced like conversation to the situation in a world of a speaker. Poetry has about it the contingency, the inherent qualification which arises when we view speech as a function of a concrete situation in being. There is an inherent skepticism in poetic discourse which we enter into and affirm when we try to bring poetry to mind in conversations which exact of us that we say what we can say, rather than what we *should* say.

H   You remind me of the idea that every lyrical poem is, in a sense, a dramatic monologue, but I seem to recall you telling me that you didn't think that was a very useful idea in the criticism of poetry.

G   I now think your observation more useful than I thought it to be at the time.

H   At last I've wrung a concession from you!

G   I think, in fact, that the importance of a real historical self which sponsors the poem is more vivid to me and more compelling than it was when I first met you.

H   Does that mean that now you are more aware of yourself than you were in earlier years as a person in transit from one place to another, one way of seeing to another?

G   That's certainly the case. I am more aware of myself as a poet in the process of growth, and I am more aware of poetry as a kind of truth that is immediately obligated to the historical and psychological circumstances of a speaker. I now think that the particular kind of truth conveyed in lyric poetry is a function of the separated individual who undertakes, by means of this art, to speak with the utmost seriousness about the totality of what he experiences.

H   And to escape ultimately from that separated condition.

G   To *enter into it* would seem to me a better way of describing the task. The new poems which I am now writing are best understood as speculative integrations of the totality of my experience—a whole world—so far as my consciousness can include it.

H   Now, in your present historical circumstances, you are a professor. So it would seem to be implied from what you say about your intention of becoming conscious of your historical reality, your biographical reality in your poems, that your poems should reflect some of your ideas about teaching.

G   Not only my ideas about teaching, but something of the history of the motive to teach that lies behind my life as a teacher. I see in looking at my new poems that my first impulse to teach was the powerful desire to instruct my mother.

H   What did you want to teach her?

G   I speak of her in "Bow Spirit" as unteachable. I address her, "unteachable Beatrice." What I wished to teach her was, of course, to acknowledge me, to construct that picture of myself which I required in order to be a person. I believe the distinction between the self and the person, which we came upon early in our discussions, arises in my personal history as a distinction between a disintegrating and unacknowledged child who does not feel secure in the eye of his mother and that value-bearing person which I aspire to be and which I aspire to make others to be, the valued person that a child becomes when he is known by the first teacher of us all, the mother, in whose eyes we *are*, if we ever can be.

H   Now what you're saying begins to sound like a struggle I'm familiar with, the typical struggle of a child with his or her parents. Yet the metaphor (what I would call a metaphor) of teaching that you select to describe this struggle does not seem like a metaphor I would have chosen. Conventionally, to say that one teaches means that one already has something thoroughly understood, thoroughly learned, and then conveys it to the other.

G   There are teachers whose business it is to transmit the instruction which they have received from their master; but I am another kind of teacher: the kind who has had no master, the kind of lover who has had no lover—indeed, in a strange sense, the kind of poet who has had no intuitive predecessors. The strangeness about my motive to teaching lies in its effort to do for others what I cannot remember having been done for myself. That accounts both for the somewhat dark passion that colors my presentation to students and also the sense of extreme urgency which characterizes my manner of addressing them.

   In my poetry there is an endless effort to instruct the mother to speak the words that she should have spoken to me in order to raise me from a self-indistinguishable being into the bright circle and first light of acknowledgment. The poet in what is called the high style is characteristically searching for a proper teacher who will give him the world—he is searching either for a mother who will give him his personhood or for a language which will persuade her to do so.

H   I wonder to what extent this demand upon the mother is a matter of the individual identity of your mother and the special nature of your relationship with her, or to what extent you regard this as archetypal in the relation between mother and son.

G   I feel that it is a general archetype for persons of my generation. It is *our* peculiarity that we have exhausted much of our motive to art in the effort to re-obtain fundamental ontological confidence more primary than anything sought by the writers who preceded us. It is a peculiar characteristic of the region of Postmodernism that the world seemed to have to be reconstructed as if from the beginning. That is why men and women of my generation are given to theory. Theory is the deep dream that precedes the description of a reality, the preconditions of which it constructs. There is, in other words, a primitivity that underlies the poetic motive of many writers in this age of theory.

H   Well, we talked before about Postmodern poetry, with Theodore Roethke as one example, and we spoke of the need to find some minimal irreducible ground for identity in a world where identity seemed thoroughly threatened at every level. As I try to understand your sense of your family's relationships, in fact, your family's failures in regard to your nurturance as an instance of and also a metaphor for more general and archetypal problems, I wonder— one thing I wonder is why this demand is addressed to your mother and not to your father.

G   This is something I do not myself understand. The patriarchal gift and the matriarchal deficit are a region of gift and deficit that I am only now bringing to mind. At the beginning of my book called *The Woman on the Bridge over the Chicago River*, there are two poems: one, referenced to my father Louis, and the other to my

mother Beatrice. The poem about my father is, in effect, a pro-
thalamion; that is to say, a poem which announces my marriage to
my father, who is called "Father Dust." In bringing to mind my
mortality, I have grown closer in imagination to my father, who is
still alive though he has lost all memory, and I grow somewhat
more free in relationship to my mother. I believe that when I become as full a poet as I can become I shall be absolved from discourse about mother and father, having written my book of mother
and father and therefore be free in the truth which arises for any
man when he has understood this aspect of his history.

My mother is associated in my mind with my discourse, and my
father with the fatality of my body. This is the reverse of the traditional association.

H I was just thinking of a cliché about parental roles which I've heard
many times and which I feel has some kernel of truth in it when I
look at my own family experience and the experiences of my
friends. The cliché is that one's mother loves one for the person
that one is, but one's father only loves one for what one can do. It
would be an injustice to my own father to say that I felt that was
entirely true in my upbringing, yet I feel there is some truth in it,
and I feel, as you say, the reverse of what you recall in your sense
of your relations with mother and father. My use of language to
define myself and to distinguish myself as an important original
person was something I felt essentially to be learned from my father and to be recognized by and rewarded by my father.

G Yes, in the "normal" state of affairs, anyway since the Renaissance,
one leaves the mother tongue, which is referenced to the earth
and which does not require to be learned, and makes one's way
through education toward the father tongue. One goes in brick, as
Rome did, and comes out marble, the finished and artificial thing.
My experience has been the reverse of that, or has left the process
incomplete. The tongue that I speak as a poet is the mother
tongue searching for the cultural significance acquired when one
enters into the larger civilization normally identified with the father. But since I received the culture in distorted forms from my

mother, and not from my father whose relationship to me was wordless and incomplete, my poetry is in many ways an unconscious seeking its structure, rather than a structured mind seeking access to its unconscious. That is why some of my poetry borders on what has been called surreal, as in the "Villa Malcontenta," for example.

H   That is one of the poems in your last book that seems most difficult to me and, I think, to most readers. I hope that one thing we can talk about today is the difficulty of poems and the kinds of value that can be derived from poems that are or are not quickly accessible to a reader.

G   The unconscious has, until it has found its cultural significance, no countenance. That enormous personal need which I have expressed as a cultural need in our previous conversations, arises in me from the passionate impulse both to acquire a countenance for myself, and for others to confer a countenance. The "Villa Malcontenta" is about the grieving mother so preoccupied with her own mysterious wound that she cannot look with the creational grace, which mother must practice toward her children, upon the many deformed beings of her great house. The effort of my poetry is to find a countenance for the formless and unmanifest unconscious being who has a destiny in countenance and must write that destiny, for a destiny is just the one story that makes sense of a self. Difficulty in my poetry is like that broken countenance that has so much to say about a reality so profoundly complex, energetic, and troubling that the face is deformed and grows unrecognizable as a human face.

H   And yet the energy in your poetry, you're saying, presses toward the recognizability of a face—the creation of personhood that will be, once it is achieved, understandable to others.

G   The origin of difficulty in poetry lies very largely in the problem of perceiving a self and a world which has not yet become an interpreter of itself. The difficult poem delegates some part of its construction to the reader as the interpreter. The function of difficult poems is to exact of the reader that severe and intelligent activity which is involved in the construction of the meaning of things. The mechanical character of many difficult poems arises from the fact that they require of the reader the re-construction of a world that is already eccentrically devised to be discovered in its structure by the poet, who has devoted himself to mystic or other extraneous ideologies. The merit, if there is any, in the kind of difficult poem that I have written is that it requires of the reader that he or she engage with the poet in precisely that cultural activity that is involved in the acknowledgment of a person. I have been quite careful, despite the peculiarity, especially the theological peculiarity, of my learning, not to seed into the poem the potentiality of the construction of a world that is already ideologically pre-formed.

H   In other words, there is no secret code lying behind your poems. There is no other notebook on your desk that contains the key to all these images, if only we could get hold of it.

G   No, you're absolutely right. There is no such code. The code lies in the reader's capacity for love and in the history of love, which in its deficits and its graces I am attempting to make sense of in my poetry. That history of love is referenced to myself and therefore to yourself. I think that the difficulty which you have with my more recent poetry does not lie in the remoteness of the cultural allusions.

H   I would be happy now if we could search out the concrete implications of these ideas in your recent poems, and perhaps you can help me with the difficulty that I have found in some of them, for example, the long poem "Of the Great House," that we will get to later in this conversation. You remind me, however, when you express a desire to reach cultural clarity from its roots in unconscious life, of a passage in your poem "A Little Sleep," in which the effort is to find a language that is cognizant of the pain of your younger self, which does justice to that pain and yet which would be understandable, coherent, to that younger self.

The bed stands between the wall and window.

On the bed lies a shadowy boy who must
Be consoled,

      and also a man who must
Believe the consolation, which should be
A sentence he can say that the boy can
Understand.

      The boy is the man when young,
And I am the man now, remembering the
Branches high up, perhaps with wind in them.
There seems so much to say about the few
Branches,

      which might be anywhere, in this
Or another time, seen through the affront
Of light by this man or boy,

      lying in
The ache of his left side (weary of much
Turning) who remembers the visionary blank
White wall, flaking to red, so near his eyes.

This section presents a teaching relationship; there is an analogy
between the older self—the man—and a teacher, on the one
hand, and the younger self—the boy—and a student, on the other
hand.

G Yes, Mark, here is a poem which describes a man lying on a bed
and turning restlessly from his right side, lying on which he sees a
wall, to his left side, lying on which he sees a window. In this
poem about the reality of the body as it affects perception, and the
intimate reality of the body as it is affected by thought, I have
undertaken to provide an intra-psychic model for teaching. My
own career as a teacher is impelled by the desire to teach myself
what I could not learn from another. In my recent poetry, the elder
self is attempting to teach the younger self about his mortality and

about the limits which reality places upon his desires. That is to say, he is attempting to teach his younger and still unreconciled and hungry self about sexuality, and inside sexuality, love.

H   I'm interested in your desire to write poems that recognize the psychic reality of your younger self, partly because it is one of my ambitions to write poems of that kind. But I think that my central desire is not the same as yours. I'm not conscious of a desire to console and bring, in some sense, into adulthood the younger self, but rather a desire to admit to, to confess and give a candid account of the presence of that younger self in my mind today.

G   Yes, here we see the peculiar inverse harmony between our two enterprises. The speaker in the poem called "A Little Sleep" is trying to bring into the more mature acculturation of the elder male mind a younger self, which like a formless unconscious to which he had not previously had access requires the addition of the intelligibility of the older speaker's more resolved sense of the world. As the teacher-person in my poems grows more confident of his patriarchal inheritance of order and presence and name, the younger unreconciled self, not yet a person, grows more apparent to him and becomes a student who can increasingly be addressed with the expectation that he will be attentive. This is a poem about my growth toward what is, I think, correctly and also commonly called integration.

It is important to me to note the greater objectivity of the poetic procedures in this poem: the clear metricality of the line, conceived according to a syllabic pattern of a conventional sort, and the elucidated relationship among the grammatical parts of the sentences.

H   Elucidated by the use of line breaks that drop half a line.

G   Yes, vertical spacing is a strategy by which I feel myself to record a greater clarity. You have observed that the criterion the speaker in this poem lays upon himself in his address to the child is a criterion which includes the intelligibility of utterance. It is as if a lucid, present mind were addressing his own unreconciled obscurity and attempting, while not abolishing the strange energies of that older self, to draw it into the realm of what we must call the *true* younger self, that is to say, the latest self evolved, rather than the earliest self born.

H   You know about and I've already spoken about my resistance to claims that metrical decisions have semantic content. Sometimes I admit the truth of such claims, but more often I resist them. I'd like you to say more about how the metrical patterning of this poetry differs from the poems in *A Harlot's Hire* and why you feel that this patterning contributes to the clarity of the utterance.

G   The metrical pattern of this poem and others of my more recent poems differs not only from the metrical pattern in *A Harlot's Hire*, but also from the metrical patterning in my other books: *The Recluse, And the Dew Lay All Night Upon My Branch,* and even *The Woman on the Bridge over the Chicago River.* My sentiment about the metrical practice exemplified in "A Little Sleep" is that it withdraws the burden of participated *subjectivity* from the relationship between the writer and the reader. My management in "A Little Sleep" of the ends of lines (the count is regularly ten but the semantic termination is unemphatic) shows a willingness to allow the line to function as a possession held, but held loosely, in common between the writer and the reader.

H   Rather than being entirely the possession, emotionally, of the writer.

G   That's right. I believe that the poem should be given away to the reader as an instrument of perception which the reader can employ to possess his world without the participation of the passion of the writer. One of the evidences of a withdrawal of authorial anxiety from my poems is the way in which the enjambments—the prolongation of the grammatical sequence over the end of the line as metrical sequence—is managed.

H This alarms me because I feel that my work is to get more and more of my real voice onto the page, and it would seem that the direction you're working in is to drain the personal speaking voice from the page entirely.

G The conception of draining anything is pejorative, or at any rate, implies the withdrawal of some good and generally—

H Vital juice.

G —fluid thing. My sense of the poem in this matter is different from yours, but your sense of my sense is not accurately stated. The goodness of the poem in my project lies in the degree to which it is un-owned by the author and a completely devoted possession of the reader. The means in my practice for obtaining the true magnanimity of the gift, which is, of course, the disavowal of ownership without the disavowal of the lovingness of the giving, is the progressive objectification of the poem; and one of the means of that progressive objectification which feels right to me is the increasing externality of the metrical procedures, which make of the poem a true common space where I may come as a reader and meet you as a reader, but where there is no owning.

In this impersonalist ambition, I do not have any difficulty with the notion that what I do is vastly more like what the High Moderns do, whose intention was deeply involved in the universalization of poetic utterance. Many, many of my contemporaries and yours are in the process of drawing poems closer to their own presence in the world. The extreme fragmentation of the poetic community at the present time and the multiplication of practitioners attests to a very general sentiment that there is something to be gotten out of poetry equivalent to social presence in the world. I do not believe that one can obtain from poetry legitimation of the author's personal presence in the world and at the same time do the business of the poetic art, which is to give the world to another, rather than to arrogate the world as an adjunct of the insufficiently validated selfhood of the poet. I feel a sadness about the widespread resort to poetry to mend directly injuries with respect to social acknowledgment. It is only by (a sometimes bitter and a sometimes joyous) indirection that I believe that that injury can be mended at all.

H   And that would have implications for parental love as well as for other kinds of love. That is, in this section from "A Little Sleep," you are modeling the love-giving, nurturant love-giving, of a father to his son. You are trying to imagine how that could be achieved. I am used to thinking of love-giving as necessarily a personal act, and expecting it to fail insofar as one person or another in the relationship tries to remain impersonal or distanced.

G   Love-giving, particularly parental love, must be, indeed, personal, but it cannot be self-referenced. In that sense, my model, insofar as there is a family model here (and I have adduced the family model as a good model for reading elsewhere in these conversations), is a parental model. You will note that in this poem, as in others of my recent poems, I have tried to explore the availability of fathers to my mind.

H   Fathers whose love-giving is not really self-referenced?

G   I have written, and they are among the poems which I value the most, poems about men who were seekers after truth. My writing about them was, really, an effort to seek out on my own behalf the truth of the male parent.

H   You're speaking of two poems that I know: "The Department," in *The Woman on the Bridge*, which is about Professor Boime, and "The Prothanation of a Charioteer," a more recent poem, which is about David Zilberman.

G   Yes. These poems, about men whom I did love and whose language moves inside me and gives me the poems which lament their deaths, call attention to the hunger inside that person in me who writes poetry to affirm a father. These fathers, however, are destroyed by the alienations which their peculiar sort of knowledge imposes upon them. They are countenances which have disintegrated in the very process of the possession of their own natures.

I think I have written one poem which does accomplish the writing of "the book of mother and father," which indeed the High Modern poets have obligated ourselves, their successors, to write—because their peculiar form of impersonalism, which constructed a history of the language and the art but omitted a history of the self, has obligated us, certainly me, to write what they did not write. My effort at this is a poem called "Of the Great House."

H I think "Of the Great House" is a very difficult poem. I'm not sure to what extent that difficulty arises from this impersonal voice that you speak of, but I do think that this poem focuses more than most of your other poems the question of difficulty versus accessibility that has separated us in other discussions.

G Mark, often when you use the word "difficulty," you are referring to those features of my poetry which are impersonal in character. I think you are describing your sense of a kind of discourse which is not specifically referenced to the private circumstances of an individual self, and you are disabled in your response by an inability to identify in the ordinary way with the speaker. The making of poems always involves a conciliation of the competing claims of accessibility, on the one hand, and truth on the other. The capacity to conciliate these severely antagonistic claims is, in my view, virtually the same as the genius which is poetic.

"Of the Great House" speaks on a scale which does promise a more general description of the world than is ordinarily available in Postmodern and post-Confessional poetry. It calls upon the reader to recognize cognitive and affective expectations in excess of ordinary experience. You have at various times commented on the density of the grammatical matrix which this poem arrays. My intention with respect to grammar is to exact attentiveness to intelligibility at the point where grammar opens out the limbs and otherwise darker regions of what intelligibility can bring into consciousness. At the level of verbal texture, I regard a certain density of surface to constitute a demand not only on the intellect but on the sentiment of a reader; for it is my desire that my poems place the reader in a wider horizon of intelligibility, on the one hand, and in a richer world of sentiment, on the other.

H   Yes, but for readers like me, it is precisely the syntactical density, and also the semantic density, of this poetry that, in some passages at least, tends to prevent me from gathering the sentiment of the poem. But let me insist for a minute on this issue of intelligibility, which you've said—in fact, which you say particularly in the section of "A Little Sleep" we have looked at—is desirable. Intelligibility is factored by time. I think of James Joyce, who said he sought readers willing to devote a lifetime to the reading of *Ulysses*. I want to ask you how much work you think a reader must engage in to absorb the meaning of this poem, "Of the Great House"? Specifically, let's take the example of a reader who has read other poems by Allen Grossman, but who has not read these interviews, who has not attended your lectures, who is not familiar in a theoretical way with your worldview: how hard is this poem for that reader, assuming the reader is intelligent?

G   Every poem must be lovable. It must be capable of an amiability which makes reading worthwhile. But it is my ambition to open my throat, and by doing so, to open your eyes as a reader, to bring you to recognitions that are not merely the repetition of previous recognitions. In order to do so, I must address you, robed in the difficulty which any worthwhile novelty has for the mind, and I must fight against the social repressions which I believe are, frequently in your responses, hidden inside the demand for access.

We are here talking today about "Of the Great House," because it is a poem that we regard as worthwhile and also a poem that we regard as difficult. The authority of poetry has as its good outcome the arresting of the attention of the reader even before intelligibility has been established. The poems that are read today in public and published in the press have almost universally withdrawn from the habit of making claims upon readers. Our audiences have been conciliated to the point where they are no longer instructed. Poets, because they so profoundly seek social honor, have ceased to engage in the risky business of instructing. Poetry that pleases by immediate recognitions, but does not instruct by the setting of hard tasks, seems to me poetry that is treasonous with respect to its own authority.

H   You would describe "Of the Great House" as a poem that sets tasks for the reader. I take it you mean not only the task of understanding the poem, but also tasks in life that would follow from an understanding of the poem?

G   Since the interpretation of poetry requires the penetration of language, and since language is our only secure access toward the world and our own minds, the capacity to secure for the self a new poem which has inside it a sufficient account of the real trouble in experience has consequences for the life of the reader outside the scene of reading.

H   I certainly share that hope, and I share the impulse to write poems with such effects. Therefore, we certainly agree that *some* level of accessibility is necessary for the poem. But I am conscious of two kinds of difficulty in poems that I see in the world: I would call them irresponsible difficulty and responsible difficulty. "Of the Great House" is a poem, I think, of responsible difficulty; that is, a poem whose complexity is caused by the poet's honest effort to say what he means, which is a difficult meaning. I feel that many of the poems we see around us published are irresponsible in their difficulty. That is, their density does not flow from realized intentions in the poet.

G   What you call irresponsible difficulty is difficulty that arises when the poem is ill-made. My feeling is that the crisis of evaluation centers upon those classes of poems which *do* have the prestige of well-making. Our critical concerns, I believe, should be directed toward the most powerful facts of our civilization rather than those candidates for status in the civilization which are inherently disqualified by craft defects.

Among the "difficulties" presented by the powerful and canonic poems of our culture, I discriminate those difficulties which can be mended by learning. Much of the scholarly response to High Modernism has been a quest for sufficient information to recapitulate the referential matrix of poems like the *Cantos* and *The Waste Land.* Where information can redress ignorance and enable response, I feel no meaningful difficulty has been found. Difficulty such as I regard as important for the civilization arises where the reference of the poem is toward facts of *experience* which are not normally or perhaps not at all susceptible to representation in language. Such facts of experience may at the present time be just those facts most important to effect our orientation and safety in the world. Indeed, in the history of my personal consciousness, I have found that those facts least accessible to my capacities for discourse at any given time have proved to be the most important aspects of my experience. The difficulties which I think the poet *must* solicit, with whatever consequence for the response of his reader, are just those situated upon the business of confronting either the inherent limitations of our social language, with respect to reference, or the conventional limitations of our poetic procedures, with respect to the range of experience and the range of human cases they can take in. It is this latter sort of difficulty I would regard as not merely sanctioned, but obligated by the ethical implications of the poetic work.

H   As a teacher you spend a lot of time helping students gain access to poems. Do you agree that as a poet it is also good to help your readers come to terms with your poems?

G   Poems always come adorned with explanations. There is no perfect reader of a poem, and I would insist that only in conversations of this sort, in which persons are obligated to one another and conscious of the purposes of one another, is explanation truly significant.

H   Rather than in an essay that a poet writes about his own work?

G   Yes, unless there is strong and continuing integration of the poet into the community whom he addresses by his explanations. But here I think it entirely reasonable, given the fidelity of our relationship, for me to read my poem with you. The poet is another reader, instructed both by his concern for his own intelligibility and his concern for the self-interest of the friend with whom he is discoursing.

H   Then let me ask you to help me with this long poem by giving me an overview of it in terms of its five sections, because it is a poem which, even when I am feeling at home on one page of it, I find hard to hold in my mind as a whole.

G   The totality which this poem should offer its reader is the continuity and integration of the voice in which it is spoken; for it is at the level of voice that the cognitive success of the speaker in a poem is registered. The integration of a poem has as its particular form of manifest truth the personhood of the speaker who proposes to speak it.
    This poem undertakes to establish a process of understanding marked by five stages, in which process the speaker exhausts his obligation to unworkable tasks and phantasmal truths, and penetrates to the actual state of the world in which his renewed life can become possible in a way different from the way in which it has been conducted before.

H   In that case, this poem can be seen as a thorough working out of the process which is only imaged in your shorter poem "The Thrush Relinquished."

G   Yes. This poem attempts to fulfill the promises for discovery that my earlier poems make.
    "Of the Great House" begins with an address to the poets. Its first words are a four-fold invocation of the great imperative, let: "Let let let let be." This succession of imperatives constitutes the establishment of permission with respect to a reality that does not know the mind of the speaker, and a summoning of the intention

of the speaker toward the construction of a human, and therefore intelligible, world. The opening of the poem, addressed to the poets, distinguishes the sighted singer, in a passionate, laboring house, from the blind singers, content to mediate an unconscious world without obligation to the integrations at the level of consciousness, which seem to me the only prize of poetic making.

The poem establishes a continuing metaphor: the great house. This house, as the poem makes plain, is mind, but as mind it is also the world. It contains the whole of the life of the speaker: the Night Room, with the stars above; the Day Room, where the life of the earth is conducted; the Winter Room, which is the realm of confrontation with the unconscious, both as personal and as collective past; and that strange and beautiful place, the Summer Kitchen, a death room, set apart, where the ideal condition of a life which has obtained consciousness comes to rest and to be inscribed, a point where life and death are indistinguishable one from another. The voice of the poet is drawn through the length of this poem by the urgency of an inquiry, an inquiry that is equivalent to life itself, the search for *the only thing that is*, which must be sought in all the regions and rooms of the great house of mind and world.

The poem then proceeds, in the third section of the first part, to assert that we must all recapitulate our personal origins and enter into and include our mother and father. This has been a peculiarly urgent Postmodern obligation, for the reason, as I have suggested earlier today, that our Modern predecessors were incapable, under the overriding burden of universal reference, of bringing the immanent life of the separated individual into the realm of their poems. Louis and Beatrice are my parents. The speaker in the poem finds himself afflicted with an anxiety with respect to continuity at the point of the imagined death of his mother, in whose mind are all of the predecessors, doomed to be extinguished at the extinction of her consciousness, and in whose mind also is the life of the speaker, who must escape from her consciousness lest he perish with it. This is a speaker who must be *born* in order to be free from the fate of the parent. At the end of this poem, the speaker, in a catastrophe of thunder and lightning, registers his birth and the beginning of his new Word.

As the first section of the poem proceeds, the speaker recalls a succession of moments, when he has committed himself to the labor of continuity which, as you know, I regard as the principal enterprise of the poet, indeed, the principal function of the presence of poetry in the human world. He vows, as the speaker in the title poem of my previous book, *The Woman on the Bridge*, does also vow, to write a book against our vanishing; remembers a moment in his past when something utterly ephemeral became the most precious fact of experience: that one thread in the plume of the seed of a cottonwood blowing across a summer road. I vow in this poem to give the fruits of this making to my father, Louis, and it is toward the succoring of this father, who is my own male self, that the most affecting (to my mind) parts of this poem tend.

H   The second section of the poem, called "The Dream of Rescue," as I understand it, tries to imagine a succoring of the mother. It offers an extended metaphor involving warships in danger of sinking, a picture of the plight of female figures who are in danger of drowning in speechlessness.

G   Yes. It is a metaphor, but it is also an action. My most precious intention for poems is to invest them with the urgency and disclosure of something *done*. This poem is also, as you say—this part two of "Of the Great House"—a picture, one of the many pictures which slowly, in the course of the five parts of this poem, become dissolved as a consequence of the cognitive penetration of their relationship to the will of the person who speaks the poem. The speaker finds a self undertaking a task commanded him by the central grief of all being, which for him is the mother's grief, the grief which he imagines her to have experienced at the violation of his birth. This grief informs all grief in my poetry and stands as my privilege of access toward the grief of all persons whom I can bring to mind.

The process of this section tends toward the discovery that the task of recuperation or rescue defined by this grieving sentiment is impossible to perform and undesirable to complete. It is this task which has burdened the style of this speaker, and it is toward the cleansing of this style that the poem tends. The extinction of the obligation to this task will constitute the *integration without solution* of the problem set by the grieving mother. At the end of this section of the poem, the speaker discovers the truth, namely, that this is a picture—and the further truth, as yet by no means a secure or sufficient truth—namely, that it stands before him, this picture, in the place of (that is to say, instead of) and, at the same time, as the only manifestation of, what he knows.

The third section of "Of the Great House," called "The Throat of the Hour-Glass," takes up the problem of men and boys, and by implication, the problem of the father. Its central metaphoric reference is to the pastoral world of the shepherd boy, who sings his song against the background of the sound of the universal grasses—the endlessly attested mortality of all persons. The speaker discovers this hero, whose language is like the life-sustaining organ of the body, the heart, and confesses his affinities both to the "stony wind" and the "watry fire." In doing so, he declares the business of poetry as in my poems I understand it. That business is to make apparent beneath the beautiful and cruel life that appears the life that does not appear, namely, the life that persons make for themselves in the world, which has as its sign the loved body, neither me nor you, but ourselves in our being with one another under the vast sanction of the starlight, the eye that knows us. "The Throat of the Hour-Glass" ends with sentiment directed toward the Other invested as the great wandering reference, the pilgrimage pronoun, you.

H   The fourth section of the poem, "At the Shore," as I understand it, shows by metaphors the vocational taking on of responsibility by the new poet imagined in the previous section, the poet who can speak the new language, the new heart-like language, and shows also in the wonderful metaphor of the baking of a new loaf of bread an image of the shape of such a new poem in this new speech.

G   This bread is the Sabbath bread, the Sabbath announced at the beginning as signifying the end of human making, that is, the making of a world of relationship responsive to the desires of the person. This section presents to Louis, my father, an image of the conduct of the father that I imagine, the old man who practices the ceremonies of the intelligibility of the world habitually and therefore with the more gracious outcome, putting the cup of offering into the hands of the divinity herself. The making of bread is, indeed, the making of a world from which violence is not absent but in which the destructive processes of culture, the mill, are administered *on behalf of* the community of persons rather than against it. The central passage of the section ends with the striking of the differences of all the parts of being into one lovely skin, as the strings of the great harp are struck into one handsome melody.

The fifth section of the poem, called "The Only Thing That Is," is an epiphanic moment. In it the life of mind is characterized as a *danse macabre* in which no human hand holds a human hand except when it acknowledges the interposition of a dead hand; but the relation of the living and dead is here not one of mutual erasure, but rather, in the ceremony of a dance, imaged. A storm now begins: the thunder of memory, which I've written about before in a poem called "The Field, Her Pleasure." In that thunder, the great pain of the mother is heard and then lost; the unfinishable task of rescue is announced, in the sirens which accompany the storm, and then forgotten. The world is begun again with a new "Let be" and the speaker is born in the birth storm, which has overwhelmed and changed his consciousness in the way growth, rather than transformation, establishes change.

At the end of the poem, the previous facts of consciousness slowly cease to burden the vision of the speaker. The facts of consciousness which are here extinguished are not truthless facts.

H   They are facts which disappear not because they are abolished, but because they are taken in and become part of the speaker.

G They are neither tasks finished nor are they tasks ignored. At the
   end of the poem, the house is destroyed and the world becomes
   the place of the life of the speaker, who vows at the end through
   dance, which is a kind of flowering in the night of a world, to
   enter once again and under new auspices into the tasks to which
   fully human action obligates the soul. As the first words of the
   poem echo the beginning of the Hebrew Bible, "Let be," so the
   last words of the poem are the last words of the same book: "And
   go up" toward the Jerusalem of the life which cannot be escaped
   and can now finally be entered as a sighted singer.

H Thus it is a profoundly hopeful poem. The person imaged at the
   end of the poem is newly enabled and can go forth into the world
   toward new actions, and presumably will be able to write in a new
   way.

G I am struggling to establish for myself a rest profound enough, a
   Sabbath as deeply accomplished as the Sabbath here desired.
   What one is capable of in poetry one as yet only hopes to become
   capable of in experience. A poem must not be regarded as a moral
   accomplishment until the poet as person has made it a moral accomplishment. The poet is like the reader. Nothing is done for the
   poet or the reader by the poem. Culture does nothing *for* its participants except to add to their means of doing what they must do
   for themselves.

H Yet that itself is an action. It is an action that has effects, and in
   that sense, I believe you think that the achievement of the poem,
   the willing of this truth into visibility, is a kind of step, although
   perhaps we will withhold the adjective moral from this step; it is
   still a kind of step toward the moral achievement.

G It is a step, but I must insist that the culture of poetry is not a
   culture which undertakes to do anything on behalf of another.
   What a man accomplishes as a moral person in the presence of an
   art he accomplishes as a consequence of his own will. Neither as
   the makers of poems nor as the teachers of poems can we do any-

thing on behalf of another, except insofar as knowledge in its broad poetic sense constitutes an addition to the moral resources of a person. But even then, those resources are the resources of *that* person and not resources that have been contributed by the poem or the teacher.

H   Yes. I think that we are bringing out that there is more than one sense of the word "for" in the phrase "I do this for you," because I know you have said it is a farther ambition of your work to become the poet for a nation, but as we were saying when we spoke of your mother as a kind of last remnant of this imaginary nation, it is not a nation that appears in the world today.

G   What can that nation be? Earlier in these conversations I expressed sadness at the inability of my mind to grasp the fundamental affinities, the nationhood, of my personhood. The historical nation, America, is disqualified, as is any nation state, as a principle of advocacy. Ethnicity, and Judaism is an ethnicity, is also merely another violent phantasm, out of scale with human life, which drives us against one another in conflicts so dangerous as to be unimaginable as a desirable state of affairs. The poet speaks *for*, in the complexity of that word you have just now introduced, a nation, just as he or she speaks, not the idiolect of a separate individual, but the dialect of a collectivity. At the same time, the speaker must possess membership in that nation, and the effort to equivocate the difficulties of obtaining membership, either through learning or acts of the hopeful will, and to ignore the historical inevitability of conflict between nations—between immortalities—is not poetically productive, nor is it safe. As witness to this, I call attention to the proliferation of Jewish poetry and, indeed, parochially sponsored poetry of all sorts, and the tendency of even our most powerful poets to disqualify the resistance of things by projecting vast and forgiving universes, such as we find in Ammons' marvelous skepticisms and Merrill's fantasy eschatologies.

Mark, I have come to the end of what I know. It's upon this problem that I believe myself to be situated now, and it is toward the solution of this problem that I address myself in such poems as I now write and shall write in the future.

H   Yes, it seems that this problem of defining, locating this speculative nation—which is not America and which is not the Jews,
which is not any collectivity we can now give a name to—places
you as a poet in search of an audience and raises the question,
which we have touched upon before: to whom are your poems
addressed? What body of readers can you hope for who will benefit
from the poetry?

G   My poems are addressed to some state of the persons around me
other than that which they currently find themselves in. My
poems should be addressed, are intended to be addressed, not to
the present powers, but to the future powers of my readers. I believe that poems should not be addressed to the already possessed
states of consciousness of the persons who read them. Poems
should have an empowering strangeness about them which summons its audience rather than receives its audience.

H   And this must have consequences for your own judicial responses
to the poems of others today.

G   Because I believe that the goodness of the poem is something to
be discovered in the strenuous activity of new making, I am less
certain than many of my contemporaries about the problem of the
value to be assigned to each new poem. In the sense in which I
am a skeptic who views the knowledge most necessary to our
avoidance of suffering as knowledge not yet obtained, I am also
hospitable to the large range of possibilities of poetic practice
around me. I do not believe that our world has yet discovered
structures responsive to the facts that bear upon persons at this
present time. Consequently, I feel the problem of judicial sorting
of a poetic community not to be the major problem which confronts the critic.

H   It would be in spring that we would decide which plants and flow-
    ers and vegetables to cultivate, but for the time being, we're in a
    cold spot.

G   It's in the spring that we see what seeds were in the soil.

6. OF THE GREAT HOUSE

In a dream to wander to some place where may be
heard the complaints of all the miserable on earth.
      —Hawthorne, *The American Notebooks*

I.

To the Poets

Let let let let be

        to the poets

                    praise,
And shame.

        To the sighted singer, in a
Passionate, labouring house. Praise!

                 But
To the blind singers among sleepy harvesters,—
Everlasting shame. . . .

         ·   ·   ·

Of the great house I have in mind I dwell in,
The world,

At night in the Night Room, hung with the stars;
By day in the Day Room, with the high doors;
A Winter Room, where storms continually wreck;
The Summer Kitchen, my death-room set apart,
Where stands a black stone written on,

                     "Establish.
Establish rest. Establish rest profound,"

Hunting, lifelong—
The only thing that is, from room to room.

   .   .   .

Everyone must write a book of mother, and
Father;

  but who could imagine how lonely
In their cold beds Louis and Beatrice are
Searching the chronicle of old memory,
By the secret lamp of pain?

      —Now, Beatrice
Is dying; and the great house fades with her
Fading mind; and her children are without
Hope,
A whole nation

    on its knees

      in the high
Courtyard, where the Fountain of the Arts is dry
As the sky above darkens, and shrinks—a grim
Page of which the sense is lost,

      where the dear
Names, like birds of the air, devour one another
In the dark. . . .

    .   .   .

I stood in the Avenue, and vowed

      this book
Of mother and father against our vanishing—
As before in childhood

     I stood at curbside
Of the summer roads, and saw: What was it?
One seed with its plumes. What was it within
The plumes? One plume, and the threads of it.
One thread, and the thread's tip.

                                   Mother Beatrice,
Give me a very distinct cry.

                                   There is
No singing without a woman who wants
An answer sufficient to her injury—
Such is the muse. . . .

Hear it, father Louis! This harp is struck
By a hand,

        a great harp, for

                the nation:

            •   •   •

Beautiful poems, like flowers! Beautiful
Poems—like webs, like seas working, like
Wind webbing black water blown flat with gray

Flowers of the foam. Beautiful poems risen
Against the granite cliffs in waves, exploding
The flinty shingle upward through the high

Window of the tower light. Beautiful poems
That I vowed, darkening the world,
Thronging the Avenue with the sweet sanity

Of profound tone, blind beautiful poems—
My servant animals, hunting the object of
Desire equal to mind's desire of an object—

Ringing and ringing through the midnight house,
Like an harassing phone call: Who is there?
Breathings only; and, behind that, the obscure

City of perpetual cry, whose citizens are
All mute, all dying, all enraged—
Beautiful poems. Beautiful, beautiful poems.

2.

The Dream of Rescue

Lighter out enormous anchors to the svelte
Dutch warships, each ship with its swarm of ghosts
And signals

    the wind molests

        in the shelterless
Offing—like unmoored planets, painted less
And less by the sheer, exalted stormlight of
Distance

    (Too far, O planetary, too far
From the sun)

      one anchor with all its cables to
Each dark lighter, whelmed to streaming gunnels
By the horned iron

    Hope,

        as in the dream
Of rescue;—and no rescue!

      Lighter out
Enormous anchors, where the slender mothers are
Luffed there upwind; and all unscarfed labour
Into the wrecking storm, each

        with her whole heart
Of grieving.
And the strayed lashings, like tear-wet locks, escaped
In loops, and ray-like cometary whips,
Betray the

    torn skirts of

      her vast secrecy
To the unsheltering light, and grief-song imperial—

Commanding tasks, impossible to perform . . .
Undesirable to complete. . . .

                                Whence the
Burden of this life,

                     the charter of this perilous
Cry;
As upward from beneath, toward the sea-bird
With a thousand voices—ocean's dove
Of long meaning—

                   a giant sea-beast, like
A drowned shield rises.

                    —But the truth is this
Is a picture—the mothers in irons in the
Unsheltering storm, the sun throwing down gold.

Night and day it stands before me, in the
Place of what I know.

     3.

The Throat of the Hour-Glass

On behalf of the sadness of men and boys,
Sing on the hills the

                long deferred poem of
The third dimension. Sing on the hills, Shepherd!
While the universal grasses sound, a bass
Pipe of vast bourdon, the note

                    of the world—:
As from the throat of an hour-glass, the voice
That remembers
A man who has no horizon,

              the hero
Whose language is a heart, the strong heart

Of a bridegroom, who runs in the sun's brightness—
Wide-eyed, thinking. . . .

      ·   ·   ·

      —The night is the studio
Of my art. In the Night Room, the immense
Air of the void opens; and closes my book.

I am not entirely human,

        writing in
Stony wind, and watry fire,
Pressing the strong heart of night's song against
The broken heart of mortal Hyacinth:

Beneath the life that appears—greatly beautiful,
Greatly cruel—is the life that does not appear
The poem makes appear,

Outered from the throat of the hour-glass, that
Cries the bridegroom with beating heart to
Sentient rest—

      loved body,

        found in starlight,
The wide-travelling starlight, with all its eyes.

      ·   ·   ·

On behalf of the sadness of men and boys
Sing on the hills

      the shepherd song,

      as of
White-flowering trees, attacked by running fire
Flowering transparent in full sun, blowing like
Birthstorm backward upwind, against the trees
In their flowering, flamelike flowers blackened
By the flowing flame—

and left for us to see;
As when

rowing across a lake (Beatrice was
In the boat, and I was rowing) against
The distance,

unvanquished tide, I heard
The bass note of the waves, like grassy wind;
And saw the universal sky

of this
Dusk page, by the pain-lamp of a low sun—

As through the mael-strom throat of the hour-glass,
The torrent of the image,
This poem of my love, pours out on you.

4.

At the Shore

And, then, he put the cup into her hand
—Quick, vine-scribbled,

silver, chalice of

offering—
With perfect luck, as the hand that is ready
Does see of itself

the goddess is there,
Athene amidst her honouring for it
Has never ceased, beside the holy sea,
Night or day—;
The old man, Nestorian, habitual as the sun
And moon,
Across the gray foam-flowered threshold of
The Seen

greeted the

            viewless, the gray-eyed:
Addressed the deep Unseen,
In the onlooking of ancestors,

                —knowing
Every grief is a person.
Praise! Though she came in the rags of our body,
He put the cup into her hand. . . .

And, then, he took the Past, Louis; and the Passing,
With quick hands;

             and What Is To Come! and made
A loaf for the good day

             —beautiful poem.
Cast wet and dry of worlds in a green bowl:
Water of the air, and some salt of ocean;
And bright sands of the field, in its ebb season,
The reaping

      of a gold

          reading of earth
In the good sense of the mill, and

               poured in
Seething the green yeast that lives forever, but
Flowers in our world, the

          power of rising
And his hand struck the difference of these,
Like the strings of a harp, into one lovely skin:

      •   •   •

. . . The question is at ease on a sunny stone
In the great Sabbath heat that makes it fit—.
This is my body to which the wonders come,

Beautiful poem, sweet mixture; and the truce of
All the strings. Louis, as the lamp brightens, the
Chronicle will show a whole nation sings

I imagine you.

          —There is a storm on the beach.
In truth, it is like my world after all;
But there is enough. Beautiful poem where

There is enough. Everyone has a body. Look!
At eighty, suddenly it was discovered Louis
Wished to be held in arms. Beautiful poem

Of a very old man in the nurse's arms.
Rest, reliable spirit. We are so little human—
So stony, so water-like, who built the great

House at the gray shore.

           —But this is the last
Age of silence; and, God willing, the first of
The unmistakable voices to which we say, "Yes, you."

Rest, rest, reliable spirit, frail and light.
The waves sing three syllables, woe-man-grief.
The mothers take you in, except they die.

Beautiful poems. Beautiful, beautiful poems. . . .

    5.

The Only Thing That Is

From room to room, my servant animals
These songs, her body, lifelong have led me
Hunting the object of desire equal
To the mind's desire of an object

            —dancing,
As thinking is, a dead one holding the left
Hand, and a dead one holding the right hand,
Whose left hand holds another living hand:
No living hand holds

a living hand in
The dead dance on mind's cold mountains, or
Through the rooms of the great house at the shore.

. . .

In truth, it is raining. There is no moon.
And the thunder comes: the restless daughter
Of a restless mother, casting away worlds—
Mother of a restless song.

First, I saw
The acetylene signal, across the ocean far away,
The lightening with its white, white hieroglyph
"Let be,"

rip-tooth of the birthstorm;

and heard
Beatrice, following in thunder, from childbed
Rise with all her scars, casting away worlds.

. . .

Let me tell you how the thunder grew,
And seemed mingled with familiar women's voices;
Sirens entered, then,

and in rain were lost,
Or overtaken by the unmistakable word-
Streak of birthcry;
And the white, white lightening—wounds as they are
Known to God—
Inscribed one stroke on the black stone above.

Now, there is nothing in the place of what
I know,

the only thing that is,

                              the world
With winds and rivers.
The house is first a torch, and then a ruin,
And then a sweetening field, quiet after storm.
Songs flower in the night by whose light we dance
And go up.

The Summer Conversations
(1990)

Contents

1. Criteria

*After ten years, questions about beginning, revision, and the
direction of revision. Mark Halliday's poem "Location," 137. In
the interest of what kinds of value is revision undertaken? 142.
Two kinds of criteria: con-textual and extra-textual, 145.
Wallace Stevens' poem "World Without Peculiarity," 149. The
competing criteriological claims on poetic practice of immanent
experience and transcendental principle, 147, 154. The ethical as
the fully narrated account, 153. The representational rationality
of the repression of the ethical, 156. Emily Dickinson's poem
"Again—his voice is at the door—," 158. The criteria of the
ethical and the admissability of the category of the inevitable,
162. The problematic of the authority of the teacher, 165.
Conflict between the criteria of wisdom and the criteria of
representation: an essentially contested issue, 168, 170.*

2. What Must the Poet Do?

   "H" and "G" are like gods, seeing the beginning and the end of
   narratives, 173. Segregation of poetic practice from cultural
   analysis in this decade, 174. Allen Grossman's poem "Mary
   Snorak the Cook, Skermo the Gardener, and Jack the Parts Man
   Provide Dinner for a Wandering Stranger," 175. The purpose and
   characteristics of a comic poetics, 177. The problematic of
   continuation, 179. Two strategies: "faith" and restoration to
   great mind; or the faithful reconstruction of mortal narratives,
   183. Thomas Hardy's poem "At the Railway Station, Upway,"
   187. The problematicity of secular meliorism. Satisfaction; or the
   critique of satisfaction, 190. Questions about the cessation of
   poetry, and the poetic work of the redistribution of
   representational privilege, 193. Poetic representation, as the
   rational and joyous desire of the continuation of the world, is a
   fundamental good and will never come to an end, 194. The
   criterion of efficacious love, 198.

3. Two Poems: Mark Halliday's "Springtime for You" and
   Allen Grossman's "The Life and Death Kisses"

G   Mark Halliday, it's been ten years since we last talked in this office
for the purpose of making sense out of poetry. Will you read me
one of your new poems?

H   Okay, I'll read a poem called "Location."

Location

You could begin by saying "This summer in Philadelphia . . ."
But then you might instantly feel a gush of weariness
and think No, no—something else—not
"this summer," not "Philadelphia" . . .
The thousands of men in sleeveless shirts
who never bother to disturb your suspicion that
they are all awesomely stupid.
The teenage girls chewing green gum outside pizza joints.
Pavement so crudded yet seeming without history . . .
Heat clotted on the skin of all the Phillies fans.
Not this.
But what?

Winter? In Chicago?—You could work that up
and it might have a cleanness of outline:
a crisp wind in off the lake,
great block boulders rimming the lake,
deep blue of that chilled lake so far from here;
hard-edged pedestrians wearing dark scarves;
a sense of tough bold swagger involving
Carl Sandburg, Saul Bellow, Buddy Guy and Junior Wells.

Snow packed solid on the stern roofs
and someone moving bravely through the canyons of the Loop.
. . . There is that option.
And yet with it the nagging of how it isn't
this, isn't the mess on hand.

Lord, let me not write poems whose little events or non-events
seem to take place in Europe, indeed in some quaintified
          Europe
of 1938 or 1928 or 1913, for the sake of naming
European streets or beverages. Let me not do that, Lord.
I will fail in my ways but not so cheaply as that.

This summer in Philadelphia
people on their front stoops glanced up at a jet
droning toward the airport (one more thing beyond their
          control)
and bent down to grasp today's thumb-smudging *Inquirer*.

G   This poem is particularly attractive to me, Mark, because in it a
    speaker is considering the problem of beginning. The problem of
    beginning any lyric requires that the speaker and, underneath the
    speaker in some clear way, the author, decide what there is of value
    to say: what region of the world, what class of language, what
    system of judgment is appropriate (by appropriate I mean truthful)
    to constitute the language of a poem. Would it be correct to say
    that this speaker addresses another poet with respect to the ques-
    tion of how a poetic speaker should begin to construct the world?

H   Yeah—I often find myself writing poems with an implied audience
    of people who also write poems, or might want to write poems,
    people who are conscious of the issue of what you have to do to
    write a poem today. Now this is an aspect of the poem that I'm
    both nervous about but also, in a way, proud of: namely, the way
    in which it does come under the general heading of poems about
    poetry, poems that explicitly allude to the writing of poems.

G   As such, Mark, it is an extremely didactic poem. You are addressing others whose business it is to make poems, and that may mean
every human being who lives and who is subject to the obligation
of giving an account of a world. And you presume that that other,
who must also be concerned with the judgments that poets make,
may "begin by saying 'This summer in Philadelphia . . .'" and then
may also withdraw from that inherently propositional act for reasons which you specify. The expectation, that there is some difficulty about giving an account of the world at hand—"This summer in Philadelphia"—is, to my mind, fraught with your
sensibility with respect to the obligation of poetic speakers, a sensibility which also contains some notion as to where truthful
speaking should be located and what world it should represent.

H   I seem obsessively to return to the idea that the most important—
most truthful—poems by me or by others will be, in some relatively thorough or inclusive way, about the real world of the poet's
experience. "Location" arises out of the sense that I ought to be
finding the poetry, the important poetic truths, available in my
immediate surroundings. I've lived now in Philadelphia for seven
years. This poem has in it a revulsion against the subjects and
images and textures that I see around me, especially in the middle
of a hot summer, in my own immediate, real world. Though I
repeatedly tell myself and others that the poem ought to arise out
of the immediate reality of the poet; nevertheless, in the Philadel-
phian summer–feeling this poem reflects, immediate reality seems
terribly inauspicious.

G   So the poem begins by situating the speaker who would begin
speaking upon an undecidable issue: on the one hand there is an
imperative which is ethical in character. That imperative states
that truth is constituted of witness or experience, and that the
poet as the representer who, by his or her privilege of craft, gives
presence to a world must address the world witnessed and at hand.
On the other horn of the dilemma lies the disposition to repress
the world at hand, to address in effect a world that is *not* at hand:
to counterpose to the world at hand another world which may be

paradigmatic of an outcome to which the world at hand should be brought, a world contributed by poetic representation as part of its empowerment toward the civilization. Not to write about the world at hand is to betray the world at hand, the only world that is. To write only of the world at hand is to leave the world as it is given, uncompensated or without the supplement of alternative realities.

H   Yeah.

G   As your poem proceeds, it presents one very vivid alternative reality, the one called Chicago, characterized by cleanness of outline, by hard and distinct edges, by an inland sea, which is not only given form by freezing, but also has a secure boundary, a world that is written about or sung by Americans in the twentieth century—by the high cultural Bellow on the one hand and also by the heroes of popular culture, Buddy Guy and Junior Wells. In this world, unlike Philadelphia, it's possible to move bravely. Nonetheless your speaker continues in his self-revising dialectic to counsel himself, in the presence of others, saying, "Lord, let me not write poems whose little events or non-events / seem to take place in Europe . . ." Why this disavowal of alternative realities?

H   It's interesting to me the way you suggest that in one sense the disposition to insist upon immediate surroundings can be cowardly rather than brave. I see that is true, and I recognize what you say as an important kind of challenge to the disposition I cited as an origin of this poem and as a disposition habitual to me. In other words, I see that there is a kind of work for poems to do which is to posit, or imagine, to create outlines for some better, or even ideal state of affairs. And I recognize that that can be a courageous thing for art to do in that it resists the merely given, the merely at hand. And yet, most of the time, my inclination is the opposite of that.

My inclination is to suspect some form of cowardice or evasiveness in the turn toward an ideal state of affairs, or another world that is somehow preferable to the immediate world. As I look into myself, it seems to me that the brave thing to do, I mean not just brave in some macho sense, but an ethically courageous thing to do, will be to come to terms with as many aspects as I can of the world that I see and touch around me. So I'm trying to say that I recognize that there can be more than one form of ethical courage; but the one that has seemed most necessary for me is the one that insists on turning toward what is at hand.

G In "Location" you engage with two kinds of poetry; and in a narrative characterized by the progressively self-revising action of the speaker you reject one, and assign the privilege of your own act to another. The poem ends with the commencement which was problematized, and for the moment rejected in the beginning: "This summer in Philadelphia / people on their front stoops glanced up at a jet / droning toward the airport (one more thing beyond their control) / and bent down to grasp today's thumb-smudging *Inquirer*." The two kinds of poetry which are here in question, between which a judgment is made, are (first) the kind of poetry which functions as a negation or contradiction of a present state of affairs and therefore promises to contribute a supplement, an alternative reality such as your "Chicago," and (second) a preferred poetry which is the heroic captive of the world at hand, and which, by representing that world also changes it in some way—a poetry which explicitly rejects the use of terms that do not arise in the description of the world as it is given.

H Like the word "angel."

G Like the word "angel," like the word "God," like the word "idea." Your narrator enacts a self-revision which rids the world of such terms. So I would like to return for a moment to the self-revision of the narrator in this poem. Prominent in this poem and in many of your poems is the capacity of this narrator, your narrator, to enact self-revision. Why is self-revision an action which is important to represent?

H   Okay. I think I know what I think about that. When we had our conversations ten years ago the word "self" was a problem between us. I think you saw my notion of the self as not skeptical enough, as if I were too confident that there is some unitary essence in each individual to which that person has, or can have, unmediated access. Maybe I'm more sophisticated now. And yet there's a difference between us on this that I think will remain as we talk today. Self-revision *is* something I like to do, something I need to do often in poems, and I think the way I can understand that is by saying that one's self, my self, the Mark Halliday that I claim to know, is a dynamic interrelationship between possible modes of self-presentation and expression. In other words, a poem that is a picture of me is likely to be a poem that has more than one and perhaps, in its best form, a large number of attitudes, modes of expression, and attitudes toward expression. And yet I will persist in claiming that the picture made by the poem as a whole nevertheless does represent a "self."

G   Mark, may I interrupt you for a moment. This self-revision we are talking about has a direction. And I would like to try to specify the direction of self-revision as a central problem. Self-revision is a narrative which forms a substantial part of the presence of your poems as it does of religious poems. The narrative of self-revision became a lyric trope in English poetry in the seventeenth century—for example, George Herbert. Herbert continuously finds himself wrong about his account of himself and his world, and continuously corrects that account until in the end his account of himself and his God's account of reality become identical. That is the moment at which the Lord intervenes—and that intervention is a gift which results from the successful enactment of a noble enterprise, the matching of the self's account of itself with the Creator's account of the self, as the Maker of the world knows it. How would you characterize the direction of revision in *your* poems, and in the interest of what value is revision undertaken? I think it's an ethical as well as a merely narratological issue.

H The example of Herbert interests me because I love many of Herbert's poems. You just made me think of his famous poem "The Collar," and it occurred to me that many of my poems could be described in their shape as "The Collar" without its ending, where he hears, finally, the voice of the Father. My poems, since I am unwilling to accept any transcendental rescue, have to find some other ending, some other resolution. I'm not really answering your question though. In my poems the direction of self-revision points toward no climactic or final resting place or solution to the problems of the self, but nevertheless seems to be in the direction of relatively more honesty and clarity and communicativeness between a speaker and possible listeners, for the sake of more humane and vital interaction between them.

G Now the poem "Location" ends with the word "inquirer," inscribed or reinscribed as the name of a newspaper which is the record of the events of the day. So the question that is explicit is whether the direction of inquiry (either the represented self-revision of a speaker or the revision of a text by a poet in the action of composition) is the direction of a reality which you wish to call important and to which in the making of your poem *you assign a prior or superior value,* and whether the knowledge of such a reality is possible without terms of a transcendental character. Remember, Mark, "fact" is in itself a transcendental term, something not ourselves, to which we assign prior existence and to which our minds tend when they tend toward the truth. The question of revision has brought us to the question of the purposiveness of poetry altogether. One answer to that question is to *find the real,* or to give an account of a mind engaged sincerely in its discovery. The other possibility (toward which the middle of your poem directs our attention) is that the purpose of poetry is to *supplement the real,* to disclose something not at hand which it is the business of the poetic speaker to supply. And I would add, something not at hand which it is the particular empowerment of *poetry* to supply, as it supplies to natural discourse a further order of discourse.

H   Okay, wait a minute. The thing about Chicago being in the middle here as an image which seemed preferable to immediate experience: the way that it is actually embedded in the poem does reflect a desire I have. In other words, the poem really does not confine itself to a simple rejection of alternative worlds or alternative visions. It purports to partake of some of the pleasure of asserting such a vision, while at the same time insisting that the poet cannot merely live in that vision. There are reasons why we go on vacations, and why we need them, and I mean on the minute-by-minute level as well as on the month-by-month level. But one knows that one's real work resides back home after the vacation. And at the end of this poem I want to locate myself back in Philadelphia, and to try to pick up the materials of what some more responsible, truthful poem would be made of.

G   A poem therefore has, among its obligations, to distinguish between what is and what is only desired. A poem which substitutes an alternative reality for the reality at hand is a poem which gives up on its moral obligations. From your point of view the poem *measures the relationship between* the world at hand and alternative worlds, and allows for the introduction of alternative worlds under the index of.repression, the index of unreality ("you could work that up . . ."), the index which states the mere statability of what is not at hand.

H   Why do you call that the "index of repression"?

G   When you declare, first of all, that the mind does not wish to dwell in Philadelphia, and then, having established that there is moral importance in confronting Philadelphia, the world at hand, you declare subjunctively that one "could"—that's the grammatical mode of alternative reality—one *could* supplement the world at hand by another. When you do these things you measure or regulate the relationship between the world at hand and alternative realities, and at the same time allow both provisionally to exist.

H   Okay.

G   "Location" is a poem seeking location, the location of mind with
    respect to its own purposes. It is engaged in the business of revising
    its own disposition with respect to its subject matter and therefore
    with respect to its choice of desirable terms and morally sufficient
    reference. The "you" with which the poem begins is the writing
    person who, in one way or another, sponsors the text of the poem.
    The question as to what direction self-revision is driven in, and
    the related question as to what conception of truth or value deter-
    mines the direction of self-revision, are fundamental.

       In order to answer such questions I think we must produce *cri-
    teria*, that is to say, terms which specify the right shape and the
    right reference of "privileged speech" such as poetry. We live in a
    world in which poetry is extensively taught. There are more than
    four hundred graduate programs in creative writing in the United
    States and Canada, and their principal concern, the instruction
    that they sell, is revision. The fundamental problem of revision is
    of course the problem of the paradigm, or model, the ideal or pre-
    ferred contour, with respect to which revision takes place. We can
    model revision in two ways. First, we can speak of revision as tex-
    tual reconstruction (contextual revision), that is to say revision in
    terms of the consistency, rationality, and order of each separated
    text, and, in a larger sense of the word context, revision with
    respect to the kind or genre of poem which is to be composed.
    Second, we can speak of revision as cosmological reconstruction
    (extratextual revision), in effect the effort to produce in the actual
    world of the specified and unexchangeable written text some like-
    ness or simulacrum, some realization of a virtual model, which is
    not text itself, but which is like the figure of Christ in Christian
    thought, or the idea of the "Good" in Platonic discourse, or the
    idea of the citizen in a Rousseauean account, an ideal, or an extra-
    historic pattern. It is my disposition to suppose that revision can-
    not take place in a fashion consistent with the importance which
    I assign to poetry, without reference to a criterion of the second
    sort.

       In any case, Mark, questions about the representation (as in
    your poem) of the self-revising speaker bring to mind the same
    class of questions which our teaching of poetry raises, namely: in

the light of what conception of value-bearing form do we choose
to shape and reshape the texts which we intend to be poetic texts?
What is our destination? And how do we know about it? And what
words help us to express its value?

H   Of the two kinds of criteria for revising that you sort out, I certainly would locate myself as thinking in terms of the second kind,
as you do, but I suppose that most poets, most good teachers of
poetry would say that also if forced to choose. At any rate, we'll
have to say more to establish the differences between us than to
say that we both understand revision as requiring a model of goodness and value outside the mere formal beauty of the aesthetic
object.

G   Mark Halliday, would it be reasonable in the light of what you just
now said to add that what the poet must know is not fully accounted for when we have spoken about poems?

H   Yes.

G   In other words, what the poet must know by the nature of poetic
knowledge lies outside of the poetic text and the poetic discourse?

H   Sure. You've made us think in terms of a poetry workshop and a
poet trying to help younger poets revise their poems. How does he
or she know in what direction such revision should proceed? I
don't think it's a question merely of the formal coherence or beauty
or perfection of the object, though I know that some activity in
workshops seems regrettably to settle for that level of concern, or
that kind of criterion. But rather, I think you and I would agree
that somehow the teacher or poet has to have a conception of the
"good person."
    What is the good person? The healthy adult. The person who
has learned enough about life so as to be able to function, in relation to himself and in relation to others, in life-affirming ways,
moral ways. If I'm sitting with a student who has written a poem
that I think is not good enough, whether I reveal it directly and

candidly to that student or not, what I'm really doing as I try to coach that student toward what I claim is a better version of that poem is trying to help the student find the most mature and healthy version of himself or herself that is compatible with the subject or scope of the poem that he or she has written.

Now I realize that the challenge to the teacher implied by what I've said is frightening and exhausting, because the issue perpetually arises, as you insist today, that it's difficult or impossible or very mysterious to arrive at a consistent or firmly reliable standard by which to decide what form of person one's students should become, or indeed, what would be the most mature, healthy, good, moral version of one's self. It's a mystery. But what I'm going to be saying more than once today, I think, is that it seems to me the mystery we live in. It's the existential struggle that a teacher or poet or anyone lives in every day.

Now the fact remains that one does make decisions about the poems by this student or about one's own poems. In what direction does one push revision? Well, you have an idea about the best version of yourself, learned in many cases from your parents, also from your friends and teachers. There's a kind of accumulated, gathered image of the healthy self that I think we all work on and try to build up; and a teacher should be someone who, partly just because of chronological age, maybe also because of sustained effort and concern in a certain area of life, has gone further in the direction of clarifying that image of health than the student has gone. What I'm saying doesn't change the fact, which I know to you is a very distressing fact: that two teachers of poetry sitting down with the same student might indeed press revision of that student's poem in divergent directions, because those two adults or older poets carry with them different images of what the healthy, good, moral, adult person is. I see no way out of that problem.

G   The very nature of the poetic tradition seems to me to propose to us not only that the problem which you have now identified is the crucial problem which poetry addresses, but also that poetry by its nature supplies a way out: an origin of discourse (the "muse," let us say) outside of the system constituted by family, by secular instruction and social formations, from the point of view of which "outsideness" it is possible to introduce into the exchange between mortal persons a kind of knowledge which is not vulnerable to the bitter ironies of social construction and vernacular particularity at any given moment in social space and time. The conception of poetry as having its origin precisely in that region which is not determined by the history of families and in general the *history* of acknowledgment, functional and dysfunctional, points in my view to the most powerful benefit that poetry can confer on persons.

The traditional account in the West of poetic vocation, for example, is a story about a social person whose mortal voice is replaced by a transhistorical and, in the language of the West, an "immortal" voice. The rule is that mortal persons cannot by mortal means speak immortal language; and the social expression of that immortality is the continuity of a tradition, always older and other than the history of any moment of poetic practice, that constitutes an alternative genealogy to the genealogy contributed by the mortal family. This "outsideness" or transhistorical "newness" of the poetic voice to the moment in history seems to me to constitute the value of poetry (without saying how to name that value) that the poet takes in hand, that the reader of poetry receives and the teacher of poetry undertakes to disseminate. The value which I am in search of when I revise a poem of my own is such that the poem cannot be said to be complete, to be satisfactory to *this* maker, unless it contributes knowledge which is *new* to the historical moment. By new knowledge I mean knowledge derived from an originary alienation which contributes to a given moment, not what is already encoded in that moment, but what contradicts that code or what decodes the discourse given by history in some new way.

It is, as *you* say, "mysterious," though I do not respect the word "mysterious." Such knowledge seems to me as concrete and apprehensible as the most immediate fact to my consciousness, indeed it seems to be more concrete and apprehensible than the immediate facts of my empirical knowledge. Hence my sense of the power of poetry in history as a model of other kinds of power structured in the same way toward history. The transhistorical character of poetic practice in the West assures us that when the source of *poesis*, the voice which summons the poet, whether Hesiod or Caedmon or Shelley or Yeats or whomever, is present, power of that kind is also present.

H   Power of *what* kind?

G   Power which reproduces the form and value of the person.

H   But Allen, I don't see how what you've just said would help anyone rewrite a particular poem. The right thing to do now—the healthy adult thing—is to discuss a poem. Let me read you a poem by Wallace Stevens.

World Without Peculiarity

The day is great and strong—
But his father was strong, that lies now
In the poverty of dirt.

Nothing could be more hushed than the way
The moon moves toward the night.
But what his mother was returns and cries on his breast.

The red ripeness of round leaves is thick
With the spices of red summer.
But she that he loved turns cold at his light touch.

What good is it that the earth is justified,
That it is complete, that it is an end,
That in itself it is enough?

It is the earth itself that is humanity . . .
He is the inhuman son and she,
She is the fateful mother, whom he does not know.

She is the day, the walk of the moon
Among the breathless spices and, sometimes,
He, too, is human and difference disappears

And the poverty of dirt, the thing upon his breast,
the hating woman, the meaningless place,
become a single being, sure and true.

H   This is a poem like many by Stevens that attracts me and troubles
    me in ways that I feel driven to complain about.

G   You are given to complaining about poems, Mark.

H   Yes. I'm going to speak of this poem as one of those in which
    Stevens seeks, and too easily wins, release from the pains and dif-
    ficulties of acknowledging persons: all the trouble that people ex-
    perience in dealing with each other. Okay, this is a poem in which
    at a series of moments, the man being referred to, the "he" (who
    is, I think we feel, the poet himself) is conscious of two things.
    On the one hand, he's conscious of his present physical experience
    of the day or the night, conscious of the natural weather of his
    present. On the other hand, he has memories. Memories of his
    father and of his mother, and also of, presumably much more re-
    cent, unhappy interaction between himself and a woman who is,
    as I take it—though I admit this is not specified by the poem—
    the wife of the poem's hero.

G   Mark, can I interrupt for a moment to ask a question? I normally
    expect short poems, which I call "lyric," to be in the first person.
    This is a poem in the third person. Can you help me understand
    the consequences of the difference that arises between the lyric
    poem written in the first person and the lyric poem written in the
    third person, here called "he"?

H   Okay, if I ask why Stevens makes that choice, I think the answer
    is that what's being described here is really a hypothesis, a hypo-
    thetical version of self. It is a man who Stevens wants to be.

G   So then the poem in the third person produces a speculative rela-
    tionship, not only hypothetically between the writer and the per-
    son in the poem, but also between the reader and the person in

the poem. In effect, this practice of the short poem in the third person opens a space of thought as well as identificatory participation.

H   Wait a second. You seem to suggest that the possible identity represented by the pronoun "he" here is made more open as a possibility to the reader than it would be if it was in the first person?

G   Yes. I feel that the third person establishes a sort of common place, a *locus communis*, where persons can gather to address a problem of thought. When the poem is written in the first person, reading becomes a competition for participation, not only between reader and reader but between hypothetical author and reader. So that I do feel an openness, a gathering in of selves, an unowned character to discourse in the third person.

H   Yeah, okay, I hear you, but I sense that I, if we were going to push the discussion on this point, would have to resist, because I think of poems that I write in the first person, and I don't want to admit that they are in competition with the reader's reality. So I think we're on the edge of a difference between our senses of what a poem does to a reader.

G   And a difference in our current practice, since most of my recent poems are in the third person or some discursive equivalent, and most of your poems are in the autobiographical first person.

H   Yeah, and this will turn out to be significant in our very different responses to this Stevens poem. Because, as I said, I want to complain against the evasion of autobiographical truths that this poem performs. Now let me say that I value this poem. I'm glad that it exists. Nevertheless, in trying to understand what Stevens achieves, which is always a matter of also understanding what a writer has not achieved, and has chosen not to do, I think it's important to bear down on what is being left out of this poem.

G   Okay. Let me, Mark, talk for a moment about what I see in this poem. I see a succession of states of affairs in the first three stanzas in which a speaker declares that there is a person, not himself, who has suffered a disruption in experience of enormous importance and consequences. That disruption takes the form of a separation of the human facts of the world from the great, inhuman, cyclical, and transcendental facts by which the person in the world was previously rendered invulnerable to time and change. In the first stanza, the father is shown to be separated from the "great day"—which is the father's sign—and has died and now lies in a place initially of deficit, that is to say, the dirt. Similarly, the mother has been separated from her signs and symbols, from the terms by which the maintenance of *her* being in the world was previously assured. "But what his mother was," a bitter inversion, "returns and cries on his breast." Similarly, the woman of whom the speaker speaks has turned cold, thus has been separated from her great and perennial signifiers, which are "the red ripeness of round leaves" and "the spices of red summer."

This sets a task for the discourser who speaks this poem: the task of re-establishing the value of the perishing mortal who is also in profound pain, pain as a result of the withdrawal of significance, the loss of acknowledgment or love. That task is formulated as a question: "What good is it that the earth is justified, / That it is complete?" The implication being that the earth has ceased to be meaningful because it has become separate from its term of significance, the human being who previously rejoiced in its providence. The last three stanzas of the poem seem to me *somehow* to repair the state of affairs which I have just now described as a disruption of the relationship between the person and the person's transcendental signifiers, the person's powers of maintenance; and this restoration becomes quite final in the last line of the poem, where the person has "become a single being, sure and true." But I am troubled by the last sentence of the poem. There is an equivocation of the very conclusiveness that is stated. The poem elides the redemptive process that the last three stanzas presumably offer us.

H   I need to know what you meant by "elides," because what I mainly have to say about this poem concerns the elision or the omission of crucial steps between the problem set by the first three stanzas, which is brought to a focus by the outcry of the fourth stanza, and the recuperation or rescue claimed by the last two stanzas.

G   Can I interrupt again? We are speaking from the point of view of practice. As poets, and as teachers of poetry, we are in a position to view the tradition as subject to our capacities to reconstruct it from moment to moment. Indeed, as poets we are obligated to change the tradition by contributing to it. And as teachers of persons who write poetry, we are entering into the fundamental encoding of the tradition, and rendering it subject to the criteria of value, knowledge of which constitutes our legitimacy as teachers of poetic writing.

H   Yes. Right. And if I were indeed in a teaching relation to the author of this poem I'm sure I would find myself pointing to the jump or skip in the poem's thought that occurs at the word "sometimes" in the next-to-last stanza. This is a poem that chooses to jump from the regrettable condition of dividedness to a sudden and dangerously charming account of a healed condition of unity.

G   Why dangerous?

H   Because by saying "sometimes" he dodges the work of saying *when* the good condition can arise, and if he can't say when then he can't tell us *how*.

G   And if he can't tell us how, then there is no ethical dimension. Right?

H   The ethical dimension is in fact what's elided. The transition comes in the fifth stanza, where Stevens makes a kind of strategic move by which he distributes the words "human" and "humanity" away from the unhappy condition of the man described in this poem (the "he") toward the earth, toward Nature, toward that realm of leaves and ripeness and strong day that the man has felt divorced from in the first three stanzas. By doing this, Stevens is able to imply that the more true, more real, more human condition of this human being will be that in which he recovers his at-homeness in the realm of day and night and summer. My proposed revision would be focused on the idea that indeed the *human* experience of this person being described is that in which he has an unhappy, unfruitful relation with the woman he has loved. It is the "peculiar" condition in which he is haunted by the ghost of his mother, and by troubled feeling about the mortality of his father. His humanness is in that divided condition. The poem's real problem was to be the examination of that unhappy condition, which would involve ultimately some more painful, painstaking account of the relations, whether in memory or in the present, between that man and his lover, mother and father; so that I can easily imagine myself pushing, you see, the young student whose name is Wallace toward a kind of unpacking or expansion of this poem to fill in, so to speak, the gap that appears at the word "sometimes" in this poem.

G   I think it's important that we are not addressing the young student named "Wallace." We are in fact addressing a formidable and privileged fact of our poetic inheritance which it is appropriate and necessary to interrogate. Stevens at many times affirmed that the good of the earth *is* justified, that the world specified conventionally as "earth," the empirically recovered world of fact, is complete in itself and satisfies human need, is "enough." From *my* point of view the problem posed by the last three stanzas is the problem of obtaining for the person subject to the inevitable divisions as between self and world (marked by the death of those upon whom one depends—father and mother—and by the distance, which does not grow less for thinking about it, between one person and another) power sufficient to compensate these inevitable, indeed fatal losses. From your point of view, to become a single being is simply to transgress against the fundamental value of being human at all, for to become a single being implies erasure of that interactivity of person in which alone persons become real. From my point of view also the idea of the single being constructs a world of persons bereaved of the fundamental resource by which a human

being is constructed and compensated for loss; but for me single-
ness is bereavement of that power or term, not Earth, and not
human, by which human relationship is founded. As I see it, Stevens is working with the paradox that the founding relationship of
which I speak does result in the elision of the mortal facts of personal relationship. You see this as a fault. I see it as the central
human struggle.

H   A word that was important to you, in our earlier conversations,
    especially, as I recall, in reference to your poem "Of the Great
    House," is the word "integration." Integration of aspects of one's
    being, so that one becomes a more enabled, more coordinated
    being in the world. That is a possible thing, that is an outcome
    that can be again and again achieved by people, sometimes
    through art, sometimes through other activities. What I object to
    is the way this poem jumps to its evocation of that condition. I
    think that there are peculiar materials in relation to father,
    mother, and lover that would need to be examined for the poem
    to achieve the transit that this poem seems to want to achieve.

G   Well, let us ask the question: What is the loss of peculiarity
    weighed against? By what benefit is that loss compensated in this
    poem? What drives the repression or elision to which you make
    reference? Now this is a poem which is struggling to maintain its
    self-consistency in the presence of facts which are unaccountable
    in terms of its speaker's ideology, belief, or previous structuration
    of the world. The fourth stanza is a cry. "What good is it," cries
    the speaker, "that the earth is justified?"
        The last three stanzas undertake to maintain the integrity of
    the speaker in the face of facts which seem to contradict the very
    structure of reality as the speaker, who has spoken so long in Ste-
    vens' work up to this moment, understands it to be. The repres-
    sions of fact which you perceive I wish to propose are in aid of the
    production of that self-consistency required to maintain the pres-
    ence of this person who speaks. Precisely that region of the poem
    which I elided in my description, and which you regard as the site
    of the repression of the ethical, is the point where there is regis-

tered the cost of that self-consistency upon which the speaker is insisting. Now that self-consistency is, in effect, the generative life of this poetic project. As Stevens has often insisted in his construction of earlier poems, precisely this abstraction, precisely this repression of particularity is the cost of this class of text, this civilizational accomplishment. I think what we find here is a repression of what *you* profoundly value in the interest of another outcome—the maintenance of the presence which we call "Stevens."

H   I disagree with what you're saying, if I understand it. Are you suggesting that it is only because he has been able to attain the state evoked at the end of this poem that he has in fact been able to write these poems?

G   Yes. The poem engages the question of how the facts of the world can be rendered consistent with the belief or account of the world generative of the discourse of which the poem is an example. What I am saying is that "World Without Peculiarity" is a poem engaged in the characteristically civilizational brutality of the repression of that which, given the structure of Stevens' poetic project, must be repressed in order to obtain the outcome which is the poem.

Having said that, I wish to raise the question as to how, or by what authoritative legitimacy, you and I can argue for the replacement of this poem by another. For the poem which you lament the absence of here is, in effect, not a revision of the poem which is presented to us, but a poem of another kind, one might say a work of another kind by another hand. There seem to me two kinds of revision that we can ask for: one is the revision of a text in terms of its own self-consistency; the other is the revision of a text such that the conditions of the production of the text in question are no longer affirmable from a moral point of view, no longer permissible or even constructable. And it's that latter kind of judgment that I think you are here bringing to bear.

I have observed that the repressions which you lament are in the interest of the maintenance of the self-consistency upon which in my view the continuity of Stevens' poetic project depends; *with-*

out these repressions this voice could not continue to be heard. How then can I reconcile my own admiration for this poem with my unwillingness to sponsor its apparently inherent violence? After all, "peculiarity" is that singularity of persons which makes relationship possible, without which love and indeed discourse itself are inconceivable. We have a number of alternatives. We can— bear in mind I think it is part of our freedom—reject this poetic practice altogether; I can (I think it is part of my freedom) reject any state of affairs, which in the interest of any self-consistency, whether it be national, religious, philosophical, or poetic, re- presses a value-bearing fact of the world. We can judge not only the artistic object in its singularity, but the very practice which produces it. Or on the other hand we can declare that the value of the artistic object is somehow in excess of the value of what it represses, and observe that there is a cultural "cost of doing busi- ness" which must be endured and is part of the weary, and discon- tented, but necessary labor of civility.

H   That list of freedoms doesn't seem to me to exhaust the possibili- ties.

G   Good.

H   There is also the response in which we would say there are different kinds of poems that we need in the world, just as there are different kinds of people that one wants to meet in the world. One wants to be free to act and write in different ways at different times. Looking again at "World Without Peculiarity," I value it in two ways, despite all I've said about it. One is that the poem is a mov- ing picture of a person—I mean the speaker of the poem—making a moral mistake. Of course we make mistakes all day. I mean it's very human for him to be making this moral mistake, so, when I put it that way, I don't intend to sound superior or condescending. A vivid, compressed, or otherwise charged or intense image of someone making a mistake, even if he or she would not be willing to describe the event in exactly that way, can be moving, valuable, instructive. Secondly, I want to note that when you reach the end

of this poem there's an outcry of gratitude. The poem, whatever
trouble it begins in, culminates in the successful expression, exclamation really, of the gratitude felt by someone who has, for whatever mysterious reason, experienced rescue from the torture of bad
dreams.

When I try to think about what is different in our attitudes and
views as a result of the ten years since our earlier conversations, I
claim that, being older, I'm more willing to admit that there are
many different kinds of poems that need to be written by one person as well as by the multiplicity of poets; so in that sense, though
I may to you sound sometimes even more tendentious than I was
ten years ago—

G You do.

H I think I'm more tolerant of diversity.

G So the precinct of the poem (by its precinct I mean all the marks
of the poem's closure which supply its form) in your understanding
anticipates the addition of other contradictory poems, and also the
presence of past poems. The poem is not an apodictic speaker (a
speaker from certainty) but rather a speaker who implicitly speaks
anticipatory of, and in remembrance of, the qualification of other
presences.

H Yes.

G As in a sane, moral life does a person. Is there, Mark, a poet for
whom a world without peculiarity is, as I think you see it, a world
in which human life is not recognizable?

H Well, what about Emily Dickinson? Let me read you a Dickinson
poem which I like because in it she confronts and even cherishes
the difference between selves, as Stevens does not.

>   Again—his voice is at the door—
>   I feel the old *Degree*—

I hear him ask the servant
For such an one—as me—

I take a *flower*—as I go—
My face to *justify*—
He never *saw* me—*in this life*—
I might *surprise* his eye!

I cross the Hall with *mingled* steps—
I—silent—pass the door—
I look on all this world *contains*—
Just his face—nothing more!

We talk in *careless*—and in *toss*—
A kind of *plummet* strain—
Each—sounding—shily—
Just—how—deep—
The *other's* one—had been—

We *walk*—I leave my Dog—at home—
A *tender*—*thoughtful* Moon
Goes with us—just a little way—
And—then—we are *alone*—

Alone—if Angels are "alone"—
First time they *try* the *sky!*
Alone—if those "vailed faces"—be—
We cannot *count*—on High!

I'd give—to live that hour—*again*—
The *purple*—*in my Vein*—
But *He* must *count the drops*—*himself*—
My *price* for *every* stain!

G   This is a poem which allows us to understand more clearly the class
of poetry which in your view is repressed in the poem by Stevens.
In this poem, as in the poem of your own with which we began,
the speaker entertains a possibility contrary to fact. You began
"Location" by saying, "You could begin by saying," meaning that
it's one of the possibilities of which you are not yet secure. Emily

Dickinson begins by rewriting an experience which in the past has been as important as life to her. By contrast to Stevens' mystified account of the disruption which arises when he and his protagonist experience the disharmony between expectation and the facts of life's outcomes, she re-writes, in all the problematical detail of which she is the champion and the martyr simultaneously, the narrative of that kind of meeting in which she invests the whole value of human experience: the meeting by the self with another whose face is "all this world contains": the face which, over and over again in Dickinson saturates sight and makes divine faces trivial.

What is particularly striking to me about this poem is, first of all, the fact that the great meeting takes place within the problematic of ordinary social ignorance between two persons deeply intended toward one other: "We talk in *careless*—and in *toss* / . . . Each—sounding—shily—/ Just—how—deep—/ The *other's* one —had been—." In the Dickinsonian re-writing of central experience between persons, there is no possibility of honoring that experience if the *impossibility* of knowing other selves is not deeply inscribed. I'm particularly struck by the end, in which, while declaring that she would give all of life to live that hour again, she nonetheless realizes the other by constructing him *as a moral person who is subject to demand* within the universe, the laws of which must be acknowledged because they were not made by either of the participants in this relationship and yet are the code of all relationships. She says: "But *He* must *count the drops—himself—/ My price* for *every stain!*"

At the end of the poem, the singularity of individuals is not overcome, but rather realized within the province of an ethical exchange in which people become real, capable of loving and being beloved, because they are objects of demand. This is a poem in which the speaker acknowledges in insistent detail the minute particulars of others who are maintained not by unification, which for Dickinson's mind and minds like hers, if there are any, is the very cancellation of relationship, but by differentiation, the maintenance of what Stevens calls pejoratively "peculiarity."

H   I have sometimes thought that a limitation of the poem might inhere in its romanticizing of the ecstasy and excitement, and a kind of romanticized idealization of her valuing of this man, this "he." But there is, as you've said, a ferocious insistence on a gap between him and her, asserted in the last two lines of the poem, that is more serious than the kind of romanticized exclamation that I might have thought we were hearing. Despite that gap, the poem is an account of a meeting that was, on the whole, happy for her, whereas the relationships between persons in the Stevens poem were painfully unhappy ones for him. Nonetheless, I think the comparison between the two poems shows here a poet who has more courage in facing up to the mysterious reality of *meeting*.

Now as you've suggested, the last stanza is the point where the poem acknowledges that the narrative of the previous stanzas is not really the present experience of the speaker, but has indeed been a re-creation of experience. The last two lines of the poem require of both the self and beloved other some continuing obligation in their mutual relation: "*He* must *count the drops—himself— / My price* for *every stain!*" I do admire the unrelaxed extension into some kind of infinite future of the mutual obligation of these two people.

G   Is Dickinson's insistence on obligation, that is to say the acknowledgment between two people, each of the other, on the grounds of ethical demand, a reason for valuing this poem? Is the poem conducted in such a way as to exemplify your sense of the ethical demand which is criteriological both for social life and for poetic practice as you understand it?

H   Yes. The poem chooses not to resort to a claim of ecstatic union between self and beloved, nor does it settle for a mere lament of endless loss and separation. I admire the way the ending of the poem points to a life in which the felt force of another person's need will continue to be crucial for both persons. So yes, it does seem to me a more ethically honest and complete statement of the self's condition than the Stevens poem.

G   Now the Stevens poem is thematically comic. By calling it comic,
    I mean that it intends a world that begins in division and ends in
    unity. By contrast, Dickinson's poem is about a tragic reality which
    produces, as tragic realities do, the irreducibility of separate indi-
    vidualities. Is there something criteriological, in your sense of
    things, about the preference for tragic construction of interper-
    sonal life?

H   That's a good question, and the answer is no, and you're making
    me see a reservation I should make in praising this poem as a com-
    plete statement about the life of the speaker. Of course no poem is
    a complete statement of the life of a speaker, but there are degrees
    of completeness, and I am trying to be the advocate of a more
    inclusive, fuller accountability of a speaker. When she says: "I'd
    give—to live that hour—*again*— / The *purple*—*in my Vein*—,"
    the implication is she will not be able to live that hour again, for
    some reason. The poem does not say why. Now there is a gap
    there, which I question in a way parallel to the kind of worry or
    questioning of an omission that I made about the Stevens poem.
    Because, you see, I write poems which reflect a social life of speak-
    ers and characters in which there is pain, there is separation, there
    is sometimes death, but there is also a tremendous "ongoingness"
    that speakers and characters continue to cope with. And I feel,
    whether with reference to Dickinson or other poets, that the im-
    plication that a crisis or failure or ending in a particular relation-
    ship between two persons is irrevocably tragic can be a kind of
    romantic illusion in itself, a failure of truth.

G   Look, Mark, my admiration for this poem derives precisely from
    the fact that it does acknowledge irrevocable laws which bear upon
    human desire and its outcomes, that are not in themselves human,
    and which it is the business of the poet in the interest of truth not
    to ignore or disqualify, on the grounds, as you have just done, of
    the imputation of irrelevance or romanticism. Dickinson here pro-
    poses that it is among the requirements of the laws of the universe
    that she exchange life for the recurrence of this profound event.

She declares not vaguely or tentatively, but clearly and emphatically, and in her work, repeatedly, that the price of true meaning (the reality of the other) is no less and no more than life itself, and that the most exquisite and profoundly human attentiveness that the other can give to the beloved is to note precisely that the consummation of any relationship, as desire constructs consummation, is the giving of life.

Now I want to stress here my sense that you repress the *context* in which social meeting does go on. In other words, Dickinson proposes that there is an economy in reality that it is her responsibility to acknowledge, and to compel acknowledgment of, by the other. I derive from your observations the sense of a mind that represses considerations of cause which are not human, as if social value, including the value of poetry and the criteria which regulate its production, were produced in the absence of all other systems of causality, such as economic systems, or such as the systems which govern the perceptibility of persons one by the other, or indeed such as the system which death seems to index that requires, as Dickinson is very, very conscious, that one will betray the other perforce.

H   Okay. Can I say something?

G   Yeah.

H   The line that I want to stress in response is: "I'd give—to live that hour—*again*—." One assertion made by that line is, as we've said, that some set of overwhelming difficulties, apparently, will prevent the reliving of that hour, but the line also does assert that an hour, not just a moment, but an hour of actual meeting between two persons did occur, and that is a possibility in the real life of this person. That dimension of life is real for Emily Dickinson. Now if she is as tragic a poet, ultimately, as you're suggesting, then she is different from me, but what I'm finding in her that I want to cherish and emphasize is that, despite her intense sense of forces that will prevent satisfying encounter or connection, let alone union, between selves, still she acknowledges and makes a space in her poetry for the hour of that real meeting, which is not undone by some tragic future.

G   Neither, however, does that hour extinguish the desire for another hour, nor does the memory of that hour secure us that that hour *was* the hour of consummation or from the desire to live it again, maybe to live it right, because it was lived wrong the first time, as there is some evidence in this poem that it was.

The business of the poet, as I understand it, is, first, to recon-struct in the artifactual space of the poem those rules resistance to which constructs our humanity, because our courage and capacity for self-evaluation are invested in our resistance to those resist-ances. And then, second, to enact the presence of the human voice, inscribed in such a way as to supply a case of the endurance and the momentary overcoming of those laws (replicated in the poem as metrical laws) which resist us whenever we undertake to meet and love. Dickinson's speaker, like Stevens' third person of suffering in his poem, leaves behind her the signifiers of an imme-diate intelligibility, the dog and even the moon, and finds herself then, like Stevens' protagonist alone, without mother and father. By contrast to Stevens, Dickinson's speaker turns toward rather than away from the constraints upon being which her passion and intelligence encounters and which constitute the transcendental validation of her art, and demands as a condition of, and as in-stance of the nature of her love, acknowledgment of a common life conducted in the presence of those strange powers, time, lan-guage, death.

We both, however, judge this poem as good. We conclude that it takes in more reality, such as we affirm, than the Stevens poem. Now the residual question which we must face is still what grounds we have for *reproducing* this preference as poets and teachers.

H   What ground do we have for teaching one poem rather than an-other? We see the Dickinson poem as taking in more reality than the particular Stevens example that we chose earlier, and it's clear that's a value for us, the taking in of a lot of reality. You ask me:

What ground do we have for teaching that? I answer simply that every person has to cope with as much reality as that person can handle. That is the responsibility of growing up, as I see it. So there's some way in which the ground, the justification for that advocacy in my teaching, seems to me self-evident, but I understand that it doesn't feel that way to you, so I want to ask *you* now: What conceivable grounds could you posit for the requirement that students learn about certain texts and not others?

G   Well, Mark, I suppose that the capacity of the student and the capacity of the teacher to bring the world to mind requires some supplement or some augmentation. In my view, the student and the teacher of poetry come together because of a common requirement that there be more access to the world than ordinary language, and discourse of another kind than poetry, affords. Consequently, the student and the teacher have a common and reciprocal agreement that two things are the case. One, that our capacity to make statements about the world requires a supplement; and, two, that the poetic means for facilitating such statements is available to be searched, and inquired of by everyone.

In the doing of teaching of this kind my *authority* derives, as I understand it, from the nature of the poetic text, and not from any accumulated experience on my part, or for that matter on the student's part, of any other reality as such. My conception of the poem is that it is required of the poet. That requirement is repeated as a requirement of the poetic speaker in the thematic of the poem and responds to the requirement of the reader that brings him or her to the supplement of the poem precisely when the will of that person can proceed along no other avenues toward encounter with what the mind needs to know in order to avoid suffering. Hence, my conception of the poem itself is as an artifact which is the result of a supplement to human powers, most specifically and most obviously, that supplement to ordinary language which is supplied when the rules and principles of poetic construction are added to the rules and principles of ordinary language to produce the characterizing feature of the poem, namely the line. And what I regard students and teachers as investigating, and as intending to

gather among their personal resources, is precisely those aspects of
the poem which intervene, interpellate, hail, call to, summon,
from the "outsideness" of the poem to both parties, teacher and
student, reader and reader, and, by calling from outside, constitute
a difference as between the experience of either party and the new
knowledge which the poem supplies.

Consequently I am not, together with the student, checking
the reality that is supplied by the poem against my experience or
the student's experience of reality. I am checking the poem as an
act against its own hypothesis of origins. The nature of poetry, a
very old human practice, and the consistency with which, across
time, and across many cultural revolutions, the human community
has turned to poetry make it necessary to note that, whenever the
poem is present, a vast history of practice is present, a history of
practice which could not be inferred, that is to say, would not be
imaginable as reproducible, from any given moment of demand.
The very structures of poetry supply a practice which cannot have
originated and cannot be justified internal to the moment of need
upon which teacher and student meet.

H   Allen, I feel, still, that what you've said so far on the question at
    hand doesn't bring us closer to an answer to the problem of revi-
    sion. We're talking about how we can know when a poem is good,
    a poem by Dickinson or a poem by you, a poem by me or a poem
    by one of our students—how can we know that a poem in process
    of revision is getting any better? What basis is there for these value
    judgments that we find ourselves making? Now I've suggested and
    I think I'll keep arguing—all day if necessary—that the only ori-
    gin really for our value judgments about poems, which are always
    statements of some kind about moral life, the only basis is our own
    experience of moral and spiritual life, as guided and shaped by
    other people, usually people older than us, like our parents, but
    also sometimes people younger than us, like our students. At any
    rate, my sense is that the only origin and thus basis of authority is
    in our experience. And when you suggest that the work of pushing
    a poem toward its better or best form and content is the work of
    checking the poem as an act against its own hypothesis of origins,

what I fear is that your argument leads toward a privileging of professional expertise in the history of poetry and poetics, which may or may not cooperate with the kind of wisdom drawn from experience that I say is the crucial thing for a teacher or writer.

If you're going to assert that your authority as teacher, or anyone's authority as teacher or poet, arises somehow from knowledge of the great tradition of poetry, I will still claim that the only basis on which you have been able to choose among all the poems offered to you as great or good or instructive or representative has been your sense of what is healthy, for yourself and for interactions between yourself and others. And that sense has come from your childhood, your life, your experience as a person among other people in classrooms and in living rooms and in restaurants.

G Is wisdom and health the same for all persons, each gender, black persons and white persons?

H I guess I proceed from the assumption—it *is* an assumption, but one that feels *necessary* to me—that all human beings have some important portion of their experience in common. The difficulties involved in having both a body and a mind, in having parents, in wanting love and achievement, in growing up, in having children (or choosing not to have children), in facing death—there is a universal element in these difficulties and there are (I feel) universal elements in what will be a healthy and/or moral response to these difficulties by each person.

G So, you are with the Wife of Bath: "Experience though no authority / Were in this world is right enough for me." But I would like to distinguish, Mark, between two kinds of knowledge that are present in the classroom when poetry is the concern. I do not feel that there is a neutral state of teaching, but that teaching always participates in the inherently dangerous and morally ambiguous powers which generate *the particular kind of learning,* and in our practice the particular kind of text, which is the concern of the teaching transaction in whatever field it may be situated. I agree that the relationship *between the student and the teacher* is gov-

erned and regulated by the teacher's wisdom, wisdom of the kind
you are speaking about which may have the qualified universality
of which you speak—that is to say, the teacher's inferences from
experience. I do feel that this kind of wisdom is especially in play
in the teacher's management of the student's transference and the
teacher's own countertransference, which, from my point of view,
is a powerful and culturally indeterminate element in all relationships of teaching and learning. But, and this is the point at which
we are at odds, I am convinced that the authority of the teacher
as a teacher of poetry derives solely from his or her practice of the
art or craft which is the subject matter that brings teacher and
student together, and which in my view is the same for all persons.
The student and the teacher together manage the supervision of
the relationship between both minds and a third thing.

H   I think "H" wins this one.

G   I don't think so.

H   Fortunately for you, there's no ultimate judge.

G   That's what you think. Look, what we are seeking when we revise
a poem is the fullest possible realization of a text *as a poem.* Our
business, in relationship to that student, is only secondarily to
obtain a truthful account by that student of his or her relationship
to his or her mother, or whomever.

H   But what will fullest mean? How will *you* know what a fullest realization is? I mean the student could write fifteen more stanzas,
wouldn't that be fuller? How will you decide what is the fullest
realization?

G   Insofar as I and the student are engaged in the production of a
poem, we are going to be able to answer that question only by
moving away from *that* poem and searching the tradition of poems
for traces of that class of integration responsive to precisely that
paradigm which makes it possible for us to speak of many scattered

and diverse texts as related to the same term, that is to say, to poetry itself. The poet intends the poem, teacher and student engaged in the revision of the *poem* intend the poem, and not a text of another kind, neither health, nor any other object heterogeneous to those classes of things which are includable in the indexical category called poetry. In other words, I wish to insist that the poetic instrument is an instrument of a particular kind, capable of knowledge of a particular kind.

Cultural modalities are inherently both powerful and dangerous, and, because they lie outside the regulative systems by which we commonly secure the maintenance of our life, our human safety, they require the closest scrutiny. God help us if the wisdom of poets as persons becomes the criterion for the goodness of poetry. But in fact, it cannot. I argue for the specificity of the instrument and the inherent danger of invoking it. We wish as teachers to make an apprentice to the sorcerer who knows the spells which regulate the art. My view is that something can be said about that regulative principle, but that it will not be derivable in the way you derive it.

H   Well, it's clear there's some deep disagreement between us that seems philosophical but, somehow beneath that, is temperamental. It reminds me of something you made me admit at least once in our 1981 conversations, that this emphasis I place on the relation between experience and the value of a poem does not account for my decision to write a poem rather than to write something else or to make a movie or to simply have a conversation with someone. In other words, I have not provided, from my point of view, a reason why I or someone else might choose to grapple with an issue or make a statement or ask a question in the form of a *poem*, rather than in some other form of communication. I think I have to admit here that there's something stubbornly agnostic in me about this question.

Clearly, I choose, again and again, to shape statements and questions and worries and investigations that I want to make in language as poems. In doing so, I want the privileges of poetry: I want to be listened to with the kind of attentiveness that some people have learned to bring to poems, and I want to feel, even if it turns out to be an illusion, that a poem of mine, like my poem "Location," will be kept, will be preserved, somehow, through time after my death because of its status as a poem. I want those privileges and yet I seem repeatedly unwilling to claim, or admit, that those privileges are bound together with a difference between the kind of wisdom or statement that poems offer, and the kinds of wise or good communications that people make between each other in ordinary life.

G   Mark, the motives to poetry you express—to speak in such a way as to be helpful to people on the basis of the best experience you can obtain, the most veracious witness and the best inferences from that witness which you can bring to bear upon your situation or the situation of others—are in my view structurally in conflict with the motive to speak words which will not perish with the moment in which they are spoken or with the person who knows how to speak them. When the criteria of *representation* and the laws which generate those criteria become a part of the same task as the obligation to speak subject to the criteria of *wisdom* useful truths about experience, there intrudes a new or third class of fact, the artifact. Between these two sets of criteria—*the wisdom criteria,* as you understand wisdom, and *the representational criteria* requisite to the revision of poems as poems—there arises a fundamental tension.

Representational criteria seem to require the repression of all that is not the poem, seem to require speech which is without alternative inscribed in one way and in one way alone, seem to participate in the ruthless economies of dominance and subordination: the poem that is your object of attention now and not another poem, the poem which is published, and not all those that are unpublished, the *poem* which is a type of discourse that has obtained dominant relationship to other discourse and represses other discourse. In my view, the problem as we have now posed it offers us two destinations which do not accord, those two destinations being truth about states of affairs on the one hand, and truths about the medium of representation called poetry on the other. As I see it, "Location" in the title of your poem really means not geographical location, but the manner in which the speaker will negotiate the competing claims of the representational system on the one hand and ethical concern on the other. The very fact that your poem ends with a resumption, on another basis, of representational activity, rather than with an intervention of a social or economic kind in the world which is deplored, suggests the dominance (not merely the presence, but the dominance) of the representational imperative. How in your view does the poem called "Location" end?

H   Well, that's a good question. It's the kind of question that worries me about lots of my poems that arrive at an apparently ethical implication. What is the speaker of this poem going to *do* as a result of having uttered this poem? The last few lines of the poem begin the poem of summer in Philadelphia that would be respectful of the reality in which the speaker finds himself and of the other people, earlier disparaged, among whom the speaker is living. So one outcome is a tentative or hypothetical improvement in the kind of poetic utterance that will come from this poet or this speaker. But, as you've noted, there is the other question about whether I imagine this poem as an efficacious action leading toward actions in the world different from the writing of poems. Will this poem turn out to be a step toward more humane or otherwise moral interactions between me and people on the street? Clearly, I want to think that my poems do not exist only in the realm of poetry, but that they are actions of mine that will enable me to behave more generously and kindly in the world of people. I also believe that the reading of a poem like this might have that same kind of wider enabling effect upon a reader. I don't admit that the effects of writing and reading this poem are perpetually at some remove from interactive experience between people in the real world, by which I mean that world outside poetry.

G   Further, you claim that the wisdom of a poem worthy of transmission across time has a certain universality and a certain permanent authority which justifies the privilege of attention that poetry demands. Do you in fact claim that the authority of the wisdom in the poem (the fruit of your experience) and also the authority of the fact of the poem (the fruit of your making) has about it an unqualified privilege which is similar to the claim of universality and permanence for poetry that lies deep in the Western tradition?

H Well I've said a minute ago that I don't seem to have a theory for that. What I have is the observation that, in my own life and the lives of lots of people who matter to me, there is this heroic willingness and readiness to pay devoted attention, over and over, to poems. I see that and I aspire that my poems will share in that. But you see I find myself shying away from the word "authority." Either I don't want to use it, or I want to bend it away from the way that you use it.

G Might we say that you repress, unsuccessfully, the word "authority."

H Well maybe, but I want to substitute a word like "rightness" or "truthfulness." In other words, it's not because "Location" is a poem that it has any right to be preserved. If anybody's reading it ten years from now or fifty years from now, it will be because in some charged form, which I admit is different from ordinary discourse on the street in ways that I have not been able to identify theoretically, the human truthfulness of this poem remains noticeable to those readers who will pick it up in years to come.

G Whether it is morally better or morally worse to have a conviction or to have a theory, it is nonetheless the case that both of us locate the imperatives which guide the revision of mind and the revision of text outside of mind and text. The question that remains for both of us is what must the poet *do* in the light of what the poet knows about his or her art in America, in this new decade, the decade which we are now entering.

2. WHAT MUST THE POET DO?

H   In 1981 there was a prevailing sense of dark seriousness that colored a lot of our talk. That seemed to be why it was right to call
the conversations "Winter Conversations" and to dwell on meanings of the word "death." Well, we're ten years older now and we
both feel that our talk has changed. And your poems have
changed. There is a texture of diversity and a kind of discursive
hopefulness in many of your new poems, along with more frequent
comic elements than in your poems up to 1981.

G   We are in the presence, Mark Halliday, of both the beginning and
the end of narratives as we sit here today, like gods. I remember
the end of our conversations in '81. At that time, we anticipated
that, because it was winter, spring would come, and that we would
in the course of time learn what was in the ground when we saw
what flowered in the spring. We can now see what was in the
ground.

When we talked in the winter of 1981, I was acutely conscious
of the murderous conflicts on the site of the educational institution
which had occurred in the late sixties and early seventies in America, and which seemed to me a demand upon those of us who
conduct education in America to consider the relationship between the culture which we transmit and are paid to maintain,
and the civilization as a whole. Much of our discussion was about
the question whether this civilization itself was safe, whether it
was a civilization of credit or discredit, and whether the violence
which was enacted in the space of education was continuous with
that education or was an intrusion into it.

Since we talked last, questions of this kind among academic
persons have been displaced away from the study and practice of

"literature" as such and toward analysis of the culture as a whole. In a manner characteristic of the organization of thought in America, there has arisen in the last decade an ever more rigid segregation of the scene of practice where poems are made away from thought about the civilization as a whole, which is now called "theory" or "cultural studies." One of the purposes of my work, now and henceforth, must be to rejoin the poet who dwells in the scene of poetic making with the extensive collective discourse going on in the civilization about its structure and the violence enacted in it, perhaps by representation as such. Academic thought has never been more penetrative of the basic structures of civilization and yet, at the same time, never more isolated from public life; and, ironically, the poets whose work is *by its nature a part of public life* have rarely been more isolated from the most strenuous thought in their time about the problems of civilization which are properly their concern.

H   Allen, what you're saying about the 1980s makes our situation sound worse than ever. And yet your practice as a poet now strikes me as less driven by a sense of threat and danger than was true before. This is partly because there is more humor in the new poems. Why is that?

G   The public situation in America today is identical with that of 1981. The difference for us lies in the success of the repressive cultural forces which have rendered inaccessible to the scene of poetic practice precisely the questions which most concern poetic practice. We seem to live in a world which knows everything but just that thing the knowledge of which would make it possible to begin the labor of mending and keeping, as teachers, poets, and the other appointed custodians of civilization can mend and keep, the human world.

Our conversation yesterday was an effort to make a beginning toward redressing that state of affairs, an effort to enter the mysteriously guarded site of representational activity, seeking at the level of microscopy the precise point in the evaluative act where the principle of poetic construction must in the interest of poetry be interrogated. Thus we dealt with the problem of grounding that evaluative activity which is inescapably the obligation of the poet. Such an inquiry leads, as we found, not merely to differences between us, more urgently defined than we found differences to be in 1981, but exactly to differences which put in question the ethical tolerability of the representational act altogether.

If I write poems now, and I do, I write with the intention of discovering new knowledge about the system of representation itself. In aid of that intention I see no human use in lamentation. The poem I'm going to read to you now is, in my view, a revision of what was said before in my poems, and constitutes, in my experience, a new knowledge, the implications of which I would like to display to you as we talk today.

Mary Snorak the Cook, Skermo the Gardener, and Jack the Parts Man Provide Dinner for a Wandering Stranger

There is as much holiness now as there ever was
And there is as much fire now as there ever was
And as many locusts in the desert and bees
But there is no hope for the oaks. The winds fall
From a greater height, a heavier burden on their streams.
And the day darkens. When it grows too dark to read,
The sun having set, we begin to write—for *that*
We do not need our eyes—and continue still
The history of the stranger, Mind, that spends
His force on the immortal seas in search of a companion
Who is like himself, and finds nothing like himself.
Island after island. Welcome him! Welcome him!
He is the only stone that can be solitary
In the universe: a man of stone on a sea of shadows,
Worthy of a history inscribed in the dark.
By day he reads the Book of the Wandering Stranger
To regulate desire, until the dark comes on,
Turning the dead leaves like a restless wind.
All through the afternoon, at ease among faint recognitions,
He pronounces the syllables. "The beauty of it,

The beauty of it all." By night he swims
On immortal seas and visits the world
(Temples, towns, seaports, ponds, and wells)
A man of stone, subject of histories,
And yet how changed, how fallen from what he was.
The Mind is fallen, and travels in a blind disguise
(Above him the maelstrom of the holy ocean
And beneath a storm of fire in the skies),
Companionless wanderer in the dark.—Welcome him!
An undistinguished fragment of the greater thought,
A common flower on a barren hill, or stone by chance
Discovered at the shore—for no clear reason
Carried home—and somehow lost—forgotten on the sill
Of a summer bedroom or given away to an indifferent guest—
And now witness to the Millennium:
A stone of witness to the one world that is.
—Who will make the dinner, then, for the man of stone
And who arrange his pastoral? How is it done?
The gardener supplies the food, the "wreckage" of his hoe,
A person almost mute, not a reader, name of Skermo.
The cook is cheerful, dressed in a printed sack
(*Pillsbury Flour,* 500 lbs.). Her name is Mary, Mary Snorak,
So fat she sneaks out *sidewise* through the doorway
When she wants a smoke. Mary is in love with Jack,
The parts man, who likes his dinner (in fact, the only guest),
Good for a joke. For after all the Mind must dine alone
And find nothing like, until dawn breaks with a crack
Against the seashore where he lies among the stones,
Dreaming of the immortal ocean, and reading in the
          afternoons
The Book of the Wandering Stranger written in the dark.
Holy, holy, holy is the lordly host
And holy is witness Mind, "historic traveller," and guest.
But holiest of all the fools who arrange the feast,
Skermo the gardener, the parts man Jack, and sidewise Mary
Snorak who loves him as he is, and can take a joke.

H My first response to this poem is that I like it. It appeals to me in several ways.

G Thank Heaven.

H Intuitively, I feel that it's a warm poem, a kindly poem, a generous poem. Like others among your newest poems, this one is written in relatively long lines and full, or rich, discursive sentences. The voice has at its disposal a lot of words that flow more readily than before. Of course, being Halliday, as I irretrievably am, I can't help being drawn to the lines about the cook, the gardener, and the parts man. I liked them in the title, and I like them when they show up later. In '81, I was happy about the presence of Pat in "Pat's Poem," and the presence of a couple of other particular and particularized individual persons in poems such as "The Protha-nation of a Charioteer." I feel encouraged when fat Mary and her dress made from a flour sack appear in this poem. Now the poem concludes with the claim made for those working-class people that they are the holiest of all, so the poem begins and ends with an apparently unironic, thus happy or even beatific assertion that there is an abundance of holiness in the world. That claim of abundance is in keeping with the quality of this poetry that I might call cornucopic, by contrast with the available resources of syntax, vocabulary, and sentiment in some of your earlier poems.

G This new poetry is a comic poetry, a summer poetry. It enters into the abundance of things, and intends a resolution which affirms the powers of the world such as serve and establish the person. Like your poem "Location" with which we began, this poem is also a journey, in which the mind wanders, always adorned by its in-evitable solitude, toward a greeting and a confirmation of its ground of being. Unlike the Stevens poem, with which we both had difficulty, though different difficulty as between us, this poem does end in recovery of those affirmed and beloved persons: the cook, the gardener, and the parts man, who are irreducible, atomic elements of the universe. Though they are related in love and by ceremony—dinner as it happens—they do not become one thing, and their difference is not only unresolved, but undesirable to be resolved. They are the undefeated companions of mind in what you are inclined to call "interpersonal relationship," among whom is constructed the possibility of being at home in the world and of having enough to be human, and therefore, to think and love.

But these persons are not *particular* in the sense in which I feel persons are particular in your poems. They are in fact working-class people, but they are people characterized by their trades. Their names do not realize, I believe, social individuality in the ordinary sense, and indeed the language of this poem is pitched toward a generality that I think contradicts the canons of taste, sentiment, and feeling for reality, human and social, which is a very large part of the moral advocacy of the work you do.

H   Well that's true. I mean I understand that someone called "Skermo the Gardener" is representative of some category of experience or humanity. I understand that there is a generic or symbolic force to those people named in the title of the poem. Still, when Mary is shown as having to go out the door "sidewise" when she wants to smoke a cigarette, there is one of those sudden, convincing glimpses of a real person such as give me great pleasure in Whitman.

G   I would like to say something about generality in this poem, and about the nature of persons here, and therefore the nature of this poetic enterprise. I believe now that, in order to address tragedy in our world, it is necessary to draw upon that "cornucopic," that ever-flowing resource I feel within me of acknowledgment and love, in order to do two things: the first, and most difficult, and also the quite common thing I want to do, is to provide models or instances that will be paradigmatic for our personal formation in proportion as the poems can convince the reader that the poems are drawn from a world as difficult as the world in which the reader lives, and also from a humanity as rich as the humanity that the reader does, or can learn to, recognize in herself or himself. Sec-

ond, this poem and the other poems of my recent making are
poems concerned, not merely or simply with the maintenance of
a social world, but also with the reproduction, the rediscovery of
the means by which poetry *capable* of that maintenance function
can be constructed.

This poem I regard as a kind of speculative instrument, a narrative but also a narrative about narrative, a narration of histories,
but also a speculative history of narration. Mind, just so, discovered journeying in its unovercomable solitude raises the question
of what we call the "problematic," or the question of the questionability, of *continuation*. What I am deeply conscious of in this
poem and wish to make others conscious of is the deferral for so
many lines of that meeting of the wandering mind with those
great, early, and powerful persons that the mind so deeply loves.
In my view, the work of the poem devised as a speculative instrument at this moment in history lies in the region of the problem
of continuation, the capacity of the poet to raise truthful questions
about the questionability of the ongoing of things. The solution
to the problem of continuation, of which the poem would be evidence, performed by the poet in all consciousness of the laws by
which reality constrains us, is the most powerful and timely con-
tribution the poet can now make.

H   Let me try to understand better. Do you then intend that there is
a kind of hard-won victory for the poem in its eventually arriving
at the opportunity, and by implication the capacity, to represent
in the poem these remembered people?

G   Yes, not merely to represent them, though finally that's what it
must be, but to discover them, to devise the luck by which it is
possible to be thus greeted. I more and more feel that the act of
making poems consists in the discovery of combinations of elements, such as constitute the effect of personal presence, which in
ordinary experience cannot be seen to be contributory one to the
other. So that the narrative of Mind, initially unable to anticipate
the meeting which in the poem finally befalls, seems to me the
kind of narrative that can and does restore confidence, my own

and by the example of my own the confidence of others, in the inherent rationality of the human world, and in the intentionality within that rationality to supply what Stevens would call "enough."

H   So the surprising arrival in the poem of Mary, Skermo, and Jack is felt by you to be an unpredicted, lucky recovery of presences whose capacity to be present to you is not explained by your preceding account of the condition of mind.

G   That's correct.

H   You refer to these three characters as early; I take it that these people *are* persons from your own childhood memory.

G   They are persons from my own childhood memories, selected from a vast number of such persons.

H   Okay. But there is an issue here of the relation between the present mind and its deep past.

G   That's right. There's no question here but that Skermo and Mary and Jack are the richness of the deep past which cannot be anticipated by the mind in any conscious present as still alive and still making dinner, but which in this poem is found by a kind of luck I wish to make paradigmatic of the luck which awaits everyone. I intend Mary, Jack, and Skermo to be the early persons in a sense that is general and abstract: irreducibly singular as their names are irreducibly singular; irreducibly powerful as their relationships are ceremonial and interlocutory and impossible to be fused and impossible to be mistaken for one another; and at the same time *general* because they are never not among the potentialities for luck of any mind.

H   Well, I'm glad that they are so irreducible in the poem, though it also seems sad to me that the Mind in this poem, though it recovers images of them, and the sense of having been cared for by them, still Mind does not attain to interaction with them. Jack and Mary have a way of relating to each other that seems outside the experience of this mind now.

G   No question about that. The mind finally is alone, and any truth about relationship must include that first truth. Interaction never passes into intrasubjectivity, the being of selves within other selves. I hold with Dickinson in this matter, that *keeping apart* is the expression by the conscious will of the fundamental nature of mind preliminary to any relationship.

H   Okay. Can I give the Halliday response to that?

G   Yes, please.

H   When you speak of this solitude as a first truth, a truth preliminary to any further negotiations between selves, what I feel is that that is so clearly the case that the statement seems to me much less interesting and useful than it apparently seems to you and, for example, to Wallace Stevens and other writers. That is, when I encounter in a poem (or in a piece of criticism) the idea that people are inevitably and perpetually alone, what I always feel is that that should be not at all the end of some statement, poem, or analysis, but only the beginning point.

G   You will notice that it is not the end of this statement or this poem, but it *is* the beginning point. I differ from you only in this matter: that it is not only the beginning, but it is an unavoidable feature, a morally criteriological fact of any good ending.

H   Maybe so, but not the only fact! Because—

G   Let me interrupt just to irritate you and to observe that the lyric is always the speech of the mind alone. In whatever way the lyric may invite another speaker inside it, or make reference to other persons in relationship, there is finally only one sponsor of utterance in lyric.

H   Yes, but my response to that is to say calmly, *of course*. At the same
time, though, there is such a thing as interaction—or else what
are we doing here today?

G   The best we can!

H   Allen, the speaker of your poem observes that the Mind's condition is somehow diminished, fallen from what he was. I'm not sure
why that is, and perhaps this poem does not take upon itself the
burden of explaining why that has occurred in some history that
lies behind this Mind. Another feature we must say something
about is the injunction to the listener of the poem to welcome this
companionless wanderer, the Mind. If there is some meaningful
action of *welcoming* felt to be possible by the speaker of this poem,
that could be performed by listeners of this poem, would it make
up for what the mind has lost?

G   The protagonist in this poem is indeed Mind. And it is also Mind,
in another state, which speaks this poem, the returned survivor,
and happily the beneficiary of the sustenance of the dinner prepared for him. The civilizational problem which the poem confronts is the historical sense of collective loss of access to the resources of mind which make civilization endurable and safe. Such
is the fallenness of Mind, "how changed, how fallen from what he
was"—the phrase is from *The Aeneid* and is uttered in the presence of the great domestic hero Hector when seen in a dream with
his wounds unhealed and his death upon him. Mind has fallen like
Hector from a prior heroic state, fallen from a state of competence
but, above all, fallen from a state in which the mind can be in the
presence of itself, as Hector has fallen from the heroic Trojan estate or Satan from his angelic estate, in which he was in the presence of himself as divinity. That is why Mind journeys—and
reads.

H   Do you mean to suggest that, in the childhood of the speaker who
once knew Mary, Jack, and Skermo, there was a capacity for mu-

tual presence that has then been lost in the particular history of that speaker's mind?

G   Not at all. I wish to assert something quite different. The mind is not a child of any particular birth, as I understand the mind, and as I discussed it in our first conversations. The mind has a history longer than the production of any particular birth. From my point of view there is individual experience, and there is also a larger collective experience in which that individual experience is embedded. The narrative of this poem asks the question whether it is possible to work with history, the inherited state of affairs, whether there is anything particular life contributes that can empower the fragment of the great Mind of which I view us all as fragments toward a restorative experience of the whole. The confidence of this poem in the face of the possibility of change which the millennium signifies—that opening, that crack of dawn, where new things are potentiated—intends to contribute a resource, such as I can affirm *because I can narrate it convincingly*, which will change the inheritance of inevitable fallenness and render other than inevitable the repetitions which are recorded and may, in fact, be repressively recorded as the "tradition."

H   You speak of the poem's confidence, and I want to notice that the crucial moment in the poem comes where the question is asked, "Who will make the dinner . . . who arrange his pastoral . . . how is it done?" and an answer immediately follows. Now, as you know, in thinking about Thomas Hardy and other poets, I have praised a kind of poem I describe as a truth-seeking journey.

G   Yes.

H   You've spoken of *this* poem as a journey, but as I look at the lines about the supplying of this pastoral feast for the Mind, I have to say that this looks to me like a story *about* a journey rather than an unfolding venture enacted on the page. The answer to the poignant question comes immediately as if already known by the speaker of the poem.

G   This is crucial. It is precisely this strong objection you have artic-
    ulated in relationship to the *elision* of mortal processes in the Ste-
    vens poem. It is your criterion of judgment, which requires the
    registration of the whole mortal process of any affirmed outcome.
    The question who will make the dinner then for the man of stone
    and who arrange his pastoral is situated precisely at the crisis of
    continuation. The Halliday model for continuation, the Halliday
    criterion for valid knowing and for a logic which he can affirm
    because it is truth-bearing, is a stepwise procession of mind or en-
    counter in which all of the causes are present, and all of the mortal
    participants are precisely and realistically accounted for, so that
    anybody can get from where they are to that place. The steps are
    known and in the process of the journey nothing is repressed, and
    therefore nothing human is misrepresented or lost. By contrast,
    this poem proposes that continuation requires a kind of confidence
    which, in an older world, and another social formation, would be
    called "faith." A faith in the richness of things, a richness which
    cannot be effectively brought to mind in the logic of that stepwise
    process. Such faith is *another criterion*. My poems stand as a wit-
    ness to the reliability of substantial being, a reliability toward the
    supply of what is needed for the life which we all desire.

H   So, this is a poem in which what I would call an epiphany occurs.
    Whereas for me, usually the most important poems try to show
    forth a process, as you say, "step by step," whereby a speaker's
    thought gets from point A to point Z, or at least point Q. Now, of
    course, the subjects of interesting poems are not confinable to log-
    ical procedures; nevertheless there is a way in which a thinking
    mind does move in what can feel like a continuous arc or itinerary
    from one thought or image to another. So, I have this wish that as
    many stations as possible along that route should be exposed in a
    sequence. Can you say more about why it is that for you the most
    important poems are ones in which that kind of continuous se-
    quential discovery does not seem to be the required thing?

G   I'll tell you what I think the poet who writes the most important
    poems today must do. That poet is obligated to questions which

have been raised with respect to the truth of poetry, and the safety for the human community of representation as such. That poet must undertake a poetry which takes representation itself as a fundamental concern. The question then arises: *Can* a poet, consistent with the requirements of representations that take a particular form when those representations are poetry, also find an outside from which the representational process can be viewed?

There is a considerable abstraction in my poetry: the journeyer has not yet or has no longer a name, but is Mind, and the discoveries of this journeyer or Mind seem to me to be prior to the representation of particular states of affairs, hence the effective generality or even abstractness in this poetry, and, incidentally, the use of a long line in this case which, in my sentiment, is long enough so that it is possible, from the point of view of that line, to look back upon the central or modal line which represents a social interaction in our tradition, that is to say the line which stops at ten, ten being conventionally the distance between one person and another. It is my view that the writing of poetry must now take place in that theoretical position prior to the continuation of the effort to assign a human value, either to the fact of individual life, or to the facts of the world which constitute that life as a continuous narrative. What the poet must do is to think in every way possible with the intention of bringing to mind the constraints upon representation which flow from obligation to the dominant causal argument of our civilization, which is narrative itself.

H   So my advocacy of the linear narrative of particular or local human realities that I am drawn to in poems seems to you naïve in its expectation of benefits that will be won just by representation of that kind?

G   Not naïve, Mark, wrong. That is to say, it is not a question of your personal disposition that we are discussing. We must be discussing a state of the world.

H   Okay, but you feel that poets like me are much too sure that the description, for example, of someone like Mary Snorak, or of someone reading a newspaper in Philadelphia, will confer upon such a person some lasting value?

G   Yes.

H   What we've been talking about for a while is the issue of what gets put in and what is left out by the putting of that in, so what is the cost of putting in what is put in. I want this texture of credible, local, present reality in poems. Is there a sense in which what I'm doing, if I write a poem about summer in Philadelphia, is violent? I recognize that every choice to include something is a choice to exclude other things. If I write about tall, handsome people in Chicago, it could be said that there is a kind of violence being inflicted against shorter, less well-endowed people in South Phila- delphia, because there's only so much time, only so many pages in the world, and I'm taking up some of them for Chicago, and leav- ing Philadelphia out of account.

There's a kind of nightmare version of my poetry project, and that of other poets who are in this respect like me—what you might call the nightmare of endless linear narrative—in which my job would be to write billions of poems. You know, there would be a poem for every trip to the supermarket, about the pathos and beauty of the particular young woman at the checkout counter; and frankly, sometimes I can feel excited by the prospect of living for another twenty or thirty years and writing lots of such poems. However, I do at other times sense that there's something increas- ingly frustrated and frustrating about the project conceived in that way, because there are too many supermarkets, with too many cashiers. There are also, for that matter, too many people who are friends of mine, for each of them to have his or her strongly con- vincing poem. So I recognize that there are satisfactions that will not be reached by the wish for the vivid particular representation of all human reality that seems to fuel my writing. The problem, though, is that I am not convinced that you or anybody has a satisfying alternative.

G But look, Mark, the very conception of poetry includes the conception of representativity. The poem is a whole which, in addition, totalizes or takes in a whole. The implication of art is, of
course, that it stands not only for what it refers to, but also for an
entire world in which the reader, or the viewer, is present by the
very way in which the artwork indexes itself. I say this because,
when you speak of putting persons or the precious facts of the
human world into the poem, it seems to me that *you elide the
medium* or space, which, like a private domain, or like the civil
precinct of any city or nation, has its peculiar rules. When something is put into the poem, it is not put into a neutral medium,
but into a particular medium subject to rules, and rules that can
be questioned.

H Let's look at another poem. The poem is "At the Railway Station,
Upway," by Thomas Hardy, and what I want to ask you about this
poem is to what extent you find it satisfying as an act of representation. It is certainly, like all such acts, as we've been saying, one
that chooses a certain subject at the expense of other possible subjects, and one which delimits its representation of people different
from the speaker in quite severe ways, this being, even for Hardy,
a relatively short, relatively simple poem written at a considerable
distance—across a railway platform—from the lives of its characters.

    At the Railway Station, Upway

    "There is not much that I can do,
      For I've no money that's quite my own!"
      Spoke up the pitying child—
    A little boy with a violin
    At the station before the train came in,—
    "But I can play my fiddle to you,
    And a nice one 'tis, and good in tone!"

    The man in the handcuffs smiled;
    The constable looked, and he smiled, too,

As the fiddle began to twang;
And the man in the handcuffs suddenly sang
With grimful glee:
"This life so free
Is the thing for me!"
And the constable smiled, and said no word,
As if unconscious of what he heard;
And so they went on till the train came in—
The convict, and boy with the violin.

G   Mark, I am rather moved by this account of two persons in very different states of social destitution who are able to enter into a moral exchange on the basis of a means of representation—that is to say, the violin, which gives rise to the song. A train station is a place where narrative time is particularly present. The trains run on time or not, and the train as a mobile path through the world, riding upon the great abstraction of the tracks, might very well be the type of the narrative reconstruction of reality. There is a figure who administers the law, in the absence of whose mind—"unconscious of what he heard"—an escape occurs. The boy contributes what childhood and minority can—that is to say, the music—and this music makes it possible for the convict to contribute what the captive person can, a song, which is a negation or reversal of what we would call his actual state of affairs.

In the time of their union, which is not railroad or narrative time, there arises a song—this song is the result of relationship and is not in conflict with it, and suspends time or establishes an alternative or countertime to the time of the train, as a consequence of its happy obedience to alternative laws, the laws of the instrument and the laws of the voice. In the last line of the poem, the convict and the boy are together by the privilege of the instrument, with the naming of which the poem concludes as if that were the last and defining fact of their reality. The constable is, for the purposes of the truth of the poem, no longer remembered. After the end of the poem, the train, or narrative time, will once again assert itself, as I must suppose, but that now makes less difference, or a different kind of difference.

H Yeah. In many ways I think your account of the poem rings true.
   This is a poem of a kind I could aspire to write. It's a poem I'm
   grateful to have found in the world. What I'm getting at is that a
   poem like this seems closer to being enough for me than I presume
   it is for you.

G Is it a violation of the poem from your point of view for me to say
   that it is the discontinuity between the social servitude of the
   child and the convict on the one hand, and the violin and song
   about freedom on the other, that constitutes their momentary
   power, for it is the violin which makes the pity of the child socially
   effective? This is what I deeply want to say about the necessity of
   establishing the poem in an "outsideness" to the social world.

H But the violin is part of this social world. If it is a poem about
   something good that is achieved through song and thus, in a sense,
   a poem about poetry, I want to say that it's a poem of the "H" kind
   rather than the "G" kind. It's one in which we see the practice of
   art or song enacted in a social world, and attaining to a good,
   moral, compassionate social effect—very brief, terribly limited in
   its impact upon the convict, but still something good has been
   done here that is an action in the real world.

G Certainly there are few more beautiful relationships in the real
   world than that between voice and song; and the violin, as I feel
   and as you feel, makes efficacious what would otherwise be meaningless and isolated sentiment; namely, the capacity of the child
   for pity. The child pities the convict and would not be able, without the violin, to make pity, a sentiment, into an act.

H I don't accept that. It's true that the poignant effect of this poem
   has to do with the presence of a song in it, but I resist your statement that the child's pity would be a meaningless and isolated
   event if he did not have this instrument of expression. If the child
   had brought the prisoner a cup of water, instead of offering music,
   this too would have been a meaningful action. I don't at all want
   to find myself proposing that this poem—with, among other

things, the passivity of the implied observer who watches this little trio of people on the platform—is the only rightful kind of response to an event that involves oppression. But I do want to remain the advocate of this poem as an act of acknowledgment which gives its reader a portion of satisfaction. It is perhaps a small portion of the kind of satisfaction that seems to me possible in poetry.

G   But it is precisely the *critique* of "satisfaction" that we are engaged in when we discuss criteria for the value of poems, the revision of poems and perhaps the revision of the very work of poetry and the medium which is its technical privilege. Poetry feeds upon the deprivation of others.

H   Yes. At least I see that the word "satisfaction," which I used, is a dangerous and volatile word, because it may be translated as complacency. What I feel, though, is that a reader of this poem is encouraged and moved toward an increasingly compassionate response to other people, that will eventuate in more sensitive and humane behavior toward others, represented here by the convict and boy with the violin.

G   But isn't it precisely the difference between the situation of the reader and the situation of the persons here described that makes it necessary to *allow* the collaboration of powers between the child and criminal, and at the same time to *disallow* any satisfaction in the restricted social ground on which they have obtained their relationship? It is precisely because this poem gives satisfaction, but does not constitute a critique of satisfaction, that it seems to me subject to censure. What we encounter in this poem is not a boy and a criminal. What we encounter is the representation of a boy and a criminal. Representation is always intentional. At very least it intends attention, and in that way it circumscribes attention. It provides occasions for satisfaction and in that way it specifies and limits satisfaction. The unwillingness of this speaker to engage the reader in a critique of satisfaction seems to me entirely congruent with our disposition to elide the *representational* status of these persons. It is precisely that critique of representation which is the revisionary addition that I think it necessary to bring to bear upon our concerns just now.

H   I want to argue that the satisfaction attained by Hardy and offered to the reader in contemplating this event at Upway is not the same as complacency. Still, I am troubled by the fact that this poet, Hardy, to whom I'm so drawn, does not characteristically write the poem in which the speaker, or a voice or character who seems close to Hardy himself, intervenes in the lives of others. When I think of Hardy's work as a whole, of course, I contemplate this succession of hundreds and hundreds of short poems which do, I realize—especially as I look at them from your point of view— seem to settle for the intractable conditions they describe, in the sense that they find, finally, no more to do about them than to lament them as pointedly and perceptively as possible.

I'm reminded of what I called the "nightmare vision" of my own work, in which there is this mere succession of tiny acknowledgments ad infinitum proceeding to the horizon, the horizon being, of course, the death of the poet. I am worried by the suspicion that a career of writing poems with that kind of limited ambition— whether or not my sense of life is as consciously or explicitly fatalistic as Hardy's—may be one that finally does not achieve what I most want to achieve. At the same time though, as I think about your accounts of *what the poet must do*, I find again and again that you imply that, if only the poet could do something that would be manifested by some new kind of poem, then his or her work would be finished. There would be an end point, and some newly integrated and empowered human life could begin, or continue on from there without art. Now that does not seem imaginable to me. It seems to hypothesize a life I would call inhuman or beyond human experience. This is an impasse that we hit a couple of times in our 1981 conversations, especially in discussing your poem "The Thrush Relinquished."

G   Maybe Hardy is not a fatalist, but, as has been said, a *meliorist*: one who expects that the exchange of information about the in-

terior states of others, as between social persons, will in fact slowly
bring to pass a state of affairs in which people will not, because
they cannot, others being like themselves, commit violence
against others. You are right about me in a sense. The desire to
inspect and qualify the privileges of the medium of representation
has about it a totalistic and indeed a totalitarian character, represses the possibility of mediate outcomes—the mere accomplishment of humanity against the background of forces not within its
control—and is open to the accusation that what it represses is
repressed in the interest of a perfection that is not consistent with
humanity. Nonetheless, let me make one last argument in the
light of an understanding of your positions and my positions with
respect to what poetry can do.

H   First, Allen, I want to emphasize a way in which we're in agreement about the relation between art and the life that we live each
day. I think we agree that whatever we do with our poems will not
suffice to make us good persons, or morally mature individuals.
Even if it is true that for me the project of an artist is necessarily
endless, whereas for you some ending must be sought, still, what
we share is the sense that moral behavior among people away from
the text, away from the page, will always be required for a sufficiently moral life, and indeed for good art.

G   I agree with you that the poem does not begin nor can its purposes
be said to be ended with the production of the poem. But the
poet's work seems to me more dangerous, or dangerous in other
ways than the work you assign the poet, beautifully open though
it be to the stream of particulars, as long a task as life, and a task
not in any way designed by reason of its purposes to preempt or
change anything in the world, but rather to convey the world to
others, to construct an exchange of news which will help the self
and others to know and also love the world as it is.

H   Well, that kind of help, to my mind, *does* constitute change, albeit
small change, nonapocalyptic change.

G Okay, Mark, but that's not enough for me. I see the work of poetry this way: I think it obvious that the kinds of conflict which are most common in our world between gendered persons, within families, between social formations of all kinds, and certainly within and among nations, are in some large part a result of representational deficit. To take a case at hand, conflict between classes in America seems very specifically to be conflict generated by deprivation not of wealth but of honor, the designed scarcity of the privilege of acknowledgment which it is in the power of the dominant group in any socioeconomic formation to perpetuate. The representational problem most urgently presented to my mind is the collective task of redistributing the fundamental wealth of social visibility. In this work, the poet participates as a co-worker, bringing to the cultural vector of this redistribution such powers as the poetic instrument can contribute.

H And what is the ideal state of that redistribution?

G The ideal state of that redistribution would be a state of the representational problem—which will not then have disappeared— in which the *pain* of representational deficit will either disappear (because of a representational equality among persons) or be ameliorated by the consensual redistribution of such inequality as the culture finds to be attendant upon the very fact of representation. In the latter case, scarcity of acknowledgment generated by representation itself will be distributed as a common burden, and not as a burden assigned by one class to another, or by a dominant gender to a subordinate gender, or by a dominant race to a subordinate race.

H Okay, so there is a value here of equality, or in a sense as much democracy as would be allowed by the problem. Now I want to grab this chance to ask you a question that you troubled me with yesterday. *Why is equality desirable?*

G I regard equality as desirable for the same reason that I do not precisely ground the value of persons in history or experience. I regard equality as valuable because, in fact, it is commanded by, and a contingent requirement for the social functioning of, the hypothesis of "humanity," which is constructed by the human kind itself and is its greatest and most laborious collective artifice, its poem. It is my nature—that aspect of my nature very particularly which is different from yours—that I regard that imperative (this evolved moral logic of the human kind) to be indicated by the collective possession of an abstract conception of the person (I call it the *eidos*), which is stated in religion as the image of God and which as a counterculture, as a culture supplemental to the central religious or transcendentally grounded philosophic or civil culture of the world, has been the commission and obligation of the poet to display throughout Western civilization. It is in fact the "lordly host" of the poem we started with today. The poet states that the human image is sponsored from the outside of human history and that the capacity of persons in history to acknowledge this originary or paradigmatic representational structure encoded in the principle of poetry has contributed the capacity to check violence short of such lethal savagery as would erase that image.

H   But still, I want to insist that you *choose* to abide by the demands of this art, poetry—poetry which seems, in the account you've just given, to take the place of or share place with divinity. What if someone says to you: "You're being silly, you could have more fun if you forgot about poetry"? It seems to me if someone says to you: "How do you know that you are thus obligated?" ultimately your answer is as intuitive as mine, and it involves your intuitive valuing of human beings.

G   The conception of intuition as an arbitrary preference, or a preference in the light of some "mere" calculus of personal pleasure and pain, seems to me inadequate to the issue. The pleasure and pain of a man such as myself derives from the contemplation of the continuation of humankind and a world in which it is possible for this man's works and this man's children to survive across time. I cannot, speaking for myself as a man who teaches and therefore undertakes to reproduce human consciousness and as a father whose pleasure is in his children, have other grounds for pleasure, intuitive or rational, than the continuity of that great image, the world-poem of which I speak. The singular task, as I have said, of the poet in the face of problems of continuation is in the penetration of the structural characteristics of a poetry which can produce continuation or the ongoing of the poem, and by analogy the human world, in new ways as demanded by history. I feel that the continuation of the human world is subject to threat, and I also feel very strongly (and I think virtually everyone in the West does) that models for renewal which may have served in the past, such as violent revolution in history and linear narration in poetry, are no longer viable models. In short, new knowledge, new strategies for continuation, whether in the poem—the laws of which are like the laws of social life—or in social life directly addressed, is required.

The crisis of representation—which is posed by the economic inequity, misdistribution, class hoarding, hoarding by whole regions (for example, the West) of the wealth of representational empowerments—indicates a dysfunction in the representational system which the poet must address in his or her search for new strategies of continuation. Implicit in this, you must note, is the notion that representation is a fundamental good, the capacity to open the self toward acknowledgment is worthy, and the capacity to reciprocate in an empowered way the claims upon worthiness of others is worthy. *I view representation as a known good, as fundamentally empowering, and I judge that as the reason why those who are in power require it.*

But the question that you press me to answer, Mark Halliday, is what would be the state of representation if, in effect, its social maldistribution were overcome? Look! At that moment, representation will, I think, take a third form, not the form in which we find it, nor the form which I intend it to take, but another form— a form which I cannot imagine, my mind being so intent upon the second that it is incapable of contemplating the third. But I am powerfully convicted of the notion that representation will never disappear. There is no way of conceiving representation, in the light of the human condition, as "coming to an end."

H   So, then, is that your answer to my question about poetry having
    an end point?

G   Not really. Because when you worry about poetry having an end
    point, you are speaking to my discourse about the necessity of pro-
    ducing a discontinuity in practice. Discontinuity, I agree, is dan-
    gerous to solicit, because it interrupts long-continuing successes in
    fundamental interpersonal regulation, but *necessary* to contem-
    plate from my point of view, because of the singular character of
    our historical moment and its urgent claims upon all the resources
    of maintenance in the civilization, including poetry. But I believe
    that beyond the historically driven obligation to negotiate discon-
    tinuity by devising new forms of social continuation—forms of
    continuation which do not reproduce the structures that lend
    themselves to that particular kind of representational tyranny we
    see everywhere about us—there is obviously a further unending
    task for representation presented to us by the enemy who is not
    the *social* other. The limit of the social construction of reality *can*
    be discovered, and one of its names is death.

    I argued for the inherent joyousness of the work of representa-
    tion from what I think to be a rational desire for the continuity of
    the world, a desire, however, which I think also has a fundamen-
    tally irrational source. As I have said, there is encoded in the idea
    of poetry an idea also of the abstract human image. Whether it
    has come to be among our possessions because of the evolution of
    the species in its immeasurable ancient collectivity, or whether it
    derives from another source outside that process, is irrelevant to
    the work at hand. But it does not lie directly in experience, and it
    is, by its nature, not an inference from experience—as meter in
    poetry is not an inference from experience, and as, in fact, none
    of the specific practices or criteria of this art could be reconstructed
    as an inference from experience.

    But let me ask you one last time to help me to an understanding
    of how *you* come by your terms of value. At one point you said
    that it was finally a "mystery," this value which you assign to that
    state of the person which you privilege, the mature state of the
    person, the healthy state of the person, and you might even say

the wise state of the person—one capable of conducting education, and therefore authorized to do so, one capable of conducting
fatherhood, and therefore authorized to do so.

H   Well, yeah. There is this way in which a successful poem seems to
me a picture of a successful person. I mean to say, a good person
in a given context.

G   Good for what?

H   I would say, just as *you* say, good for the continuation of life. Life
that is as healthy and even joyous as possible, given the physical
conditions of our lives. No matter how we seem to disagree about
the original source of these values, we, like all the other humanists
around, share the desire for a life that goes on that way. I'm a
father now, and you are a father.

G   What do you mean by "humanists"?

H   Well, it seemed to me that about eight minutes ago I had you
exposed as a humanist, though you don't want to lean on such a
flimsy support, as you see it, as the idea that we must simply value
the human because we are human, and nothing else will take care
of us. You spoke of Hardy as a poet finding it good and/or necessary
to value persons apparently different from himself, such as the convict, or the boy with the violin (who may or may not be a beggar),
or indeed the constable, because of Hardy's sense that ultimately
those persons are *not* different from himself. I think that's close to
my insistence on sympathy for other persons as a value sought by
and solicited by poems. In a way, I guess that's the more rational
component of the value judgments implicit in poems I write and
the poems that I tend to praise. Rational in the sense that self-
interest seems more rational than behaviors that may aspire to be
considered altruistic. I want to perpetuate myself and therefore I
want the world to be a propitious place for beings like me. There
is in that a kind of logic that feels rational as a justification for
trying to honor others. But I also feel, and I guess this is where

the idea of "mystery" more immediately flows into my talk about this, I also feel that there is a propensity, or at least a potentiality in the human soul, to irrationally love other human beings across perceived differences between the self and other. Why? Because of some sense, which many people seem to be born with, that humanity in any form, in any shape, is a good thing.

G   Mark Halliday, when you talk about all these givens, the possible, happy circumstance that some persons are born in the world to love one another, I see a difference ever deeper and more fundamental between our positions. I believe that you view the world (and I should be happy to do so, but I cannot) as constituted of worthy particulars, known and unknown, which precede the representation of them, and are not fundamentally dependent for their establishment upon the human collective capacity to represent them and assign value to them. The world, as I view it, requires a supplement; that is to say, requires a source of its own worthiness other than itself. Persons are constructed traces of that source, and poetry, whether it is in service of religion or not, is engaged in the iteration, the perpetual reconstitution of that grounded worthiness by reason of poetry's capacity to contribute to any given present, and to any given particular, something that is not inherent in that present or in that particular. Hence the crisis, as I perceive it, of representation.

H   But I don't feel that what you say describes your relation, for example, to your sons and your daughter. The word "inherent" is a crucial hinge in our debate. I think, and I feel that *you* feel, there is something inherently worthy of preservation in your sons and your daughter. It seems to me that that love precedes anything that the culture has conferred upon them.

G   If there is such a love, it is a love which does not have the power to effect its purposes in itself. If it is meaningful to speak of that love as inherent, then it is a love which requires a supplement to its powers toward nature and history, in order to make it efficacious love, to make that passion, in the language of Christianity, an efficacious passion.

H   Maybe so, but that's still a different matter from the worthiness of the particulars.

G   No, it isn't in my view. I believe that love, insofar as it assigns worthiness to particulars, assigns worthiness only in conjunction with an empowerment. The terror of deprivation or poverty of the particular kind of representational empowerment that we often account for in terms of honor or goodness is all the more terrible in view of that state of affairs. I think the purpose of poetry (which I regard as an inherently irrational, an inherently painful task, a task fundamentally so difficult that it should not, in fairness, be a task of any mind) is to construct that additional possession which the heart requires in order to make its love effective love by means of the poem's mediation of a power not inherent or intrinsic or immanent in the world. Why else would you think to add to Philadelphia, at the end of your poem called "Location," a description of Philadelphia?

H   I thought I claimed that the point was partly to help myself think about a respectful relation to others in Philadelphia so that I might then enact away from the text itself; and, secondly, to help those persons who might be willing to listen to my poem to contemplate such modest local improvements in their moral lives.

G   These are hard problems in hot weather.

H   Hard problems, Allen, yes, and we've engaged with them in more generalizing and abstract ways than is my habit, as you well know. I recall, though, that when we were talking about the Mary Snorak poem you had to admit that there's something more comfortable about the voice and style of your newest poems; that is, more (as I would say) at home in the world, somehow happier and more free in relation to language, and also in relation to a variety of the elements of experience. Thus, remembering again a certain shadow of grimness that was present in many of your remarks in 1981, I am glad to say once again that you seem a happier poet now, notwithstanding all the difficulties, and fears, of the approaching millennium.

G The idea of the millennium is a dangerous opening which nonetheless fills me with the profound hope of change of the kind that I have specified. It requires me to speak from that confidence with respect to continuation which I intuit and trace, as you do, in the mystery of the beauty of the particular, a faith rather than an argument—in effect, to subside upon the wealth of my nature, which is the same as the wealth of any other nature. Stylistically, the question of continuation is a question of discovering ways in which disparate facts of the world, such as threat and hope, can be brought together in the utterance of a person who possesses, by right of that collective construction which is not the function of any given moment in history, the power to produce the image of the person as the fundamental and always new knowledge by which history can be, strange as it is to say it, cured.

H To my mind, there is a way in which the ending of your poem with Mary and Jack is like the last line of the Hardy poem in that his poem comes to rest on the assertion of the image of persons— "The convict, and boy with the violin." I just want to say one more time that this movement toward, as I think you called it, the wealth of the particulars, though in one sense it is a subsiding upon the action of mind, need not be conceived as a defeat. It can be a healthful kind of rest.

G I think so, Mark. Healthful in a profound, reconstructive sense, in which rest is referred to health. It is, in my view, a Sabbath, which it is our desire to make, and which is part of the commission of our art. The poem about Mary Snorak and Jack and Skermo ends:

But holiest of all the fools who arrange the feast,
Skermo the gardener, the parts man Jack, and sidewise Mary
Snorak who loves him as he is, and can take a joke.

We haven't had many jokes, as between us, this time we talked.
Why is that?

H   It's because of my attempt this week to impersonate a grownup.

G   But that would be to be "mature," right?

H   I guess you've got me there. I do worry more deeply about what
maturity is now, because I have a son who's almost three years old.
I want him to think the world is a good and happy place. But that's
not always true, and it seems my task to help him figure out how
to deal with both the adequacies and the inadequacies of our life.
When we play baseball, as we do, even though he's not yet three,
he's inclined to think I should never tag him out when he tries to
steal second base. I feel obliged to teach him that sometimes the
best ballplayers get tagged out, and they have to learn not to cry
about it.

G   And I would like to know how your work and my work as a poet
would help you teach him that thing.

3 · TWO POEMS

Mark Halliday's "Springtime for You" and
Allen Grossman's "The Life and Death Kisses"

Springtime for You

You had an experience. It was the night
you and Zahra saw "Divorce Italian Style"
at Cinémathèque, you both sipped lemonade,
Zahra's eyes were dark with her thinking about
her father. I can tell you remember it.
Judy sat in the dappled shade of the mimosas
and myrtles watching you play tennis and laughed
like music when you tripped over your racquet;
it was the morning after the call came from Kentucky.
Later her arm brushed against your arm in sunlight
and Jim Friedman drove you back to campus.
I'm sure it meant something to you the way
the car was blue and *Tonio Kroger* lay on the floor.
A cooling wind came off the nearest mountain
and what you felt was not romantic love but
something more interesting. That's what you thought.
Jim talked about Churchill and Roosevelt
while you studied photographs by somebody,
not Walker Evans but a woman, those wooden
walls, and faces, those textures of seriousness
(as you said to yourself). It was that night.
When Tommy's father played a record by Peggy Lee,
of all people, you said something that was just right.
Springtime; and you are the one who was there.

The Life and Death Kisses

    ibant obscuri

The chroniclers ceased, they ceased . . . until I arose—
Out of the infinite unborn, one of the born who lived,
And out of the number of all who have lived and died,
One of those yet alive,
And among all who are yet alive, one of us not in the greatest
Pain, not demented, not buried and awaiting rescue without
       hope
Under a cruel weight, and not mourning inconsolable losses
Night after night, or enraged by the treachery of women,
Or subjected (not for *this moment*, thank God!) by the evil
Power of J—

Arose, in truth, because it was time, punctually,
At three in the afternoon, from where I was sitting without
Thought on an obdurate bright bench of varnished rattan
In the last car of a train—leaning and slowing as on a curve—
Beside a honey-blond woman of indeterminate age whose
Eyes were strange—
Amidst the blandness of air and the thin light of destination.
It was in the middle-western state of X—Land of Lakes—,
Somewhere on the western, unbuilt limb of the central city
Where lordly factories, and highways, and nursing homes were
Transparent with hesitation between then and now in sunlight
Whiter than it should be

Because the foul windows of the old train were crowded with
Papery faces—like bleached leaves fallen to the bottom of
An empty pool, one upon the other; or like ocean waves
       blown down
White by the silent hurricane, waves breaking out of sight of
       land,
Unsurvivable by ships—
Human beings with the faces of leaves or fallen water:

Near at hand the faces that *can* appear, and behind them also
The ones that *cannot* appear, in their multitudes, white faces
Receding into the whiteness of the light and the flat landscape
Of the Great Plains of the dream.

I rose to get down, for the train had stopped and it was
Leaning in the light. And I looked on my right hand to the
          woman
Who sat beside me—the stout, blond woman with strange
          eyes—,
Thinking, "She will know the way. This is her country."
But I saw she was blind.
She was blind. I knew by the hesitation of her body as she
Lifted it like something very large with separate intentions
In another world. She took hold of me and we entered the
          dark end
Of the car, and then she kissed me with life and death kisses
Amid a great rush of air mingled with odors of metal,
And the slamming of doors. And out of her mouth a stone
          passed
Into my open mouth.

"This is the stone of witness," she said, "that stops every
          heart."
Thereafter, I turned to the left hand and went down. In the
          sunlight
A Spring snow was rising and falling on the plain, and the
          rails
Where the train had been
Were brimming with silver. I would have lingered in the light
For the interest of the empty scene, but I was wearied out
By the silence of life and death, and the kisses of the Fate.
And I lay down among the leaves like a young soul bewildered,
Beneath a sun that was as a stare of the finest eye. And then,
The life stopped in me, and the witness-stone divided my
          throat.

II. SUMMA LYRICA:
A PRIMER OF
THE COMMONPLACES
IN SPECULATIVE
POETICS

Introductory Note

My purpose in the *Summa Lyrica* is to bring to mind "the poem," as an object of thought and as an instrument for thinking, consistent with my account of poetic practice in the foregoing conversations. In particular, I intend to facilitate (and exemplify) *thinking* as it may arise in the course of inquiry directed toward the meaning of poetic structures. The *Summa Lyrica* proceeds by stating—aphoristically—some of the commonplaces by means of which poetry and poetic purposes are accounted for in the West. As a primer or handbook of commonplaces, it is designed to befriend the reader of poetry (always supposing that the reader of poetry needs a hermeneutic friend) by constructing a culture in which poetry is intelligible.

In aid of these intentions and purposes, the attempt has been made to make this work total (a *summa*), that is to say, to place individual analyses in the context of a version of the whole subject matter. This is of course not the same thing as attempting to make the work complete (supposing that were possible). What *is* attempted is to identify the alliances and relationships of the specific terms and situations in poetic analysis (in something like the same way that they arise in my own mind, when my mind is engaged with poetry), as far out toward the horizon as possible (an aphorism is a proposition with a horizon), and thus to circumscribe a horizon in which poetry rises up and is present *as in a world*.

The basis of order in the *Summa Lyrica* is the procession of commonplaces *(loci communes)*, assertions which are possible to be made (and generally are made) in the presence of poems. Commonplaces are not pieces of theory but points of outlook. In the commonplace (as in the aphorism), everybody can start from the same spot, because discourse is *bound* into the authority of a human presence. Theory of poetry does not participate in the nature of poetry (as perhaps the theory of something else participates in the nature of that thing)— except insofar as the theory of poetry is also something that somebody says. In the *Summa Lyrica*, an attempt is made to stay inside the business of the thing, and to use the matrix of particular personal presence as a system of paths along which to move among realms of being (for this reason there is also a web of cross-references from title to title in the text). Flowing from the commonplaces are comments (*scholia*) which show, in increasingly open styles of discourse, how the commonplaces are amplified and serve to make audible the world-wide and history-long discourse which is always going on (30.6) in the presence of the poem—with the intention of putting poetry and poetic knowledge in service of human interests.

Above all, therefore, this is a text for use, intended like a poem to give rise to thoughts about something else.

The Primer

Immortality I (14)

1.   The function of poetry is to obtain for everybody one kind of success at the limits of the autonomy of the will.

> *Scholium "in the wake of language."* Here we conceive of poetry as doing moral work, as having a function in the same way as a machine has a function but a machine that speaks. (43)

> Like language (but not identical with language)—perhaps it would be well to say "in the wake of language"—poetry makes promises to everybody and keeps its promises only to some. So when we say "the function of poetry is to obtain for *everybody* one kind of success," we are running ahead of the fact (but doing so in the name of the fact), and raising the question of *justice*.

> By "success" we mean "outcome." Poetry serves to obtain a kind of outcome (a success is any outcome) precisely at those points in experience where the natural will is helpless.

1.1   The limits of the autonomy of the will discovered in poetry are death and the barriers against access to other consciousnesses.

> *Scholium on limits.* Poetry thematizes the abandonment of will of the speaking person as speaker. "Sing, muse. . . ."

The maxim is: "No mortal man speaks immortal words." In this way poetry repeats its function as its subject matter. (This is what is meant when poetry is said to "be about poetry.")

The abandonment of the autonomy of the will of the speaking person as a speaker constitutes a form of knowledge—poetic knowledge. The knowledge that not "I" speaks but "language speaks" (Heidegger). The function of this knowledge is to rescue the natural will at the point of its death, that is to say, at the point where death arrests its intention.

Poetry is produced by the mortality of body and soul, the immiscibility of minds, and the postponement of the end of the world.

1.2   The kind of success which poetry facilitates is called "immortality."

> *Scholium on immortality.* Poetry functions as a machine for producing immortality in the form of the convergence of meaning and being in presence. (For modern immortality theory, see Becker, Lifton, Rank, Arendt, and Cullmann.) Note, for example, Plato, *Symposium*, 208, 209:
>
>> Do you think, she went on, that Alcestis would have laid down her life to save Admetus, or that Achilles would have died for the love he bore Patroclus, or that Codrus, the Athenian king, would have sacrificed himself for the seed of his royal consort, if they had not hoped to win "the deathless name for valor," which, in fact, posterity has granted them? No, Socrates, no. Every one of us, no matter what he does, is longing for the endless fame, the incomparable glory that is theirs, and the nobler he is, the greater his ambition, because he is in love with the eternal.
>>
>> Well then, she went on, those whose procreancy is of the body turn to woman as the object of their love, and raise a family, in the blessed hope that by doing so they will

keep their memory green, "through time and through eternity." But those whose procreancy is of the spirit rather than of the flesh—and they are not unknown, Socrates—conceive and bear the things of the spirit. And what are they? you ask. Wisdom and all her sister virtues; it is the office of every poet to beget them, and of every artist whom we may call creative.

Immortality may be thought of in any number of ways:

Civilization originates in delayed infancy and its function is security. It is a huge network of more or less successful attempts to protect mankind against the danger of object-loss, the colossal efforts made by a baby who is afraid of being left alone in the dark. The famous poem of Horace may be regarded as a symbol of this effort:

Exegi monumentum, aere perennius
Regalique situ pyramidum altius.
(Géza Róheim, *The Origin and Function of Culture*)

1.3 The structural definition of lyric is "that poetic situation in which there is one speaking person, who is nameless or to whom we assign the name of the author." (6.4)

Scholium on lyric. Lyric is the most continuously practiced of all poetic kinds in the history of Western representation; and also the most endemic to the present Postmodern situation. Lyric is the genre of the "other mind" as it has come to manifestation through the abandonment of autonomy and the displacement toward fiction. (For the specific *differentia* of the lyric form considered as the imitation or "fiction" of speech, see Barbara H. Smith, *Poetic Closure*, p. 122. For a beginning with genre and the lyric genre in particular, see Claudio Guillén, *Literature as System*, pp. 398–400.)

Note the following (Northrop Frye, *Anatomy of Criticism*, p. 366):

Lyric: A literary genre characterized by the assumed concealment of the audience from the poet and by the predominance of an associational rhythm distinguishable both from recurrent metre and from semantic or prose rhythm.

Frye's "concealment of the audience from the poet" is an abbreviation of Mill on overhearing (cited at 16.7). The idea of "associational rhythm" is a reference to the fact of lyric as the imitation of man alone, either as he is alone in himself, or as he might be alone before or after society. As the kind which imitates man alone, lyric is the first and the last poetic sort.

Insofar as the lyric is associated with music, the music stands for those solitudes. (For the history of poetry and music, see John Hollander, "The Poem in the Ear," in *Vision and Resonance.*) The assignment of the name of the author to the nameless speaker in lyric reenacts (repeats) the normal social process of the naming of the person with stress on the problematical nature of the naming of persons at all. In addition, the question of singular and plural attends the self-reference of the lyric speaker. For a beginning with this problem, see citation from Fox at 3 and Emile Benveniste, "Relationships of Person in the Verb," in *Problems in General Linguistics* (especially p. 203).

1.4   A poem facilitates immortality by the conservation of names.

Scholium on the conservation of names. The traditional function of poetry is the conservation of names (Note 23.1 and Scholium, and 38.8). The strangeness and point of lyric can be seen when we note that the speaker in lyric by contrast to the speakers in drama (all of whom are named) and the speakers in epic narrative (all of whom are named except the narrator) is only equivocally named, has in effect a sponsor (the author) but no name, is prior to or posterior to name, is an orphan voice. The name of the speaker in lyric is inferential (see 40) or intuitive. The speaker in lyric communicates with the past lives of the reader (Scholium at 28.1).

1.5   The features of the poem which are instrumental toward its immortalizing function are those which distinguish it from other forms of words, its prosody (for example, meter and line).

> *Scholium on poetry and other kinds of utterance.* The opposite of poetry is not strictly speaking prose but rather the "not fictional." But this would hold for the novel as well (see Barbara H. Smith, *Poetic Closure,* p. 15 and note 10). The question arises as to what stage of the distancing of utterance from its natural situation constitutes a difference, a desituation sufficient to constitute a new or "fictional" status. For another current treatment of this issue see Frank Kermode in *The Sense of an Ending,* where the difference lies between the fictional and the mythic (see 38), and see also the distinction between the radical or participatory and the aesthetic (32).

1.6   Immortality is the simultaneity of meaning and being. Immortality can be discussed only in relation to persons.

1.7   Neither immortality nor persons are conceivable outside of communities. Consequently, reading engages the reader with the community in the interest of the immortality of all persons.

Reading I (22) (37)

2.   The poem is the destiny of the reader. (9)

2.1   The reader is the destiny of the poem. (9)

> *Scholium on the circle of immortality.* Immortality as the continuity of human presence through acknowledgment is a "virtuous circle" (Goodman) on which all persons stand (writer and reader being two) in mutual dependence. Hence, immortality as presence is a collective human artifact in which the self-interest of persons converges. "Creation" is creation not of poems but of presence, or immortality, and is not an act (in the sense in which an act has a terminal moment) but a process in the sense that it is always ongoing and

only ongoing. The process of creation of human presence through acknowledgment moves through persons across time and is completed neither in the writer nor in the reader but in the mutually honorable reciprocity of both. At any moment of reading the reader is the author of the poem, and the poem is the author of the reader. The honor of creation is not with one or the other, but among them. Above all, they are intended (destined) for one another in that the poem looks ahead to the reader, and the reader (as reader) to the poem. In a culture in which honor is conferred asymmetrically on the author rather than the reader, the dominance of the image of the author and the subordination or feudalization of the image of the reader derogates from the good of reading by setting the self-interest of writer and reader in conflict and breaking the circle. Such a situation gives rise to theory.

2.2   We should not let anything enter our discussion of a poem but what we see for ourselves.

2.3   While I am doing this, you are doing something else.

Scholia on the difference of tasks.

A. *What difference does it make what other people say?* What difference does it make what other people say? The answer is: What other people say is what *they* say, each of them as it were all the time. The difference is *the saying of what is said.* In other words, what is said is first of all the portrait of the other person present because of his or her speaking. The difference that the speech of another makes is the difference of other being in its being as other. Scripture, written down speech, does not make the difference. The good book stands in the difference of the other person. Therefore, the good book pitches you away, makes a difference. Here I am trying to make a difference, working with the problem of a good book.

Whatever I do (whatever you do) has the same weight as being, has the weight of being in it. A sentence is of the same order as being; it is something a *person* does—eidetic. You can say "Yes" to the *eidos*, or you can say "Not Yet," or you can say "Not Mine," but you cannot say "No." Even if you say "No" it will not disappear.

B. *Prudence in doing an eidetic science.* The effort in doing poetics (eidetic science) is not to tell anyone anything, and not to stop speaking. The clearest (simplest, most admirable) form of an essay in criticism of (any kind of talking about) the poem must precipitate no conclusion that might be known ahead of time by either of us, must acknowledge the inutility of anything that can be taught in this matter and the splendor of anything that can be learned.

> Who is so stupidly curious as to send his son to school in order that he may learn what the teacher thinks? All those sciences which they profess to teach, and the science of virtue itself and wisdom, teachers explain through words. Then those who are pupils consider within themselves whether what has been explained has been said truly; looking of course to that interior truth, according to the measure of which each is able. Thus they learn, and when the interior truth makes known to them that true things have been said, they applaud, but without knowing that instead of applauding teachers they are applauding learners, if indeed their teachers know what they are saying (Augustine, *De Magistro*, XIV).

In the matter of poetry, everybody is *trying* to say the same thing. Your business and my business is with the commonplaces, helping one another to the world. Whether I understand what I am saying is not the important thing. The important thing is to be faithful to the event.

2.4 Reading presupposes a meditative sorting of the true situation of the self from false versions (37.5). Reading also results in a sorting of the true situation of the self from false versions.

2.5 The question "Why read?" depends for its answer on a true conception of self-interest.

Scholium on teaching and learning. Teaching and learning is the facilitation of understanding of self-interest by one person in the presence of another. Reading is an instance of teaching and learning. It is something you do for yourself in the presence of another person (whether at hand or absent) who is the living boundary of the interest which you serve.

2.6   The poem is first prior to the self (ahead) and then posterior to the self (behind).

2.7   Reading recurs. Writing does not recur.

2.8   The poem is the reader's thing (Scholium at 40.2).

Scholium on "appropriation."

By appropriation I mean several things. I mean first that the interpretation of a text ends up in the self-interpretation of a subject who henceforth understands himself better. This completion of text understanding in self-understanding characterizes the sort of reflective philosophy which I call concrete reflection. Hermeneutics and reflective philosophy are here correlative and reciprocal: on the one hand, self-understanding provides a roundabout way of understanding the cultural signs in which the self contemplates himself and forms himself; on the other hand, the understanding of a text is not an end in itself and for itself; it mediates the relation to himself of a subject who, in the short circuit of immediate reflection, would not find the meaning of his own life. Thus it is necessary to say just as strongly that reflection is nothing without mediation by means of signs and cultural works and that explanation is nothing if it is not incorporated, as an intermediary stage, in the process of self-understanding. In short, in hermeneutical reflection—or in reflective hermeneutics—the constitution of *self* and that of meaning are contemporaneous (Paul Ricoeur, "What Is a Text? Explanation and Interpretation").

Silence I (19) (Scholium 31.4)

3.   A poem begins and ends in silence. Why not call it nothing?
       (36.3)

> *Scholium on the culture of silence.* The meaning of silence is
> an implication of speech which constructs silence as a "back-
> formation" or inference from itself. As a preliminary instance
> of the culture or ethnography of silence (40), note the fol-
> lowing:
>
>> The Quakers of the seventeenth century were particularly
>> concerned to do away with the empty formalism in wor-
>> ship into which they considered Christianity had fallen,
>> and since many of the outward forms they rejected were
>> verbal forms, their distrust of speaking and the value they
>> placed upon silence assumed especially high symbolic sig-
>> nificance. Speaking was a faculty of the outward man, and
>> was therefore not as valuable as the inward communion
>> with God which could only be achieved through silence.
>> In his curious treatise "A Battle-Door for Teachers & Pro-
>> fessors to Learn Singular & Plural," which was an apology
>> for the distinctive Quaker pronominal usage, George Fox,
>> the principal founder of Quakerism, wrote, "All Lan-
>> guages are to me no more than dust, who was before Lan-
>> guages were, and am come'd before Languages were, and
>> am redeemed out of Languages into the power where men
>> shall agree . . . all Languages upon earth is [sic] but Na-
>> turall and makes none divine, but that which was before
>> Languages, and Tongues were" (Fox, Stubbs, Furley
>> 1660:ii) (Richard Bauman, "Speaking in the Light: The
>> Role of the Quaker Minister" in *Explorations in the Eth-
>> nography of Speaking*).
>
> Observe that silence is the topical space in which the scarce
> economics of speech are no longer in force, and the possibil-
> ity of relationship precluded by utterance as a means of rela-
> tionship becomes actuality. Silence is where "all men agree."

3.1   The silence out of which poetic speech arises is more or less busy.

3.2   To bring speech out of silence there must be an occasion generative of speech.

3.3   The "occasion generative of speech" is some dislocation or "disease" of the relationship of a subject and an object (for example, as between lover and beloved or a god and his world). Creation is not the speaking itself but the primordial disease or fall which thrusts me into a predicament in which speech is the only way.

3.4   The poem achieves "closure" only when some new cognitive element has been added to the relationship of subject and object. Terminal closure is "something understood." Closure brings the poem to an end as apocalypse ("dis-closure") brings Creation to an end (cf. 8).

> *Scholium on part and whole.* One way of thinking about closure is as the completion of the inventory of part-whole recognitions. A basic moral component in the analysis of the literary work is the discovery of the part in relationship to its whole. This discovery is a *moral* component because it is in effect an ethical function which carries the literary function—the immortality function—inside of it. It is the business of the reader to discover the compositional harmony of the part of the work in relationship to the whole of the work. It is the business of the moral person—the business of consciousness with itself, the literary work being in this respect a version of consciousness—to discover the ethical implication of this moment of consciousness in relationship to the whole career of consciousness; or, stated another way, it is the business of the moral person (for which literary analysis is a model) to discover the relationship between this moment of the story of *this* person and the whole of the story. Each discriminable element of the work is related to the whole of the work, and the work itself is a discriminable element in

the history of its own story (the "archetype" which has not one but many histories, as many as the explanations proposed to account for its coming to be). Analogously, each moment in the history of *this* consciousness has a place in the whole history of consciousness. *But* we observe that consciousness is asymmetrical—consciousness includes the past but not the future. We do not remember the future. Hence the part-whole perception in the analysis of the literary work is an anticipation of the mind in contemplation—*per impossibile*—of the whole career of consciousness as a completed system. In the work of art meaning is complete in a *version* of being, thus fulfilling by anticipation the state of affairs in immortality—the accord of meaning with being as a whole. For "parts and wholes" with reference to the important concept of *totality* see Roberto Unger, *Knowledge and Politics*, pp. 125ff. See also *Parts and Wholes*, ed. Daniel Lerner.

Behind the idea of wholeness of discourse is the organic analogy (see Plato, *Phaedrus* 264 C), and the organism which is assembled (the whole which is assembled) in analysis is the human countenance. Closure is therefore a form of recognition.

3.5   The speaking subject in the poem is always definable in social terms, that is to say, "is always a person" (1.7).

3.6   Loss is the principle of life of the speaking person.

Poetic Language

4.   All poems employ an artificial, that is to say, a "poetic language."

It is characteristic of artificial languages that historical mutability is precluded by their very nature. Artificial languages are devised to exclude or control mutability (Edward Sapir).

*Scholium on the arbitrariness of regarding language in poetry
as "language" at all.* Insofar as the poem is an artifact, its
words have ceased to be language and become objects, or
merely have gotten lost in the totalization which arises when
the parts of a thing are superseded by the whole which they
have become (Scholium at 35). The embarrassment of treat-
ing words in poetry as language can be seen in the effort to
identify sentences in poetry as statements. (Cf. I. A. Richards.) If sentences in poetry are statements, then they are
subject to the rules of verification and sense (such as the
Aristotelian Law of Contradiction). But it is clear that these
rules disable too many of the sentences of poetry (for example, those which employ metaphor). Further, statements
are analyzed without reference to possible differences between speaker's meaning and hearer's meaning; but language
in poetry is always language which has become the *speech of
a person,* and is therefore no longer statement, or not yet
statement, in any case. But as speech, as will be seen, the
words in poems are also in many ways disqualified. Hence,
the choice, which is always possible, of regarding the words
in poems as pieces of language in any normal sense tends to
be counterindicated. Language in poetry is an example of a
natural thing which by being framed or contextualized in a
powerful and singular way has changed its nature (35).

4.1 All poetic languages are versions of social language, that is to
say, versions of socially identifiable dialects. When I speak of
them as "versions" I mean that we encounter them as disguises
(8.4, Scholium at 38.6).

4.2 Poetic languages are strategies to prevent the meaningless use of
the human speaker—the engagement of the labor of the
speaker toward any stake but his or her own.

4.3 The feature which distinguishes poetic versions of social language from natural versions of social language is *archaism*
(Owen Barfield). Speech which manifests itself as poetic language has the authority of *prior* life (9.4).

Scholium on priority, interiority, and power. The idea of "archaism" associates poetry with the power of prior life. It should be noted in assessing the claims for poetry that priority, power, and divinity are mutually explanatory concepts in Western culture. "Archaism" associates poetry with the power of origination through which reality is established prior to conscious life, and toward which consciousness directs its eyes backward—as it were in retrospect, and subject to the irony of a mind known by a mind which (like the poem) cannot by its nature be known in the same sense. Inside each moment of poetic language there is the taunt (Job 38) "Where were you when I made you?"

Archaism also involves poetic language in the paradox of earliness and lateness; the prior thing is at once the firstborn and the infant and also the thing longest in the world and oldest. The poetic speaker is the archetypal *senex puer* (on this *topos*, see Ernst Robert Curtius). The middle ground of strong life does not belong to the iconology of the poem. "The novel is the art-form of virile maturity . . ." (Georg Lukács, *The Theory of the Novel*, p. 71).

The association of poetry and historical priority is legitimated as history by Vico as follows (*The New Science of Giambattista Vico*, in "Idea of the Work," p. 34):

> We find that the principle of these origins both of languages and of letters lies in the fact that the first gentile peoples, by a demonstrated necessity of nature, were poets who spoke in poetic characters. This discovery, which is the master key of this Science, has cost us the persistent research of almost all our literary life, because with our civilized natures we [moderns] cannot at all imagine and can understand only by great toil the poetic nature of these first men.

After romanticism, priority and power are modally subsumed by the category of interiority so that the archaic and the interior become identified. For the refusal of this position in modern structuralism and the return to the Semitic world construction which places the archaic and the prior in the exterior, see Jean Starobinski, "The Inside and the Outside":

> Making the most remote past coefficient to our most intimate depth is a way of refusing loss and separation, of preserving, in the crammed plenum we imagine history to be, every moment spent along the way. . . . There is no reason, however, why our interest in the cultural past should diminish if, instead of representing a part of ourselves, this past consisted in things other men have accomplished within a conceptual framework which is not and will never be ours, using a language in which we recognize nothing of ourselves. Leaving aside cultures which have not contributed to making us what we are, it is moot whether other cultures which have indeed influenced us form a history of assimilation rather than the contrary— a history of evictions.

This exilic conception constitutes a refusal of typology and entails a hermeneutic rather than a participatory civilization. Compare Blake's "ancient time" (Scholium at 41.4).

4.4 The route taken by the speaker in the poem through the poem's problem of utterance is (by the definition of speech in a *poem*) a unique route. Hence there is always only one poem. (All versions of a poem are poems.) The extent to which an utterance insists on its specificity as a unique event is the extent to which that utterance participates in the poetic quality. The source of the poetic quality is the risk of commitment of all being to an unalterably singular manifestation (19.1, Scholia at 22.6, 31.15, 42.3).

> *Scholium on manifestation in the one world.* The association of poetry and immortality can be constructed by observing the eidetic utility inherent in the exact repeatability of sentences. Note the following from William M. Ivins, *Prints and Visual Communication*, p. 162:

The conventional exact repeatability of the verbal class symbols gave words a position in the thought of the past that they no longer hold. The only important things the ancients could exactly repeat were verbal formulae. Exact repeatability and permanence are so closely alike that the exactly repeatable things easily become thought of as the permanent or real things, and all the rest are apt to be thought of as transient and thus as mere reflections of the seemingly permanent things. This may seem a matter of minor moment, but I have little doubt that it had much to do with the origin and development of the Platonic doctrine of Ideas and the various modifications of it that have tangled thought until the present day. The analytical syntax of sentences composed of words certainly had much to do with the origin of the notions of substance and attributable qualities, which has not only played a formative role in the history of philosophy but for long presented one of the most formidable hurdles in the path of developing scientific knowledge. At any rate, until comparatively recent times nominalism, with its emphasis on facts, its distrust of words, and its interest in how things act rather than in what they essentially are, has had little chance, and its great development has coincided remarkably with the ever-broadening development of modern pictorial methods of record and communication.

But it should be noted that all manifestation involves the risk of reduction undertaken (with more or less confidence as the state of the community in history allows) in view of the great reward of perpetualization. All manifestation, whether verbal or visual, is determinate. As Gombrich points out, we do not *see* ambiguities; we see one state of a thing and then another. (The idea of ambiguity as also of metaphor is meaningless without the fact of the constraint of presence in manifestation to univocality.) Hence in manifestation possibility is broken down. At the point where manifestation really occurs (on the outer skin as it were of representation) presence is postcatastrophic. (On poetry and the brokenness of worlds, see 31.15.) Hence the ideology of the unique language event (style) is a repetition of the nature of manifestation elevated to a moral allegory. Poetry incorporates as a *rule*, as the *differentia specifica* of its kind, the sacrificial history of presence.

Poetry thus offers a symbol of the one world which appears, as it is founded on the infinite plurality of worlds which cannot also appear. Poetry repeats in each of its instances the story about the scarcity of existence, the cosmogonic story which tells of the destruction of an infinity of worlds before the creation of this one (Leibnitz, *Monadology*, #55 ff.).

The matter is worth dwelling on. We may say that poetry, like ethical life, does not take place in the philosophical plurality of possible worlds, but in the relentless and inescapable unity of the one world as recovered perceptually.

Contrary to the Aristotelian implication that poetry is "more philosophical" than history, poetry is part of history. Poetry is one thing (an instance of that sort of thing) which actually has happened. Among all the possible things that could happen—the myths (38)—it is the one actual thing (one of the actual things) that did happen in the situation at hand. The poem as such is not the child of the experiential *esprit d'escalier*, nor does it consist of experimental counterfactuals with respect to a given state of affairs; it is the one thing that could be done by the speaker then. (It *is* that thing that was *done*.) Consequently, poetry is a hostage in the one world where finally and unexchangeably the one thing that happens (the very thing) really comes to reside.

The poem as manifestation is mounted upon the ruins of excluded possibility; and as manifestation it competes, within the horizon of human attention, for its spatiotemporal moment. In this it is like the human body. The soul is a creature of the plurality of metaphysically possible worlds; but the body, a case of representation, is bound to the one world. The body is psychophanic, the picture of the soul, competing for space in the museum of the human world. Therefore, the poem like the body is subject to the law of the one world, as it comes to mind through the eye; and the name of that law is scarcity. (Note the debate about synonymity by E. D. Hirsch and Nelson Goodman in *Critical Inquiry* 1, nos. 3, 4.)

4.5   The frame of the poem (its prosody or closure) is coterminous with the whole poem, and must be conceived as bounding the poem both circumferentially (the outer juncture with *all* being) and internally (the inner juncture, produced syllable by syllable, with its *own* being). The minimal function of closure is to fence the poem from all other statements, and most strenuously from alternative statements of the same kind. The closural frame may be more or less permeable. In Wordsworth it is more permeable (where the space outside is filled with almost audible, slightly disjunct versions of the space inside); in Ben Jonson it is less permeable (where the space outside is outer space, enemy and keeper). The quality of singularity manifested in each instant of utterance is in each case of manifestation, syllable by syllable, the frame of the poem (that is, its closure).

Scholium on frame as theater, the repetition of the sufficient conditions of perceptibility. Note the following from Barbara H. Smith, *Poetic Closure*, pp. 24, 25:

> Meter serves, in other words, as a frame for the poem, separating it from a "ground" of less highly structured speech and sound. . . . Meter is the stage of the theater in which the poem, the representation of an act of speech, is performed. It is the arena of art, the curtain that rises and falls as well as the music that accompanies the entire performance.

The poem represents the act of speech in the metrical theater which is in turn a representation of the space of appearance, the sufficient conditions or *meta-topos* of the perceptibility of persons. The theater as structure is the imitation of the space in which meeting takes place, and all its enabling preconditions.

Meter (as frame or closure) as a repetition or imitation of the psycho-social world construction which enables the *precon*ditions of personal actualization is alluded to in Heidegger ("The Origin of the Work of Art," in Hofstadter, ed., *Poetry, Language and Thought*, p. 45):

> A work, by being a work, makes space for that spaciousness. "To make space for" means here especially to liberate the Open and to establish it in its structure. This installing occurs through the erecting mentioned earlier. The work as work sets up a world. The world holds open the Open of the world. But the setting up of a world is only the first essential feature in the work-being of a work.

The metaphor of "frame" propagates itself throughout the theory of perception. As the enabling preformation of meaning, for example, it is the familiar paradigm of Gombrich, Kuhn, and others. Note also Erving Goffman's *Frame Analysis*. What should be emphasized is that *frame* is established through reduction by differentiation and is thus postcatastrophic, the "formal feeling" which succeeds upon "great pain." And framing in representation (including art) is the repetition as a subject of consciousness of the unconscious world-construction which is an automatic component of every moment of experience.

We cross the frame into the poem. But the edge may be anywhere like the border of the sacred grove. Often we note only a slight shudder of difference.

4.6   All poetic speech implies both a speaker and also a class of speakers.

4.7   There is always a sense in which the *object* in the poem (the speaker's *world*, the Beloved) is definable in terms other than social terms. That is to say, the distance which modulates the relationship of subject (always social, as in 3.5) and object in the poem is filled with ontological questions (theory), questions about the being of the object. All the Beloveds are alive in the philosophical ambience both of being and of being *that*. Such is *poetic* life.

> *Scholium on consciousness and the philosophical estate of the Beloved.* When I say that the Beloved is always in some sense philosophical I place her in the classical estate of the object of consciousness. As, for example, Roberto Unger, p. 200:
>
>> To be conscious is to have the experience of being cut off from that about which one reflects: it is to be a subject that stands over against its objects. A prerequisite of the distinction between subject and object is that the subject be capable of defining its relationship to the object as a question to which different answers might be given.
>
> On lyric as a culture of consciousness, see 16 and Scholium at 24. It is also the case that the Beloved in lyric is an image of the perceiver as perceived. What we celebrate in the Beloved is the self as known—the principle of whose life is the paradox of storytelling.

4.8   Obscurity occurs when the measure of the distance between subject and object becomes indefinite. This phenomenon takes place (simultaneously and from the same causes) (1) within the poem and (2) between the poem as object and its subject (the reader).

Value (18)

5.   A poem is always a thing of value of a given sort.

> *Scholium on the Compositional Principle.* It seems worthwhile noting that there is a common principle or constitutive rule of all compositions by reason of which they are compositions. This "Compositional Principle" manifests itself as a minimal relationship between fact and value. When we speak of "fact" in this context we are speaking of fact in rep-

resentation, or the *appearance* of fact as distinct from natural fact or fact in experience. But when we speak of value in this context we are speaking of the *same* value which we ascribe to natural situations.

The Compositional Principle may arise from the ascription of compositional status to an object from the outside. That is to say, the *mere* declaration that an object is a composition. (Prosodically this might take the form of *mere* centering on a page, or more generally *mere* framing or labeling.) Whenever "the compositional status" is assigned to an object the inherent complexity of all objects in experience makes possible the perception of relationships among parts and whole in the object. Fact and value tend to adhere to one another as soon as part-whole relationships are perceived (3.4) because the perception of wholeness in experience is a constitutive element in valorization, which like sanctification functions to facilitate orientation and perceptibility. In this sense "compositionality" is a *topos* which is always potential in objects, which comes to exist when it is *assigned* as a status to the object (not as a new feature), and which carries value with it because perceptibility, which is a contingency of topical perception, is inherently valuable.

On the other hand, the Compositional Principle may assert itself as it were from the store or fullness of the object itself, as in the case let us say of objects in Dante. The object (as symbol, then) may offer relationships (part-whole couplings) to the mind of the viewer as new applications to experience of the relationship of fact and value (in effect the coherence as wholes of facts). In this case, the object wills, as it were, its own perceptibility; in effect it glows.

Between these two possibilities lie most of the objects encountered in experience.

The idea of a minimal state of affairs of all objects that are brought to manifestation or arise and offer themselves to the eye is comparable to the "minimal teleological elements still alive in ordinary thought about human action" which H. L. A. Hart allows (see *The Concept of Law*, p. 187). Since discourse about art is displaced discourse about persons, and the value which arises in art is the same as that which is constitutive of justice, we observe that the minimal grounds of the association of persons in society for the purpose of survival is the same as the minimal association of elements in perception, which can be said to compose a whole.

5.1 What the poem is *about* (its "subject matter") points to a value of a different sort from the sort of value implied by the existence of the poem (38.8 and Scholium).

5.2 When we talk about poems there tends to arise a convergence (never complete) of these two kinds of value. For example, I am always *about to say* that the poem is about poetry. (But note 25!)

5.3 Poetry can never take its medium as its whole subject. Language always means something else.

5.4 There is no useful theory of a poem the value of which is not known.

5.5 The question of value is not a question.

Person I (13) (34)

6. All speech implies a speaker. (But not all language.)

6.1 In poetry we encounter only speech (never language). By speech we mean versions of language which have been made the act of a person (35.2).

6.2 The image prior to all other images in any work of the arts of language is the image of the person (the *eidos*). In poetry the person is prior to all worlds. Archaism (4.3) is the style or characterizing mark of the person arrayed in priority.

> *Scholium on the eidetic function of language.* "The eidetic function of language" refers to the human annunciatory or

anthropophanic (cf. epiphanic, theophanic, hierophanic) content of speech. The eidetic function of language points to language insofar as it effects presence. Consider:

> Religious awareness grows out of regard for sacred times and sacred places. But sacred time and sacred space [Eliade] are space plus and time plus. The divine presence irrupts into time and space and "inhabits" them. Presence does not irrupt *into* voice. One cannot have voice without presence, at least suggested presence. And voice . . . being the paradigm of all sound for man, sound itself thus of itself suggests presence. Voice is not inhabited by presence as by something added: it simply conveys presence as nothing else does.

> > My nerves are bad to-night. Yes, bad. Stay with me.
> > Speak to me. Why do you never speak. Speak.
> > What are you thinking of? What thinking? What?
> > I never know what you are thinking. Think.

> The distressed person in *The Waste Land* of T. S. Eliot expresses the agony of one to whom presence is denied because vocal communication is denied. (Walter J. Ong, S. J., *The Presence of the Word*, pp. 113, 114).

The eidetic function distinguishes *parole* (actual human utterance) from *langue* (whatever language may be *before* it becomes the act of a person). (See Ferdinand de Saussure, *Course in General Linguistics*.) In the process of changing *speech* into logical *statement* the eidetic function must be deconstructed. This is because the eidetic function takes all the meanings and structures of language into itself and redefines them as one meaning and structure. *The one eidetic meaning* is the same as the meaning of the sentence "Here is a man"; *the one eidetic structure* is the human face. (For the phenomenology of the face, *le visage*, see Emmanuel Levinas, *Totality and Infinity*.)

Poetry is language in which the eidetic function is prior to all other functions. Indeed, the meaning of most claims for poetic language (that it is "divine," "primordial," etc.) is that poetic language, by contrast to other kinds of language, has no other function than the eidetic function. Hence, also, language which is managed in terms of the eidetic function tends to be called poetic, and poetics is the science of constructing presence through the eidetic function of language. (Current discussions concerning the function of language [e.g., Max Black, "The Many Uses of Language," in *The Labyrinth of Language*] seem to refer to secondary functions which do not take into account the human authority of speech. Jakobson's "cardinal functions of language" [referential, emotive, conative, phatic, poetic, and metalingual], through the differential hierarchization of which speech kinds vary, all presuppose the eidetic function, though certain of them, the "poetic" and the "phatic," with greater directness [see Roman Jakobson, "Language in Relation to Other Communicative Systems," in *Selected Writings II: Word and Language* p. 703]. However, no hierarchical arrangement of the six functions produces the inner human reference of language. The eidetic function of language is primitive in the same sense that the "concept of a person" is "logically less primitive" in Strawson's argument about persons [P. F. Strawson, *Individuals: An Essay in Descriptive Metaphysics*, chapter 3, pp. 82–113]. Other modern efforts at specifying the function of language, such as those of Austin, Wittgenstein, Piaget, and Malinowski, also call attention to the necessity of presupposing a general human science, a science of the meaning-bearing speaker and the laws of such a science, prior to the linguistic science which specifies the secondary rules of construction by which the *eidos* becomes manifest in situations.)

Attention to the eidetic function of language requires extreme consciousness of a kind that is sometimes called radical. (Cf. Marx's aphorism "To be radical is to grasp things by the root. For man the root is man.") When language is conceived with a view to its eidetic function all worlds characterized by language and all consequences of all other functions become metonymic of the countenance, *the eidos*. For another exposition of the anthropophanic function of language, see Hannah Arendt, *The Human Condition*, pp. 182, 183, as follows:

> Action and speech go on between men, as they are directed toward them, and they retain their agent-revealing capacity even if their content is exclusively "objective," concerned with the matters of the world of things in which men move, which physically lies between them and out of which arise their specific, objective, worldly interests. These interests constitute, in the word's most literal significance, something which *inter-est*, which lies between people and therefore can relate and bind them together. Most action and speech is concerned with this in-between, which varies with each group of people, so that most words and deeds are *about* some worldly objective reality in addition to being a disclosure of the acting and speaking agent. . . . The basic error of all materialism in politics—and this materialism is not Marxian and not even modern in origin, but as old as our history of political theory—is to overlook the inevitability with which men *disclose themselves as subjects, as distinct and unique persons, even when they wholly concentrate upon reaching an altogether worldly, material object* [italics added]. To dispense with this disclosure, if indeed it could ever be done, would mean to transform men into something they are not; to deny, on the other hand, that this disclosure is real and has consequences of its own is simply unrealistic.

In poetry language has gone strange. The strangeness in poetic language arises from the presence of *the eidos*, the presence of presence. An exceptional act of consciousness is required to greet this presence. (The Greek word *eidos* is here used in its Homeric sense as the form or beauty of the person. Cf. Latin *species* and German *Bildung*. No implication of the Platonic-Husserlian sense [idea or essence] is here intended except insofar as the sustaining and ideal image of man is the countenance or shape of the person, the basis of human recognition.) (See Gadamer, p. 15; Paz, p. 171; Levinas, p. 200 especially.)

6.3   The person in the poem is known because he has given his *word*. He has staked his existence on the efficacity of this one promise of fidelity. Take him at his word. There is no other way.

6.4   Lyric is the mode of visibility of the speaking person "who always and at all times says I" (Nietzsche). What becomes visible is the interior portrait of intuitive humanity that harvests all worlds toward the metonymic construction of a right name.

6.5   The "I" in the poem, reposing in a ground of unknown causes (43), promulgates all its features in the same way that the apex of the shell on the horizonless sea bottom is the cause of all its whorls and colors. The shape of the poem is a self-enclosing spire which darkens its source. (8.1, 16.2, 20, 28.3, 43.)

> *Scholium on the spiral or gyre (picture of the story about the impeded will) as tree of life.* There is no poem in the realm of autonomy as there is no story or narrative. Narrative is produced by, and repeats, the situation of the impeded will, the will subject to a law other than its own, subject to antinomic laws. Narrative is omnipresent in poetry. Because all speaking is action which has a history.
>
> The conditions of the arising of narrative are the special theme of the poetic statement, and are repeated in the processes of poetic construction (1.1). The prototypal form of narrative is genealogical story in which the history of the arising of the individual from source is inscribed upon the history of the arising of the species from source (31.15). In lyric the story of a singular occasion of speaking is inscribed upon the history of all speaking which is repeated in the crossing of the threshold from silence to speech in opening.
>
> The traditional plastic form of the narrative as tree of life (genealogical story rooted in source and flowering in conse-

quence) is the spiral or gyre—the course of the right line subject to antinomic rules: autonomy and constraint, space and time, going and staying, novelty and repetition, concealment and disclosure. . . . The structure of the poem is a picture of the history of speaking as action and that picture is realized as the gyre or spiral where what discloses also encloses and therefore conceals—where the will as subject both to space and time (motion and countermotion) becomes manifest in its impediment; and wisdom consists in seeing the picture of the quest (the *nostos*, or return) as Odysseus saw it as both possible (in the spatial realm) and impossible (in the temporal realm). In the spire as symbol the complex beauty of life as manifest (poetic life) is seen.

The spiral, as the picture in the poem as structure, is the map of the *nostos* or return, the narrative of the wanderer from source, the shadow of life's tree. (See Scholium B at 36.)

Note the following by Pierre Gallais ("Hexagonal and Spiral Structure in the Medieval Narrative," *Yale French Studies* 51, pp. 116, 117):

This leads us to *unwinding* (*déroulement*), to the circle and cycle, and, far more appropriately, to the *spiral*. For the spiral alone can be said to unwind: that is its definition and its function. And the spiral is the fundamental characteristic—on our planet—of the Living; no mineral presents a spiral form: the latter appears only with the vegetal (flowers, fruits, positioning of branches and boughs) and especially with the animal; the spiral is characteristic of the fluid (liquid or gaseous), characteristic of *force*, in a word. Of the force which thrusts and seeks to manifest itself despite the constraint of form (and because of this constraint). Thus would I willingly represent all life, and all that is produced by living beings—and especially by the Living Thinking Being—by a spiral, drawn out and maintained by its double polarity: expansion and contraction, liberty and constraint, centrifugal movement and centripetal movement.

6.6   "I" in the poem looks two ways, forward and back. In neither direction does it encounter an historical (natural) human being.

6.7   The laws of life of the speaking person (1.6) are the structural features of the poem. All prosodies are, first of all, strategies toward the immortality of the speaking person; and after that, allegories of the name.

6.8   The person in the poem has come to the end of his speaking. Why did he begin? (3.2).

6.9   The notion of "person" is irreducible, logically, psychologically, analytically. Whatever can be predicated of the poem (e.g., unity, goodness, eternal life) can be predicated of the person. Indeed, the predicates of the poem are the consequence of the will of the person toward condign actualization. In the poem the person has come to judgment (36.1).

6.10   Discourse about poetry is displaced discourse about persons.

Self

7.   A poem has the same singularity as a self.

7.1   The question arises: "Why are there many poems? Why are there more poems than one?"

7.2   Stationed within the horizon of the speaking person of the one poem, we cannot say for sure that there is more than one poem.

7.3   The observation "There is more than one poem" calls to mind the historicity of the observer. As no face has turned quite round toward itself, and no eye looked into its own depth, so no speaker has seen his or her own poem, nor the marks upon it of his or her singular point of emergence in history.

7.4   There is more than one poem only in the sense in which there
       is more than one self.

7.5   There is a strong sense in which there is only one self (15).

Poetic Knowledge

8.   Poetic knowledge is intuitive (irrevocably personal) knowledge
       of the origin of the self. Being *knowledge* it is nonidentical with
       that origin; but, rather, it is a keeping of the self through *be-
       speaking* origin. As incarnation and history are stays against
       apocalypse. The life of the poem is assurance against the end of
       the world, the opening out of all the secrets. (Cf. 3.4.)

8.1   Nothing goes on in the presence of the poem which has the
       finality of truth. Poetic immortality is an arrested process sub-
       sumed within a living process that will itself end in death—
       which is truth of a sort. Poetic knowledge is an arrested process,
       in which time is kept in order to prevent the self-devouring of
       space. It is pictured by the gyre, which has two coordinates,
       time and space; not by the circle, which (having but one) is not
       a human figure. It is human not to *be*. The poem aims only at
       humanity. *Satis superque.*

8.2   A good poem is the cause of (exacts) poetic knowledge in the
       writer. A good poem is the cause of (exacts) poetic knowledge
       in the reader. Is the poetic knowledge of the writer and the
       reader the same? Are there one or several genealogies?

8.3   If the reader has one destiny, how can he or she be reader of
       more than one poem? If the writer has one destiny, how can he
       or she be the writer of more than one poem? Apparently, im-
       mortality is a task with which the conscious mind is never done.
       Presence seems to have no past or future until it is thematized
       (becomes an object of consciousness) and then it is no longer
       presence.

8.4   Authority attaches to poetic language (4) insofar as poetic lan-
       guage is the language of a collectivity or a class. *Poetic knowl-*

*edge is personal knowledge expressed in the language of a collec-
tivity or a class.* The class may be conceived historically, as
Wordsworth's "lower and middle class" or Williams' "American
idiom," or transhistorically, as the language of Yeats' aristocrats
or Jung's archetypes, or as the language of genre (e.g., Donne's
conception of the language of satire) or ontogenetically as
Roethke's language of children, or phylogenetically as with
those who regard poetry as the language of early and original
"man," or socially as the language of women and blacks. But in
all cases it is the class which is the repository of past lives. The
distance between the historical poet and the class language by
which the poet constructs poetic knowledge is the factor which
produces the transcendence of the class, the edge of difference
which is the healing power (cf. 38). There are, however, pathogenic (demonic) versions of this distance (cultural lateness,
Harold Bloom's "belatedness") which deform the enterprise.
The poet in history is necessarily a person of one class speaking
the language of another class (the rule of transcendence); but
when the axis along which the poet moves from existence to
presence, from where he is to where he *is*, becomes too long,
demonic versions of art and personhood arise. This requires
more study, but suggests that the history of art is the history of
changing access to transcendental reference.

8.5   Nothing in the collective ever lives or dies. Put another way
(Joan Berns), "The collective always lives. In the instant of
recognition it flares up in view."

8.6   The person in the poem begins to speak by addressing the origin
of his or her being as a speaker. She says, "O Muse . . . ." This
beginning is always an answering back, responding to an initial
annunciation. The biblical type of the poem is the *Magnificat*
(Luke 1:46–55). The poet knows the muse because the muse
has disclosed herself. The origin of the being of the poet as
speaker may be as in the Hellenic case the origin of speech as
medium (the scribal deity) or as in the Hebraic case the origin
of reality as a whole (Milton's Uranian muse, the Bible's God
who created by speaking). In either case, the poem is spoken *to*

the muse and not by the muse. The muse is the principle of orientation (the sacred source) by which humanity becomes a speaker. The poem is what is said.

8.7   The poem is another self with which it is possible to take liberties.

Destiny

9.   You cannot say anything about a poem unless you know where you are.

9.1   You know where you are.

9.2   Whether you read poems or not is neither here nor there.

9.3   The person in the poem is always being-for-another-altogether. The person in the poem has no sake. (See Scholium on the Collective at 14.4.)

9.4   The power of the poem is the force of prior being.

9.5   All conscious life has a destiny in its own origins.

9.6   Poems are a version of the destiny of the individual in God.

The Wedding

10.   The drama of the creator is a tragedy. He is always only a guest.

10.1   The drama of the creation is a comedy. He is always only the bridegroom.

Labor

11.   Labor mediates between the person in history and the poem.

11.1   "The work" is not reducible to the labor which accompanied its coming to be.

11.2   Labor in the realm of necessity (nature, scarcity) can be abolished. Labor in the realm of freedom (fiction) cannot be abolished.

11.3   Conceived as labor, working at art ("Creation") is totally alienating, because the work of art is being-for-another-altogether.

11.4   Conceived as knowledge, working at art facilitates the reconquest of the origin of the self—poetic knowledge.

11.5   Conceived as redemption, working at art is the sacrifice of first fruits.

11.6   Conceived as charity, working at art is the kiss of peace.

11.7   Labor was the curse upon Adam. The work of art can only be understood as the reconstitution *per impossibile* of states of being irrevocably excluded by the definitions of consciousness.

11.8   The silence with which the poem begins is the curse of God— the speechlessness of toil. (Scholium at 25.2.)

Statement

12.   A poem is a statement which is an occasion of statements.

12.1   As a statement, a poem is a statement like any other statement—only less interesting.

12.2   As an occasion of statements, it is a goad to unending speech.

Seriousness I (25)

13.   The person who speaks in lyric is always alone (1.4, 16.7).

13.1   The lyric speaker is overheard in the same way in which the mind of another person is known, that is to say, *per impossibile*.

13.2   The lyric speaker intends to be overheard conversing with the images of the origins of consciousness who are never present and never reply (8.5).

13.3   The other *enters* the lyric cell only through indirect discourse, though the other is everywhere beyond its boundaries sustaining its form.

13.4   The scope of the lyric is defined by the situation of psychic individuality.

13.5   Seriousness is the state of feeling which arises when consciousness, encompassing the circumscription of its own life, becomes centered in itself and becomes heavy with the gravity of its own solitude. Seriousness is a quality of lyric.

Immortality II (1)

14.   Immortality (poetic immanence) is the descent of the speaking person into the ground of language as a collective possession.

14.1   Eternity (religious transcendence) is the incorporation of time by a mind which cannot die.

14.2   Prosodic utterance insofar as it is "numerous" is an imitation of time. Incorporating time, it triumphs over time.

14.3   Having incorporated time, the speech of the lyric person carries time into the pleroma of the human collective. In this sense the speech of the human person in the lyric frame is the incorporation of time by a mind which does not die.

14.4   The drama of redemption, when it becomes the subject of poetry, is enacted on the threshing floor of the immortal self-consciousness of the human collective.

> *Scholium on the Collective.* Engaged with the poem, you enter the Collective. But the Collective means death.

> Traditionally, the life of the Collective and the death of the individual intersect. On society as an agreement to die, see Michael Walzer, "The Obligation to Die for the State" (*Obligations*), in which we see the necessity of death as a crite-

rion for membership in the immortality of the Collective. When Donne, for example, says "Since I am coming to that holy room / Where with thy quire of saints for evermore / I shall be made thy music," he describes death as an entering into the Collective of which God's Music (His choral or-chestra) is the image. Death is the condition of access to the Collective, and the death of the individual is the condition of the life of the Collective. "Socrates was asked to die for the common life, because he had no right to do any damage whatsoever to the common life."

Once again, Hegel has stated the point most clearly. In the society of egoists, he argued,

> Death, the phenomenon which demolishe[s] the whole structure of [the individual's] purposes and the activity of his entire life, must . . . become something terrifying. . . . But the republican's whole soul was in the republic; the republic survived him, and there hovered before his mind the thought of its immortality (Hegel, *Early Theological Writings*, p. 157).

I want to stress those last three words: of *its* immortality and not his own (Walzer, *op. cit.*, p. 92).

> The Rousseauian republic does not claim, then, to be an eternal shrine to the memory of its heroes; it claims some-thing more: to be the totality of their present exis-tence. . . . "If the citizen is alone," writes Rousseau, "he is nothing, he has no existence; and if he is not dead, he is worse than dead." Rousseau's political theory is designed to give the communal being supremacy over the natural egoist, while recognizing that in fact a tension always ex-ists between the two (*ibid.*, pp. 93, 94).

The Collective authorizes poetic speech, as in the above ci-tation the Collective in the form of the republic authorizes personal life. Its presence always entails the threat of death to the "natural man" identified by individuation on the analogy of the singularity of the physical body. Donne's poetry has as its subject the postponement of the acknowledgment of the claim of the Collective on the natural man. Christ is the natural man whom the Collective as the crucifying father God has claimed. The actualization of the marks of personal identity (singular life) in the Collective as ground is the *impossibilium* somehow obtained by reason of the poetic fact and in particular the lyric.

The social and the Collective are not identical. Total concession of the Collective to the social is one kind of tragedy for the imagination. (For "collective representation," see Emile Durkheim, *The Elementary Forms of Religious Life*, tr. J. W. Swain.) In Tolstoi we find personal death and access to the Collective (which renews value in social life) identified in the final act of love (*Master and Man, Ivan Ilyich, War and Peace* [Andrew's death]). Immortality as a personal destiny (the unending continuity of the conscious subject) is not clearly understood in the tradition as a real state of affairs. Poetry is noneschatological because it is itself the eschaton which makes its claims, not on behalf of its subject but on behalf of itself as a medium. The poet in history dies into the speaker in the poem (the citizen of the lyric cell) and is reinvented by that poet in the poem as an image.

The question of the corporate person is customary in legal philosophy. (See John Dewey, "Corporate Personality," in *Philosophy and Civilization*.) As the "I" in lyric is both singular and collective, so also the person of which it is inferential.

By analogy, in English Statutory Law (see Dewey, *op. cit.*, p. 150): "the word 'person' shall extend to a Body Politic, Corporate or Collegial as well as Individual." The analogy between the poetic person and the legal person is important insofar as both are distinguished from the natural person.

The notion of the fictional character of the legal person (the doctrine that corporate bodies are *personae fictae*) is also significant for the notion of the fictional in religious contexts, since the *personae fictae* (a concept attributed to Pope Innocent IV) were disabled by contrast to natural persons in various ways: for example, they could not be excommunicated. From this we may derive the notion of the corporate person as concessive. Note the doctrine that there is no capacity in the corporate person to act as a body corporate without positive authorization (that is, without substantiation from the state, the ultimate person). Here we have the notion of the substantiating image applied to the corporate person. All of this is in aid of the notion that life in the Collective is both privileged and deprived in statable ways, and that the Collective is a constituent element in the social, both contingent upon the social and also transcendent of the social at the same time.

The Collective as the universal or general (and therefore immortal) *persona ficta* (the republican), especially as conceived in liberal theory, can be seen in the works of Max Stirner as a lethal insult to the sense of singular being:

> One can now, after liberalism has proclaimed Man, declare openly that herewith was only completed the carrying out of Christianity and that in truth Christianity set itself no other task from the start than to realize "man," the "true man." Hence then the illusion that Christianity ascribes an infinite value to the ego (as in the doctrine of immortality in the cure of souls, etc.) comes to light. No, it assigns this value to *Man* alone. Only *Man* is immortal, and only because I am Man am I too immortal. In fact, Christianity had to teach that no one is lost, just as liberalism too puts on an equality as men; but that eternity, like this equality, applied only to the *Man* in me, not to me. Only as the bearer and harborer of Man do I not die, as notoriously "the king never dies." Louis dies, but the

king remains; I die but my spirit, Man, remains. To identify me now entirely with Man the demand has been invented, and stated, that I must become a "real generic
being" (Max Stirner, *The Ego and His Own: The Case of
the Individual against Authority*, p. 176).

(The last allusion is to Marx. See, for the king, Ernst
Kantorowicz, *The King's Two Bodies*.)

Collective man is immortal and dead; he has no specific interiority.

A similar meaning pertains to the word "common" as in "the
book of common prayer," or as in "common" (ballad) measure, or as in "common man." Note that the Sternhold and
Hopkins translation of the Psalms (made for communal singing in church) is common measure by contrast to the Sidney
psalms, which are particular measure, the metrical type of
singular (solitary, lyric, aristocratic) being. When the voice
accepts the Sternhold measure it becomes anonymous and
whole. When it accepts the Sidney measure it becomes
named and partial. Common prayer is the death of aristocratic worship (the private mass) and is the birth of religious
man as a republican in the Rousseauian sense.

Death is the Collective (Abram's bosom), the realm of cow-
ards who look all one way and sing beyond belief. (See Yeats'
"Cuchulain Comforted.") In the social realm human beings
look at one another; in the Collective they look all one way.
Language is a portal to the Collective. (See Emile Benveniste, "Subjectivity in Language," in *Problems in General Linguistics*.) The speaker in the poem enters language in a different way from the poet in history. The speaker in the poem
prays the common prayer. As *persona ficta* the speaker in the
poem is illegitimate, a *filius nullius*, a foster child. (See
Keats' "Ode on a Grecian Urn.") The Collective, death, and
the divine are equivalent expressions.

Scripture

15.   One life. One poem.

15.1   There is one poem written by God.

> *Scholium on Scripture.* Scripture is privileged text. The na-
> ture of the textual privilege of Scripture derives from the fact
> that the source of its language is identical with the source of
> reality. Scripture is the text which is the perfect whole from
> which experiential reality has departed and to which it will
> (in the "Apocalypse") return. As fixed text it is the *essence*
> of unfixed experiential reality. In relation to other texts, it is
> primary in the sense in which we think of the real world as
> primary or as the cause rather than the consequence of ex-
> perience. Scripture and poem are antithetical and contradic-
> tory terms.
>
> From a psychological point of view, "Scripture" responds to
> the latent sense in which the statement "There are multiple
> truths" is always false. Insofar as each poem is unconscious of
> any other poem, each poem partakes of this feature of Scrip-
> ture. Scripture is the paradigm of perceptual boundedness,
> insofar as the bounded generates the universal, as it is also of
> every moment of meaning-intention insofar as there is inside
> every act of intentionality the will toward all meaning. But
> note also that the presence of Scripture announces the loss
> of the god (Scriptural religion is antitheophanic). In the
> same way, the poem is the sign of loss of unmediated relation-
> ship between the person and experience (and between one
> person and another).
>
> Scripture is the model of the fixed (*literatim*) text which it is
> the first business of the community of the living to conserve
> on behalf of the dead and the unborn. The members of a
> community conserve its Scripture, first, as the final map of
> all reality and, then, as the possibility of any mapping of

reality which time and the accidents of historicity—the general rage against meaning—continuously threaten to snatch from the hand. Scripture as the one book equivalent to all being is the type of the sense in which every life includes all life. This sense of "Scripture" is the sense in which the lyric text becomes Scripture. Correlatively, Scripture answers to the desire of the mind for a discriminable meditative object which nonetheless (despite its discriminability, its finitude) includes all objects. Hence, Scripture is not read, any more than lyric.

> (Note the following: "In the sphere of religion, it is significant that the religions of conversion, the excluding religions, are all religions of the book. In the non-literate societies of Africa, at any rate, magico-religious activity is singularly eclectic in that shrines and cults move easily from place to place. The literate religions, with their fixed points of reference, their special modes of supernatural communication, are less tolerant of change. When this occurs, it tends to do so in sudden shifts, through the rise of heresies or ('movements of reform') that often take the shape of a return to the book—or to its 'true' interpretation" [Jack Goody, ed., *Literacy in Traditional Societies*, p. 2]).

15.2   At the summit of the tower the eye turned outward gazes on darkness, turned inward recognizes a multitude of kindred.

Eve

16.   The lyric is entranced in the first astonishment that it is at all, the awakening of Eve (36.2).

16.1   The apex of the shell is not in space, until the spire on its journey upward inscribes a precinct (28.3).

16.2   A poem is a fiction of a self seen from within.

16.3   Poems are fictions of the privacy of other minds. Wherever the
       philosopher says *per impossibile* the poet shows the way.

       Scholium on poetry and knots in philosophy. Consider whether
       the occasions of representation, and hence of poems, are not
       those junctures in ordinary experience across which philos-
       ophy cannot bear us. Note, once again, (1) above. Among
       the knots in philosophy at the present time is the problem of
       other minds. Between J. S. Mill and Wittgenstein there arose
       a fundamental doubt about the central argument for the ex-
       istence of other minds (the argument was from analogy). But
       it is clear that from Homer and Plato through Descartes the
       knowability of other minds depended upon the hypothesis of
       an intelligible essence for man, a soul, on the one hand, or
       a common nature on the other (such that all minds were
       knowable by each mind intuitively). With the withering of
       confidence in these hypotheses (see the final critique by Rob-
       erto Unger, *Knowledge and Politics*), the entailed knowabil-
       ity of other minds also disappeared. Hence, poetry became
       lyric overwhelmingly, because lyric was the social form of the
       unknowable singularity of the liberal individual. But in po-
       etry it is the formal aspect that effects the transmissibility of
       the world represented. As formality (prosody, line, and
       counted stress) ceased to be preferred (or possible) as constit-
       uents of poetry, the sentiment of interior being became less
       and less transmissible, and representation as lyric becomes
       caught on the same knot as the rational will.

       We have observed that the "occasion generative of speech"
       in poems is trouble. In the silence prior to speaking, there is
       a barrier to the rational will which must be defined, for in it
       lies the "meaning" of the poem. Representation completes
       the world (as best it can), which philosophy (or theology)
       cannot complete (31.14).

16.4   By these fictions of the privacy of other minds it becomes pos-
       sible to conceive of ourselves as possessing knowable inner
       being.

> It is a necessary condition of one's ascribing states of consciousness, experiences, to oneself, in the way one does, that one should also ascribe them to others who are not oneself (Strawson).

16.5   The "I" in the poem is not in time, until the voice on its journey upward inscribes a precinct.

16.6   Lyric is a mode of the soul's "rejoicing in communicability" (Jaspers).

16.7   In what sense of the word "overheard" is the voice of the speaking person in lyric (not heard but) overheard? The answer must be either as the devil (and all social beings) knows the self, by outward indications, *or* as God knows the self, through participation of personal being (Aquinas).

> Poetry and eloquence are both alike the expression or utterance of feeling: but, if we may be excused the antithesis, we should say that eloquence is *heard;* poetry is *overheard.* Eloquence supposes an audience. The peculiarity of poetry appears to us to lie in the poet's utter unconsciousness of a listener. Poetry is feeling confessing itself in moments of solitude, and embodying itself in symbols which are the nearest possible representations of the feeling in the exact shape in which it exists in the poet's mind. Eloquence is feeling pouring itself out to other minds, courting their sympathy, or endeavoring to influence their belief, or move them to passion or to action.

> All poetry is of the nature of soliloquy (J. S. Mill).

Metaphor

17.   What is *like* cannot be unique (31.13).

17.1   Metaphor is a device for reducing the unknowability of the fact by eroding its uniqueness.

17.2   In a similar way the poem by a fiction reduces the uniqueness
       (inconceivability) of personal (own) experience.

> It seems as if the elementary psychic fact were not *thought*
> or *this thought*, but *my thought*, every thought being
> *owned*. Neither contemporaneity, nor proximity in space,
> nor similarity of quality or content are able to fuse
> thoughts together which are sundered by this barrier of
> belonging to personal minds. The breaches between such
> thoughts are the most absolute breaches in nature (William James, *The Principles of Psychology*, 1, p. 226).

17.3   What is *like* cannot be identical.

17.4   The function of the particle *like* in metaphor (all metaphors
       being reducible to some form of the sentence "A is like B") is to
       enable the perception of a relationship by *distinguishing* its
       terms.

17.5   The fundamental metaphor substantiating human presence
       (the *eidos*) in Western civilization is "Man is like God"—en-
       abling the perception of a relationship by distinguishing its
       terms.

> *Scholium on God.* The first constitutive rule of image con-
> struction (eidetic substantiation) is the distinction of realms.
> The most fundamental distinction presented by Western cul-
> ture is the distinction between "man" and God. God creates
> the mortal person at every moment of interhuman percep-
> tion by participating as *difference* in relationship. The imita-
> tion of this difference, inherent in the grammar of metaphor,
> accounts for the sense we have of the centrality of metaphor
> in eidetic (human-presence) discourse. The sacred is func-
> tionally a principle of orientation. This function is enabled
> by the nature of divinity as generative of boundaries. Meta-
> phor implies the experience of sanctity by repeating the con-
> straints which boundedness imposes on experience. The par-
> ticle "like" functions as divinity by keeping realms in being,
> in the same way that "space" enables perception by interpos-

ing a middle term between subject and object. The decline or foundering of metaphor indicates the decay of difference, and portends the loss of the poetic resource. Where surrogates are placed in the God-position (as in sentences such as "Imagination is God," or "Community is God"), the distinctness of the human image is eroded just insofar as the difference which the surrogational term makes is less than the difference which God makes. When difference is repudiated ("Man is God"), the *eidos* and the world with it disappears.

17.6   The prosodic feature of the poetic medium is a version of the time-experience. "Like" represents an insurmountable barrier in experience which both enables possibility and destroys possibility *until the end of time.*

17.7   The relationship of percept and experience-in-consciousness is always of the "is like" character. In other words, the metaphor of metaphor is the fundamental situation of being conscious of something in the world.

The Ontological Affirmation (5)

18.   The value of the poem for the reader of the poem flows from the acknowledgment which it enforces that something not the self is. The act of reading begins (?) with this ontological assertion.

> *Scholium on the ontological affirmation.* The ontological affirmation ("Something is.") is equivalent to the creation of difference out of sameness ("no-difference") and in theological terms is in fact the sole redemptive act. This is because it is a repetition of the creative act of God and stands for that self-creation or "cooperation" with grace which is the precondition of the experience of grace. The difference between the damned and the saved in Dante is the difference which the ontological affirmation makes and no other. The ontological affirmation is of peculiar importance for the lyric since

the lyric is the representation of mind alone. In the Scholium at 16.3 we observed that representation takes its stand where philosophy sinks down. The poem interposes itself to enable the ontological affirmation. Its "presence" constitutes a negotiation of the mind-world threshold. Reading in poetry therefore is a continual celebration of presence. The further paradox introduced below (18.1) corresponds to the theological commonplace and paradox that other-finding and self-finding are the same finding. From a theological and a poetic point of view difference and no-difference converge in the self.

18.1 The "something not the self" which is affirmed in the act of reading is the self.

Silence II (3)

19.   The silence which precedes speech is the first representational event of the poem. It is the poem's first artifice.

19.1 The *termini* of the poem (the marks of its boundedness) are the white portions of the page which constitute a morpheme meaning silence.

19.2 Some of the meanings of silence are: noise, darkness, possibility, death, "woman," chaos, ineffability, unconscious life, sin, the curse of God (11.2).

19.3 The specificity of anything is that by reason of which it is replicable in only one way. The speech of the lyric person is characterized by absolute specificity.

19.4 A poem is a voyage which is the destiny (the specificity) of only one speaker, undertaken and brought to an end with complete finality on only one occasion. Where any code will do, we call the utterance prose. The untranslatability of poetic speech is a non-negotiable aspect of its seriousness.

19.5   One function of the absolute specificity of poetic utterance is to keep out noise, that is to say, all other utterances and especially the most nearly adjacent.

19.6   In immortality nothing turns into anything else. The speaking person in lyric enacts the situations of individual life within *termini* which bound a precinct where nothing ever happens for the first time and nothing will ever happen again.

19.7   The creation of silence is the condition of the articulation of speech. Silence mediates difference.

The Vortex

20.   The basis of the poetic of lyric is the principle of continuity.

20.1   The "I" of the speaking person is the apex of a vortical system in which a storm of recurrent and non-recurrent elements at war with one another by their nature is simplified through the act constituted by the poem.

20.2   At the opening of the poem what-always-happens and what-will-never-happen-again contrive a knot.

20.3   Lyric speech authenticates its occasions by inscribing new occasions upon old under the auspices of perpetual recurrence. Lyric utterance assures a moment at which the canons of individual life and of collective life are in a relationship of meaningful continuity. Poems open *sub specie iterationis:* "Yet once more, O ye laurels, and once more. . . ." (Bruno Snell).

> *Scholium sub specie iterationis.* The first words of every poem locate the speaker in the poem at a point of recurrence in a system of cycles or at the point of recognition of synchronicity (the all-at-onceness of experience). Hence, poems tend to open with aoristic time indications such as "once more," "often," "and yet," "Let us go *then*. . . ." The recognition of recurrence, the concession to the non-singularity of the mo-

ment, is the precondition of access to the resource of poetic language. It is in effect the concession to death (and therefore the mounting toward fiction) which is entailed by entrance into the Collective. The doubling of experience (or, better, the pluralization or multitudinizing of experience) is also a precondition of the addition of meaning to being, for meaning is a double-take or retraveling (second seeing, revisiting) of the landscape. Note that the implication for the speaker in the poem of this enabling feature of poem-opening is that the speaker is seen to remember not an anecdotal, personal past but an archetypal transcendent past, which is identical with the totality of speakers in the genre or poemkind in which the speaker is speaking. Thus poem-opening is recapitulatory but in a way different from poem-close.

20.4 Established as without alternative by the *termini* which bound it within and without, the poem becomes for the reader a paradigm of the intelligible object of consciousness.

20.5 The principle of life of the speaking person in the poem is loss (3.6). He comes to judgment. The principle of life (that is to say, situation) of the reader who speaks the poem is loss. He comes to luminous patience.

20.6 Poetry is one strategy with respect to scarcity. The loaves and the fishes is another.

20.7 Useful and sweet, public and private, sacred and profane, intelligible and sensuous, transcendent and immanent, other and own, immortal and mortal, general and particular, archetype and anecdote, collective and individual participate one another in the act of speech.

20.8 When to these are added the criminal and the saint, the speaking person in lyric has been perceived (28).

Scholium on the ambivalence of the speaking person in lyric. The person who speaks in lyric is the hero of private space who both keeps and breaks central rules. His nature contradicts itself. This contradictory doublesensedness is central to his nature. He is, for example, disclosed, though his nature belongs to the class of private things which are always hidden. (Cf. the Eumenides in Aeschylus' *Oresteia* or the servant of Isaiah 53 [*non decus ei atque decor*].) He is whole as only a fictional thing can be whole, and yet he is broken completely as the fictional thing must be seen to be in relation to the natural thing. He is the truth speaker who has "given his word," and yet like the completely devoted man, the self-slain, he can keep no contracts. He is an appearance essentially and cannot withhold himself, and yet he is completely hidden and cannot be questioned. He is singular but in a sense he is also plural. He is concrete but also abstract. He is for another altogether, and yet when become demonically the speech of another he is treacherously self-same. Above all, he is defiled (28) as the perfect son of the father (his speech has become numerous, measured), and also he is the incestuous lover of the mother (he has entered the realm of poetic knowledge, the principle of continuity, at the opening of every utterance). From the point of view of the natural man, the man whom the god mastered at the beginning of the story, he is impossible. By reason of his impossibility he is both deeply desired, and deeply feared.

20.9   In the principle of continuity that reconciles contradictions at the first moment of utterance, there is no element of forgiveness. In that moment all the seasons of the sun and moon mount the stair.

Majesty

21.   The didactic of lyric flows from the example of majesty.

> *Scholium on didacticism.* Lyric is, like all poetry, didactic in nature. But its didactic is not normally the rational didactic of useful sentences, the didactic of prudence. The didactic of lyric is normally the didactic of eidetic exemplification,

which is the contradiction of the didactic of prudence (note Scholium at 20.8 and also 28). The didactic of lyric teaches the possibility of surviving the labor of manifestation in the one world, the world of manifestational scarcity. In the lyric "space of appearance" all being is celebratory. (This is true in the same sense that all representation has about it the quality of celebration.) The speaker in lyric has mastered the process of manifestation, and endured the tragic losses which manifestation entails, without being destroyed. The speaker in lyric has not lost heart. To go on speaking, not to lose heart, is an occasion of celebration and an attribute of majesty.

But majesty also implies the privileges of dominance and the solitude of sovereignty, (21.1, 21.2). In the sense in which didacticism promises the transmissibility of usable knowledge, the example of majesty is antididactic, unreal, the origin of order as the king is the origin of order, but not itself the subject of law, as kings were not the subject of law. The didactic of the example of majesty includes the didactic of the counterexample. For the speaker in lyric is also mythic and the function of myth is to repel life, to generate by differentiation. The sentiment of majesty is an occasion of the consciousness of difference. From majesty there goes forth the consciousness of difference by which the natural person is measured and made whole. The encounter with the person in lyric shatters the homogeneity of the encounters of the natural person.

21.1   Majesty is the quality which mastery of contradictory natures (the animal, the citizen, and the god) confers upon the human voice.

21.2   An image cannot be reciprocated, and therefore cannot be loved. The person we really meet and not the image is the beneficiary.

21.3   When the voice across time is attended to, the human image is remembered. In the didactic of lyric there are no teachers; there are only rememberers.

21.4   There are no inhuman uses of the speaking person.

21.5   Bent on the unpacking of the skein, humanity deals less treacherously with itself.

Reading II (2) (37)

22.   When *I* say, "Yet once more, O ye Laurels, and once more. . . ," what do I do?

22.1   I serve.

> *Scholium on reading as service.* Service is one light in which poetic reading is viewed. *Service to* is the contradictory of *use of.* The non-utility of the speaking person in the poem produces the attitude of service, and service is the reciprocation demanded by majesty which can have no use for its servants. In lectorial (reading) service there can be no color of humiliation, for service and servitude are contradictories. The humiliated servant is the disgrace of the master. Poetic service is the labor at existence under the conditions which scarcity defines for the production of existence. The service of the poem must be the chosen labor of those who will not serve their tools. The poem has an interest which is only actual in the presence of another and contradictory interest. Only a person or the representation of a person can have an interest.

22.2   As soon as I begin to read a poem, I stop talking. As soon as the hearers of a poem begin to hear, they stop listening.

22.3   Certainly it is grand to be the other for whom the poet's self became desolate.

22.4   The poem in my voice is a set of constraints toward acts of speech more specific than I can answer for. The poem explores the humanity of the speaker.

22.5   When I take the poem in voice, I enter the freedom of the rememberer by way of the service of the kindred.

22.6   "Print reminds." The voice serves, but never gives a complete version. Yet if the text is lost, the poem is lost. If the voices falter, the poem has no occasion. The poem is like a person. It has a mind-body problem. (36)

> *Scholium on the fixed text.* All poems have a fixed text, for the poem is a manifestation and manifestation cannot be this way *or* that. There is no *aporia* in manifestation. All alternate versions of poems (drafts, revisions, alternative singings, miscopyings) are alternative poems. The poem has a body by which its identity is established, as a human being has a body. The fixed text of the poem is the feature of the poem which prevents the perfect service of the poem, for the constraints of the poem which arise as a consequence of the specificity of its nature prevent its perfect actualization in voice. The voice has an irreducible interest which is contradictory to the irreducible interest of the poem (represented by the fixity of the text). In order to read the poem, it is necessary for the voice of the reader to become conscious of its interestedness, and it is the reader's confidence in his or her own interestedness (his or her own stake in the world) that is tested by the constraints toward (but never identical with) a reading which marks the poem. The poem requires that the reader assert confidence in his or her own interest in the world. That is an instance of Hermeneutic Friendship, and the method of meaning.
>
> The reader therefore becomes the soul of the poem, and the poem the body (the principle of manifestation) of the reader when the reader reads the words. In the structure of classical poetry the word-specific character of poetry (of which syllable count is one guardian and lineation another) is a fea-

ture of its bodilessness unalterable in reading. Stress is the soul element, the point of entrance of the interest of the reader, the point of openness of the open texture of all texts.

22.7   The poem summons the voice of the speaker of the poem to enact the business of the speaking person. In the service of the poem the voice of a man or woman reaches to the *value* of a person.

22.8   When the speaker of the poem enters the voice of the speaking person he or she becomes free by way of another version of necessity which says: "You are a being that speaks. There is nothing else to be."

22.9   In speaking the poem the speaker of the poem reacquires self-hood by serious reciprocity with another self. He or she reenters the situation of humanity, becoming conscious of it once again as if for the first time and without dismay.

> *Scholium on dismay.* Where there is dismay there is no poem (5). The speaker meets the poem at the limits of the autonomy of the will. (See, for example, Dante, *Inferno*, canto 1, line 60.) But the rules for that meeting are the same as the rules of grace in the high church (the voluntary rather than the involuntary tradition). The service of the poem requires cooperation, and cooperation requires conviction of a stake in being, confidence in the interest of the self.
>
> On the side of the poem, dismay is the manifestation of the "bad" poem, the thing that is not yet made. The natural person may be dismayed, but the compositional principle does not admit of dismay as a meaning, for dismay is the defeat of meaning, the abdication of majesty. Dismay solicits consideration and the poem can never solicit consideration.
>
> The culture of manifestation is vulnerable to the estate of the self in history.

22.10   The speaker of a poem is in the presence of the fathers.

22.11   Perhaps, they do not know him.

The Poet in History and the Speaker in the Poem

23.   Of the poet in history, we ask: "What is the motive to art?" Of
        the speaker in the poem, we ask: "What is the motive to utter-
        ance?"

23.1   The motive to utterance as speech (the motive of the speaker
        in the poem) must be distinguished from the motive to utter-
        ance as art (the motive of the poet in history). The experience
        recorded by the poem as sensed from within is not an aesthetic
        experience.

> *Scholium on the speaker in the poem.* The speaker in the
> poem is rarely a poet, and never *the* poet in the sense that
> the author is *the* poet. The speaker in the poem is a man or
> woman laboring at manifestation, but the manifestation at
> which the speaker in the poem labors is not the poem. This
> is most striking in the religious cultures. The speaker in
> George Herbert's poem (see "Love III" at 30.9 S) is a Chris-
> tian soul laboring at manifestation before God. The motive
> to utterance of the speaker in the poem is not, therefore, the
> motive to utterance as art. The speaker in the poem (like
> George Herbert) is serious in a way different from the way in
> which the artist in history is serious.
>
> The speaker in the poem cannot go away, which is to say he
> cannot die.
>
> In like manner, the name of the speaker in the poem is not
> the same as the name of the artist in history. For the speaker
> in the lyric has no name. Or we can say the name is intuitive.
> The name of the artist *in history* is by contrast documentary.
> If we assimilate the speaker in the poem to the poet in his-
> tory we abolish the enterprise of poetry. Poetry of the sort of
> "the poem in question" is not what the speaker in the poem
> is about.

23.2   The speaking person *in* the poem is a contingency of the exis-
        tence of the poem.

23.3   The life across time (such as it is) of the poet in history is a
contingency of the existence of the poem.

> *Scholium on biography.* Poems create poets. (See Martin Hei-
> degger, "The Origin of the Work of Art.") One of the *conse-
> quences* of the existence of poetry is the existence of "the
> poet." It is effectively the case that the existence of bodies of
> fictional writing (poems, novels, etc.) authorize the kind of
> cultural staring that takes the forms of biographies, life-
> documentation, etc. The poet is not the strongest or the
> most beautiful or the most tested man or woman of the time.
> He or she is the person who has enacted the deed of presence
> and therefore passed into manifestation. The poem sets its
> "author" in the center of onlooking. The rule is that the
> maker of images is thereby privileged to become an image.
> The poem is therefore the cause of the poet insofar as the
> poet is a person who is an object of attention. What distin-
> guishes the poet from other persons is his or her knowledge
> of the rules of manifestation. The poem is a thing made
> which makes its maker. Since, however, the life of the poet
> is a life constrained by the labor at art, it should be clear that
> the lives which come to manifestation are lives selected by
> conformity to a special set of circumstances. This is true also
> of all other lives which come to consciousness across space
> and time. (As, in an extreme case, it is the criminal or his
> victim who is selected from the whole population of a city
> for display in the newspaper.) What is displayed by history is
> that figuration of life which has accommodated itself to the
> rules of manifestation. Consequently, the manifest is a very
> circumscribed "set" of the true.

23.4   The poem summons its poets and is the principle of their life.

23.5   The assignment of the poem to a historical speaker is an instance of anxiety about cause (habitual consent to which limits
response to the fact).

23.6   The tendency to assimilate the speaker in the poem to the poet
in history in ordinary discourse about poetry attests to the em-

barrassment of the reader in time before the other destiny of the person—not the fear of greatness but the fear of death.

23.7   The image of the maker flows from the artifice toward the worker at artifice, as in theology.

23.8   Person as hero is the voice in the poem which speaks across time. His being is speaking. If he does not speak, he is not (6.3). If he does speak, he leaves all else behind. "Poet" is just that sort of man. The person in the poem has staked his life on the destiny of utterance.

23.9   What is the nature of the freedom to which the speaker in the poem is subject? The speaker in the poem is subject to nontemporal constraints (the rules of manifestation rather than the rules of history) tending toward a consequence which is either perpetualization or oblivion.

23.10   It is the self dwelling in mutuality that is here shown forth.

23.11   What of the reader? The eye that does not care about the world has him in mind.

"I" in Lyric

24.   The lyric moves from least differentiation of the self (the opening) toward most differentiation of the self (at the close), from the dark embrace before the lark to the full day of cognitive self-recognition.

> *Scholium on aubade as a model for lyric structure.* (Cf. 16.) For an example of the poem of waking as an analogy of the *structure* of lyric procedure (the direction of flow from beginning to end), see Shakespeare's *Romeo and Juliet*, act III, scene v, 1–36. The passage ends, "*Rom.* More light and light—more dark and dark our woes!" The lyric begins by awakening from the dark night of participation, the night of *having*, in which there is no speech. As light grows, differentiation increases, the lark and nightingale are distin-

guished, persons become identified and more separate. As light grows sorrow increases, as does knowledge. In this sense the direction of lyric is from participation to acknowledgment, from intimacy to strangeness, from the hour before dawn to the hour after dark. The short lyric is a dawn phenomenon in its traditional form. But the structure may be run backward (Roethke tried to make it do so) so that the conclusion is in the collective and the opening is in the nonparticipational singular. In general, however, the lyric opens with a breaking of participatory silence and closes with some strategy of reconciliation to individuation short of return to the night in which the poem first began. For the direction of lyric is irreversible. It flows from Eden toward history. Hence, the study of poetic ending is the study of the several strategies for the management of fundamental loss.

24.1 The "I" in the poem (Janus-like) looks back toward an undifferentiated selfhood which it prevents and has not wholly forgotten, and forward toward a differentiated selfhood which it enables and has not wholly acknowledged.

> *Scholium on "I."* For the study of "I" see Emile Benveniste, "Subjectivity in Language," in *Problems in General Linguistics,* esp. pp. 224–26. His maxim is "Language is so organized that it permits each speaker to *appropriate to himself* an entire language by designating himself as *I*" (p. 227). The personal pronouns are universal; they exist in all known languages, though in certain rhetorical situations they may be suppressed. Lyric begins with an establishment or founding of the linguistic man, that is to say, lyric begins with "I" and is the artistic form generated by the conditions and consequences of I-saying. Since "It is in and through language that man constitutes himself as a *subject,* because language alone establishes the concept of 'ego' in reality, in *its* reality which is that of being," it therefore follows that lyric, which always includes a history of the founding of the "I," is also always a history of the birth of the linguistic and subjective person. In this sense lyric is prior to all other forms of utterance and

assumed by them as prior. As an account of how the "other" is both present and absent, both indispensable and transcended with respect to the occupant of the lyric cell, consider the following (*ibid.*, pp. 224, 225):

Consciousness of self is only possible if experienced by contrast. I use *I* only when I am speaking to someone who will be a *you* in my address. It is this condition of dialogue that is constitutive of *person*, for it implies that reciprocally *I* becomes *you* in the address of the one who in his turn designates himself as *I*. Here we see a principle whose consequences are to spread out in all directions. Language is possible only because each speaker sets himself up as a *subject* by referring to himself as *I* in his discourse. Because of this, *I* posits another person, the one who, being, as he is, completely exterior to "me," becomes my echo to whom I say *you* and who says *you* to me. This polarity of persons is the fundamental condition in language, of which the process of communication, in which we share, is only a mere pragmatic consequence. It is a polarity, moreover, very peculiar in itself, as it offers a type of opposition whose equivalent is encountered nowhere else outside of language. This polarity does not mean either equality or symmetry: "ego" always has a position of transcendence with regard to *you*. Nevertheless, neither of the terms can be conceived of without the other; they are complementary, although according to an "interior/exterior" opposition, and, at the same time, they are reversible. If we seek a parallel to this, we will not find it. The condition of man in language is unique.

And so the old antinomies of "I" and "the other," of the individual and society, fall. It is a duality which it is illegitimate and erroneous to reduce to a single primordial term, whether this unique term be the "I" which must be established in the individual's own consciousness in order to become accessible to that of the fellow human being, or whether it be, on the contrary, society, which as a totality would preexist the individual and from which the individual could only be disengaged gradually, in proportion to this acquisition of self-consciousness. It is in a dialectic reality that will incorporate the two terms and define them by mutual relationship that the linguistic basis of subjectivity is discovered.

24.2   As the narrative structure of the poem advances toward the specialization of the self in understanding, the symbolic structure of the poem gathers the redemption of the self from the archaic source of unity.

> *Scholium.* The characteristic strategy by which the lyric manages the fundamental loss attendant upon the individuation which is the last event of the poem is the presentation of a transcendental substantiation of the separated ego which has been prepared by the prior symbolic content of the poem-stream. While the poem has tracked its irreversible course from participation toward individuation it has gathered reference to unity of another sort, which is finally announced at the close of the poem. The announcement or disclosure of transcendental unity is remarked by the reader in the awareness that the thing has become whole. This "making whole" which constitutes a management of the separated self and its losses is generally obtained through the repetition and consequent fulfillment or completion of the symbolic content of the poem-stream. The poem thus moves from a wholeness which is, as it were, internal to the person to a wholeness which serves the person by being transcendent to him. The losses entailed by speech (awakening) are thus compensated by the resources internal to speech which rescue the desolate self-in-acknowledgment by a process similar to the theological mechanism of grace.

24.3   When we say "I" we deny that we are all and affirm that we are not wholly other.

24.4   The speaking person in the poem is privileged to ascend and descend simultaneously, because he has staked his life. When the Janus gazes at us through all his eyes at once, that is *anagnorisis*.

24.5   Looking at the poem, we cannot take it all in.

24.6   A strangeness in the poem (and one fence against meaningless uses of the person) is the peculiar access of the speaking person in poems to the oblivion of prior states of the self. Luminosity flows from hiddenness.

> *Scholium on the recollection of past lives.* Speaking in general is a case of the recollection of past lives. In lyric the speaking person obtains his or her nature by reference to the verbal conduct of all other speakers who have inhabited the lyric cell. There is a haunted compulsion which attends the speaking of all persons who speak in poems. They are not quite themselves, and not quite sighted with respect to a present. Their "kind," which is not nature but the class of artifice to which they belong, speaks through them; but it is ignorant of all but the general case of their state of affairs. The recollection of past lives is the master privilege of the enlightened in all cultures; it portends immortality by totalizing the otherwise individual life. But it takes away something of the alertness of the waking self, the quick-eyed person who greets the comer in the middle distance. There is in this sense an ignorance about the person in poems which must be attended to. From this ignorance flows a sort of light.

24.7   Remembering and forgetting participate at the festival where Lordship and Bondage cease to be.

Poetry and the Scarcity of Language

25.   Poetry is of no particular importance.

25.1   In poetry the scarcity of language becomes a principle.

> *Scholium on poetic artifice and the contrivance of linguistic scarcity.* There is more experience than language and more

language than poetic language (4). In constructing poetic utterance we contrive singular and unexchangeable routes through global linguistic and, perhaps also, experiential resources. The first loss in poetic saying is the loss of the infinity of verbal strategies that are not permissible, first in this *kind* of poem, and then in this poem. This exchange of all for one thing, of much for little, is repeated at every stage of mimetic construction. It applies to the classes of persons represented (26) as it does to the class of worlds possible of representation. Saying, which puts us in touch, is either so precious that we will to lose the world to save the soul (the symbol of the person in touch) or so necessary that we resign the world in rage in order to grasp the thing that we cannot truly want.

25.2   The *topics* of lyric must first be considered as perennial triumphs over the hardness of saying anything at all. Thereafter, they must be conserved and distrusted as falsifications of experience which bear with them irreplaceable intimations of the truth denied.

> *Scholium on labor and pain* (11.8). The commonplace with respect to what the poem leaves out is labor, pain, and deformity. Poetry is traditionally a work which obtains its characteristic life by obliviating the labor by which it was produced. See Yeats' "Adam's Curse":

> > We sat together at one summer's end,
> > That beautiful mild woman, your close friend,
> > And you and I, and talked of poetry.
> > I said: "A line will take us hours maybe;
> > Yet if it does not seem a moment's thought,
> > Our stitching and unstitching has been naught."

> "A Creation" is characteristically, indeed by definition, a thing which is discontinuous with its causes. The biblical hatred of the image made with hands is a prototype of the preference for the object which has no genetic history. But

the genetic history contains inside it more of reality than the finished object attests to. An example of the falsification of genetic history for the purpose of asserting the freedom of the creator is the Priestly account of the Creation in the Bible (Genesis 1–2:4). What is not named is the anticreational forces which become the suppressed powers of history, the Canaanite, the woman, the passionate darkness of the mind, the earth's seas. More immediate examples of the falsification of reality by art—a falsification which takes the form of a suppression of cause—can be seen in the studies of Peter Laslett (*The World We Have Lost*) and Raymond Williams. See especially the latter's careful account in *The Country and the City* of the falsification of the social cause of art in the English pastoral, during the early period of transition from feudalism to agrarian capitalism.

Part of the "hardness of saying anything at all" is the difficult separation of utterance from its causes, the clarification of the medium so that it can specify a reality other than its own history. The artistic gesture must be departicularized in order to obtain its efficacy *for another*. Its semantic destiny requires separation from its effective causes. In this sense, the artist, insofar as the "artist" is a metonym of the art, is like a priest who must separate himself from pollution and deformity. The epic allegory of the constraints on reference entailed by this rule is the founding of Rome, the symbolic city, the city of symbol: the priestly semantic founder, the seed father of Rome, Aeneas, is shown the place of pain but forbidden by his nature as priest to walk the path that leads through that place. (See *Aeneid* VI, ll. 548ff.)

In traditional culture, the cognitive gains which arise from the possession of the *topoi* outweigh the cognitive loss which topical cognition exacts. At the present time, the question has arisen as to whether the exclusions exacted by topical knowledge do not constitute precisely that knowledge which is necessary for safety. The fact remains that manifestation is constructed upon obliviation, and what can be shown, and what must be obliviated to effect that showing, belong to specifiable classes of processes, properties, and persons.

25.3   The question arises: "Do men and women live in situations corresponding to the plots and arguments of poems and plays?" The answer is that men and women do not live in situations at all. As all moments of consciousness are acts of representation, situations are an entailment of consciousness, the blindness of Oedipus.

25.4   As the blind father entered the grove, so in the situations of poems and plays the consciousness of the reader approaches the bronze threshold.

25.5   There is no poem of the experience at hand.

25.6   All of this is not to say that poems are about art. On the contrary, art is about experience (in the same sense that a cat indoors is "about" the house).

> *Scholium on "art" and the subject matter of poems.* "Art" is the class of things to which poems are sometimes said to belong ("poetry" is another such class). Speakers in poems know nothing about art (and little about poetry). Poems are deeds of presence preoccupied with, sensible of, the rules and disciplines of presence. As deeds of presence they are present in the world. They are ecological, as we would now say, that is, present and *in* the matrix of other things which make and facilitate claims upon acknowledgment. The "meanings" of poems situate poems as present in a concrete horizon within the one world where, and where alone, being present is actual. Hence, we must be clear about the notion that "art" is only a classification (in general a disabling one) of poems, which the speakers in poems have an interest in disconfirming. And the "subject matters" of poems are (1) the terms of presence and (2) the horizon of an outlook on the one world, insofar as such a horizon is the beginning of the inference of the presence of a person.

25.7   Poetry is a version of the unutterable in human scale. While the poet sings, the unutterable keeps right on talking.

> *Scholium on poetry and ignorance.* Poetry by contrast to theory is a form of constructed ignorance. In this it resembles the Wisdom class of utterance in general. The strategy of poetry is *to take a stand in* the global, and therefore *unutterable,* state of affairs. By taking a stand it disavows whole knowledge. Poetry, therefore, is antignostic as it is antimystical. (A model for the relationship of human knowledge and Wisdom, and by analogy for the relationship of poetry and truth, is Job 28.) In poetry the countenance is manifested, and the realm of manifestation is a broken realm. When humanity becomes established in the whole, the ontological whole (truth) or the social whole (the collective), poetry ceases.

25.8   Patience is the *paideia* of this art. The patient man is always overtaken by the event.

Privilege

26.   Poetic art begins as the representation of privileged consciousness, the speech of kings.

26.1   The susceptibility to representation of the privileged human actor first summoned the powers of the poet.

26.2   Pitched into the world, the poet then obligated himself or herself to the honor of the inhuman actor, the poet's maker. The residual authority of the *praxis* of the divine agent (God) perpetually authorizes as a possibility the representation of the world.

> *Scholium on poetry as the honor of the world.* The first and paradigmatic privileged actor is the god. His act is the world (in Bible) or its qualities (Hellenic polytheism). Insofar as the poem is a version of the world accommodated to the horizon of a person (the horizon is a piece of the world ar-

rayed in such a way as to imply a viewer) the honor of the god is mingled in every acknowledgment of presence, for the world is the god's deed of honor and presence. All subsequent actors become subject to representation by reference to the divine actor and every narratable *praxis* is a repetition of the act of creation. The religious history of the world (as in Bible or Hesiod) is therefore the story of the establishment of the sufficient conditions of the narratability of the world, and the rules of morality are the rules of the continuing narratability of new creation as it arises. It follows, therefore, that what was not narratable at the beginning cannot subsequently become so. When the primordially outcast, the Canaanite, become claimants upon the representational privilege a new foundation, as of the world at first, is required.

26.3 Refluent on the maker of images, the susceptibility to representation of the human and divine act makes of the imagemaker an image.

26.4 Not the actor but the act generates the image.

26.5 The lyric speaker, summoned into visibility (eidetic privilege), depends for being on the poetic act. The authenticity of the poetic act is a contingency of the acts of the mighty others. Thus summoned, the poet explores his or her nature, incapable in itself of any act except the artistic act, which elaborates itself in another sense.

26.6 The unacknowledged legislators of the world are the forces of sentiment.

26.7 Like the choral person in ancient tragedy, the lyric speaker has no action (*praxis*). As a model of self-representation, therefore, lyric utterance individuates outside the circle of tragic definitions, and accommodates itself to the conservation of image of an otherwise socially anonymous (nonpractic) class.

> *Scholium on sentiment as* praxis. In lyric, sentiment is taken as a deed of presence, sentiment becomes *praxis.* In this sense, lyric is potentially the medium of visibility of the class

which, in the evolution of the older estates system, is called the third estate. This is the modern "possessing" or "middle" class, for whom the final transformation of *proprium* is the inner life, subjectivity. In the Marxian allegory of surplus value, the self which is appropriated by the capitalist from the worker is just the inner self, the growth of which the wage system, that permits only physical life, is adjusted to prevent. Capital is subjectivity.

The transformation of sentiment into *praxis* resulted from the assimilation of the many into one in the context of Christian story. Lyric derives historically from the ancient choral poems and from the chorus of Greek tragedy. The namelessness of the speaker in lyric is a residue of the name-lessness of the collective. Jesus is the great Western hero in whose person a passion becomes an action. In him manyness becomes oneness as passion becomes action. He establishes the human individual as totality, intuitive humanity, and drives out the demon whose name is Legion. Jesus individu-ates without separation.

But the secularization of interiority in art returned subjectiv-ity to the realm of the economic, and the immortalization of affect was mounted upon the dominance of a ruling class. The visibility of affect was sustained at the cost of the invis-ibility of labor, and the immortalization of the middle class predicted the obliviation of the working class. Internal to the mind which possessed it, the immortality of affect also ren-dered equivocal the meaning of its own physical processes which in the traditional estates metaphor are, as it were, the productive class of the body. Hence, lyric became special-ized, as in Romanticism, toward idealist world-pictures.

26.8   The liberation, or authentication, of all voices in society leads to madness. Toward this the lyric tends.

> *Scholium on the propagation of liberation.* Lyric is founded on the liberation of an order of being, the inner world, and a class of persons, the third estate, upon whom the inner world

devolved as a *proprium*. The dialectic of liberation of one class implies the liberation of all classes. But the conditions of the enjoyment of freedom by one class require the subordination of another class. Hence, the dialectic of freedom is at odds with the enjoyment of it. This is true so long as individuation implies separation, and until the achievement of an "organic" community in which representation can be effected in the absence of hierarchy. Such a community is not yet known. Hence, while the dialectic of liberation inherent in liberal and lyric culture continues to work, the possessors of freedom are at war with the new claimants, and the liberation of all persons is anticipated as an unintelligible Babel (the collapse of all "tradition") or madness (the final isolation of the self as a consequence of the decay of individuality toward unacknowledgeable uniqueness). This is the paradox of letters in the context of liberal education.

26.9   Once again, lyric poetry is the instrument of the self-transcendence of those selves and aspects of selves which exist only as *pathos*, or sentiment. In this sense the lyric self is a unique instrument in civilization for the representation of the unrepresented aspects of the self, the nonsocial sector of human self-recognition, and the traditionally nonpractic classes in the polity (in particular the third estate). In the imperial epic, Carthage is destroyed. The novel is the "epic" of Carthage, as it is the Bible of Canaan, and the lyric is its song.

26.10   The dominance of the lyric is correlative to the liberalization of the polity.

> *Scholium on the nonparity of economic and eidetic by contrast to political privilege.* The rise of the middle classes and the rise of the lyric are obviously parallel in modern European history. But the continuing political enfranchisement of peoples has not been accompanied by the growth of new media of eidetic enfranchisement. The noncongruence of eidetic or image privilege and political privilege resembles (in-

deed, may be exactly parallel to) the noncongruence of economic and political privilege in liberal society. The politically "equal" are not humanly equal as long as they are economically oppressed. The parallel of image life and economic life calls attention to the intimacy of eidetic value and scarcity and to the high degree of likelihood that material wealth and eidetic privilege are versions of the same substantial value.

26.11 Eidetic privilege is a historically contingent imaginal identification embedded in actual past cultural statements and administered but not created by poets.

26.12 The status of poetry as the collective representation of private (nonparticipant) experience is reflected in the "hardness" of poetry in the modern world. What is collective cannot die insofar as it holds its being for another. Inevitably it dies to itself (14.4). The hardness of being for another at precisely that place where the self is most accessible for the self, in the *topos* of the affections, is the internal version of the liberational paradoxes of lyric. As labor, lyric construction becomes in the modern world the alienation of the centrally "own." This "transmemberment of song" is mapped upon language as "difficulty." As long as the motive to individuation and the motivation to transcendence in the collective are in conflict, lyric construction will be filled either with pain or with savage, unaccountable forms of emotional scepticism.

26.13 Since the self-representation of the poet in history is authenticated as a residue of the privileged speech acts of kings, the mimetic enfranchisement of the nonpractic consciousness will never be complete. The chorus is still a slave collectivity even when the king and queen are wholly and nothing but their dream. There is no poetry but of the creative acts of kings and gods and of the servile dreamers whom they hallucinate.

> *Scholium on the one eidetic language.* The culture in which we live has produced only one language of immortal being,

only one account of the visible person. When persons of the
third estate put on immortality or assign it to states of the
world which reciprocate their claims they do so as a cosmetic
application. The felicity of visibility is still (insofar as visibility is inseparable from individuation) a function of the language which describes kings and queens or their theological
sublimations, the crowned saints. There is only one eidetic
language. Christ was enthroned in the iconography of the
Roman emperor. The great labor of the Postmodern world is
to find a second eidetic language—a labor which the atavistic modern writers postponed in the interest of their monumental *artistic* intentions.

26.14 The history of the English lyric from the Renaissance is characterized by the struggle of the lyric person toward self-representation as a man of the third estate. The antagonist is helmeted
and plumed.

> *Scholium on the history of representation as the struggle for a
> new eidetic language.* Both Auerbach and Gombrich call at-
> tention to the history of art as a struggle toward realism. Art
> has a history because of the collective human impulse to cor-
> rect preexistent paradigms or models against experience
> (Gombrich) in the interest of the stabilization of fact (expe-
> rience) in relation to value (representation), a precondition
> of meaning without which there is no human world. The
> most intransigent (because most precious) paradigm is the
> *eidos,* the paradigm which enables interhuman perception.
> In proportion as it is precious, it is guarded, by its inner
> structures, against change. The *eidos,* or countenance, first
> *appeared* as the regal *visage.* The process of correcting that
> image against the decay of estates and the rise of classes and
> roles is the central history of art, and also of poetic art. The
> fact that the *topos* of the person tends to resist the approach
> of humankind is the most important problem raised by the
> study of poetics.

Poetry as Appearance or Phenomenon

27.   A poem is an appearance. There are no appearances which are
       not appearances to someone.

> *Scholium.* A better, but less familiar, word for "appearance"
> here is *manifestation.* An appearance or manifestation is the
> likeness of a presence. ("Poetry is displaced discourse about
> persons.") All manifestation is subject to the constitutive
> rules of manifestation, which are antinomic, and the central
> contingency of these rules is the collaborative nature of im-
> age construction, the social nature of presence.

27.1   As an appearance, the poem is subject to description.

27.2   In saying that a poem is an appearance we also assert that it is
       no longer to be accounted for in terms of cause.

27.3   In saying that it is no longer to be accounted for in terms of
       cause, we assert that the poem is a version of experience which
       is complete. For example, the possibility of rereading the poem
       equivocates the asymmetry of memory. In the poem, we remem-
       ber both the past and the future. It is also the case that in the
       poem there is no possibility of further event.

> *Scholium on totalization.* Closure, which is a precondition of
> the existence of the poem (because it is a precondition of the
> perceptibility of an appearance) brings about the totalization
> of the constitutive elements of the poem, each of which has
> a history, so that the history or causes of the elements of the
> poem may be said to be lost or transformed in the poem as
> appearance. In a concrete totality, all the elements are unex-
> changeable and have come to the end of all their histories.
> The consequence of this for the reader is the possibility,
> which the poem opens out, of experimenting with the total-
> ization of experience, which the reader who has not come to
> the end of all his histories can only do by way of fiction.
> Time asymmetry is simply one of the areas with which he
> can experiment. But time asymmetry opens out the possibil-

ity, which is fundamental to the usefulness of poetry, of ex-
perimenting with the situation of *having chosen* or *having no
more choices*. This experimentation with the consequences
of *having been free*, which preempts for the moment the in-
determinacy of being, is close to the bottom of the meaning
of the management of time in the poem, and the function of
appearance as an occasion of thought.

27.4   In this sense the poem is an anticipation of death, a judgment
on the whole consciousness from within.

27.5   Nothing comes to judgment except that which has a moral nature flowing from its freedom. That which comes to judgment
has used its freedom to abolish its freedom. What is judged can
take no further form.

Seriousness II (13)

28.   The speaking person in the poem is implicated in the primordial crime. If incest is prohibited because the human species
requires that the human individual abandon its primordial impulse toward autonomy (the incest prohibition), then the lyric
person, as self-recapitulatory, is the primordial criminal.

> *Scholium on "the paradox of sociability" and on defilement.*
> The paradox of sociability lies in the fact that the marriage
> of the self with the origin of utterance, with originality, is a
> precondition of self-identification as a speaker. But this pro-
> cess portends an autonomy, a self-createdness, which renders
> equivocal the relation of the speaker with the social other.
> On the other hand, an exclusive "giving over" of the self to
> the social other compromises the relation of the self as
> speaker to the source of the speaking competence. The lyric
> speaker seems always to be a version of the self in the process
> of withdrawing from objective social relations toward the de-
> filement of the marriage with origins. The redemptive possi-
> bility in the lyric process is the meeting of all persons in the
> subliminal "I" where all origins are one origin. This is the

"symbolist" didactic. The achievement of that state of sociability in which interhuman acknowledgment is adequate to
human need extinguishes lyric by putting an end to the
trouble which gives rise to lyric. This is the *u-topos*, the uto-
pia. (For the paradox of sociability formulated from another
point of view, see Unger, *Knowledge and Politics*, pp. 215ff.)
The defiled character of the original speaker is reflected in
the Jewish idea that the central text (the text which has
touched origin) "defiles the hand."

28.1   Lyric individuation implies a recapitulation of the self from the
point of view of origins which portends an autonomy that is
antisocial in the largest possible sense. The seriousness of the
lyric person is incestuous. The abhorrence which is a feature of
the response to the lyric person (and to poetry in general) arises
from the spectacle of a face which has looked upon the body of
the mother.

> *Scholium on the recollection of past lives.* In the West, by
> contrast to the East, the recollection of past lives is a system-
> atically impeded privilege. (See E. R. Dodds, *The Greeks
> and the Irrational*, p. 151.) Genealogical story is an objective
> demonstration of relationship to origins such that connec-
> tion to source is affirmed as the authenticating privilege of
> the socially powerful, the members of the ruling group (or, as
> lineage, the members of the priestly caste); but that affirma-
> tion is such as to be removed from consciousness. It is inter-
> subjective without being subjective in the sense in which the
> subjective is the intuitive. Art facilitates the recollection of
> past lives as an intuitive resource. The speaker in lyric is
> "intuitive" and nameless because it is The Speaker, and its
> life is the same as the life of speech, the same therefore as
> the species which is characterized by speaking. One model
> for reading, to add to the other models proposed in these
> pages, is the recollection of past lives, which in the West are
> the lives of the ancestors. But note that the very idea of
> ancestors is a limitation on the autonomy of the self. The
> general sense that art is an effect not reducible to the aggre-

gate of its causes (is a totality) expresses the function of art as an instance or model of the person who is *causa sui.*

28.2 Speaking across time and bearing the marks of unforgivable knowledge the question must arise, "How has the lyric person survived?" The "divinity" of the poem (and by Romantic metonymy of the poet in history) is the quality that adheres to the criminal who has survived the retribution of the gods.

28.3 The form of the poem is principally a phenomenon of centering (16.1). What is centered shapes itself by a process of decisive negations. The centered thing (for example, the line) withdraws itself from alliances in order to return with a power which renders all relationships equivocal and unmistakable (like personhood subject to the "paradox of sociability"). The line confers upon the sentence the unanticipated implication that it is an everlasting and unalterable management of a meaning-predicament which was before merely a mythic plenum of many possible acts (19.3).

28.4 The abhorrent seriousness of the lyric person constitutes an intolerable privilege. In the lyric, privilege has been withdrawn from the hero, the aristocrat, the god, or it has not yet been conferred. For that reason it constantly propels the person represented toward a scale of being incompatible with human life. The lyric person has always in some sense refused the sacrifice of the first fruits.

28.5 In the outlook of the lyric person the horizon has ceased to be a precinct and has become a vortex (20).

28.6 The vortex in the poem is the horizon of outlook of the blind man whose eyes have been transformed: one eye has become a mirror, the other an abyss.

28.7 The speaker in the poem is the man who has usurped the right of the first night in which he was conceived. Hence the beauty, the shining of the face.

Line I (36)

29.   In English we observe three modular versions of the line:

      1. Less than ten syllables more or less.
      2. Ten syllables more or less.
      3. More than ten syllables more or less.

Scholium on line and breath. There are two breaths or breath-ings which poetic analysis takes into account: the Greater or Feeding Breath is the breath taken in, during which there can be no speech. This breath comes to an end with the *limit of expansion,* when the body is as full as can be of the nur-turant air. This silent feeding on the world to the limit of expansion precedes or prepares for *the line opening* (or, in appropriate degree, the lesser medial caesura). The Lesser Breath is the breathing out, during which speech occurs as the reticulation of the dead breath. This Lesser, or Dead, or Speech Breath explores the opposite limit, the limit of con-traction—at which limit is *the line ending.* The strong sense of the contradiction of speech and feeding lends weight to the preference of silence to speech, and adds a further bitter-ness to the paradox of storytelling.

Equivocation of the limit of contraction as in open form verse, since it involves reference to death, the emptying out of the self into the world, is also equivocation of death. Hence, it is at the line end, the limit of contraction of the self, that history records its several strategies with respect to transcendence and the facilitation of continuity.

Speech is obtained by *inscription* upon the dead breath, a meddling with the exhausted air as it is pushed from the body outward. The terminal caesura is the point of turning (*vertere*), as at the end of a furrow, the beginning of the in-breathing which carries the burden of the process from pre-ceding line-close to following line-opening.

29.1   In *the line less than ten syllables* transformations occur. The precinct is closed as by a force pressing outward from within. Alternative versions of the same utterance are very remote; not
even a faint murmuring is heard.

29.2   In *the line of ten syllables more or less,* persons address one another in human scale. The topic of the line of ten is conflict.
Adjacent utterances are very near at hand, whispering in a sort
of idleness just beyond the *termini.* When two speak, as in
drama, four or five voices are near at hand. The line is closed
with equal force from within and without. (See Scholium on
Blank Verse at 29.8.)

29.3   In *the line more than ten syllables,* the speaker in the poem
bleeds outward as in trance or sleep toward other states of himself. In the unexpected air he takes grotesque and comic forms.
Alternatively, he grows heavy with the unmanageable seriousness of excluded states of his own being. The line more than
ten is closed from without, but the *termini* are shrouded in
mists.

29.4   In the line less than ten syllables the silence around the precinct is like a vacuum. Something has been taken away, and
what is within presses outward against radical emptiness. The
line of ten floats in a social space managing its boundedness by
stratagems of reciprocity. The line more than ten is sinking into
the ground of selfhood. In it is portended the dissolution of the
self in the ground, a version of apocalypse. Less than ten speaks
of change in the mode of changelessness. Ten speaks of mutuality. More than ten indicates the troubling of form by inner possibility.

29.5   In the stanza of more than one line-length we observe the management by the speaking person of the several modal values of
consciousness encoded in the several modal actualizations of
the line. The poem of several stanzas displays the multivocality
of the speaking person by arraying a series of "openings upon"
different states of the speaker's being. In like manner, the stanza
of more than one line-length exhibits consciousness as a reci-

procity of the modal values of consciousness as defined by the
three states of the line.

29.6 The line is the first occasion in the poem when the speaker's
motive as a being-for-another-altogether acquires a meaning.
As the eye of the reader scans the line, it passes from crisis to
crisis of surmise.

> *Scholium on surmise and the scanning of the line.* As the eye
> moves from left to right in the line, it passes from a station
> where any actualization consistent with the nature of line is
> possible (line opening, Genesis) toward ever more concrete
> declarations as to the modal specificity of *this* line. Hence,
> the line is like the poem (24), moving from less differentia-
> tion and more possibility toward more differentiation and less
> possibility, from global participation toward closure and cog-
> nitive increment. As the eye scans the line, it surmises the
> outcome of the excursion, and these surmises remain as dis-
> sonance after the outcome of the linear excursion is dis-
> closed. A similar process of surmise and discovery takes place
> at the syntactic level as the eye surmises possibilities of gram-
> matical closure arising from the possible combinations of
> morphemes which do not become actual. These surmised
> possibilities remain as semantic dissonances after the actual
> syntactic structure of the morphemic string is distinguished.
> Line opening both as prosody and meaning is characterized
> by structural distinctness and semantic irresolution, and line
> close is characterized by semantic richness and structural ir-
> resolution. (See also 37.5.)

29.7 When the line has been noted, the centering of being is complete and the space in which the poem displays itself rays out.

29.8 Lineation cannot be added and cannot be taken away. When it
is present, there is no sense in which it does not specify that a
poem is present. When it is taken away, there is no sense in
which there ever was a poem.

> *Scholium on Blank Verse (the line of ten) as the modal English
> line-form.* Blank Verse, unrhymed (hence "blank") ten-

syllable strings, is the modal line-form in English, the line of ten. Blank Verse is normally taken to consist of ten vocalized syllables with alternate, iambically sequenced (that is to say, sequenced in a rising series) stress peaks. In this (normal) form it can also be called "Iambic Decasyllables." "Blank Verse" may also refer to a line-form characterized by five stress peaks with a variable syllable count. In this case, the stress peaks are taken as the principle of measure and the line is called pentameter, measured by five. When five stress peaks characterize a line which is also regularly divided into five iambic feet, the line is called iambic pentameter. Occasionally, a line is written with a rule of ten syllables and no rule of stress arrangement, that is to say, in *syllabic meter.* Then the line is merely called decasyllabic. It is continually noted in the literature that wherever the five-stress rule is manifest the number of stresses may reduce to four as a part of normal expectation.

Blank Verse in all its actualizations includes a medial caesura (a central internal silence) and a caesura before the beginning and after the end of each line. As in all line-forms this organization of the ground, the silence, for a little way out, is more or less perceptible, but always present, as a turbulence at the edge.

The Blank Verse line-form was established between the fourteenth and sixteenth centuries in English as the form speech takes when it depicts the speech of persons in social situations. Blank Verse is a regime the rules of which produce the picture of the speech of a person under those conditions of exteriority (seen from the outside) and scale (no larger or smaller than a human being as he or she is seen by other human beings) which characterize social situations. Blank Verse, therefore, is the order speech takes when it gives the picture of the well-formed social person—as in Shakespearean talk, where only "gentle" persons speak Blank Verse and only gentle persons are well-formed. The fate of Blank Verse tends to be discussed as the fate of social man. To lib-

erate verse from rhyme is for Milton to liberate from bondage, to set up the human form divine. In Blank Verse there
is understood to be represented an equilibrium between the
outer (syllabic) and the inner (stress-factored) natures of the
speaker such as facilitates social relationships, interactions
between persons in the human world of sight and sound. The
various alternative actualizations of Blank Verse (as iambic
decasyllables, or pentameter, iambic pentameter, or the syllabic actualization as mere decasyllables) should be understood to be modifications or variations of an initial interpersonal settlement. Note that line-forms, and verse forms in
general, are fundamentally discussable as mediations of relationships, as rules and orders of polities. In the line-form is
worked out the politics of presence which are normally managed by the body and the will in natural by contrast to poetic
(textual) situations. Hence, the differing nomenclature for
the pentameter line-form is merely a modest discussion about
how many ways you can rule this sort of person without his
becoming another sort.

The blankness of Blank Verse seems to have arisen in the
process of improvising an English line-form suitable for the
translation of dactylic hexameter, the normal classical epic
line-form as in Virgil. It was thus a part of a Renaissance and
humanist movement toward representation which sought a
medium the implications of which were different from the
implications of medieval prosodies. In Blank Verse the line
must "stand alone" without losing distinctness. The medieval
addition of rhyme which secured the actualization (the pre-
presentational possibility) of the Christian "infinity" of aspiration introduced as a semantic possibility together with
stress (in the fourth and fifth centuries) has been abandoned
in the interest of an internally willed finitization, a finitization which is immanent to history and effected in secular
(social) interactions—following the Virgilian civic emphasis. Blankness was, as it were, an antimedieval atavism, a
turning back to another version of the human form which

required another line-form, another lineament, for its mediation. As a result, the blankness of Blank Verse also came
to imply an epistemological critique of a former state of affairs; and rhyme became, from the point of view established
by Blank Verse, a transgression against truthfulness, an ex-
cessive claim and therefore a deformity. In this way there
arose a connotation of antimystical severity within the range
of reference of Blank Verse which determined that it could,
for example, be used by Robinson and Frost but not by Yeats.
When Pound came to boast that to "break the pentameter"
was the "first heave" of modern prosodic reformation he registered the defeat by history of the cause of the well-formed
social person, of free men in the Shakespearean and Word-
sworthian sense.

Interpretation

30.   A poem is an occasion for loving exchange of perceptions
among the company summoned.

> A. *Scholium on poetry as hospitium.* Poems pitch persons to-
> ward one another full of news about being, about personal
> life. The poem is an occasion, across vast reaches of space
> and time, for the performance of the ceremony of hospitality
> in which the stranger is greeted and the contracts of socia-
> bility are recovenanted. This is because the poem as a com-
> mon place is like a festive table where persons renew their
> relation to the substance of being in colloquy. The poem has
> no other life than the relationships it facilitates, and these
> relationships reproduce the profoundest human covenant,
> which is the covenant of language through which they give
> and obtain the world simultaneously, and only obtain the
> world when they give.

30.1   The uninterpreted text is a token of unextinguished relationships.

30.2   The interpreted text is a crisis in the community.

30.3   Interpretation is a banishing ritual. The specialization of the
        self toward cognitive apprehension precipitates a situation in
        which the self seems no longer to need to ask questions about
        the other.

30.4   Thereafter, the reconstitution of the community depends upon
        an array of loving gestures which solicit the other to ask ques-
        tions about the self.

> *Scholium on healing the bad diversity of meanings.* One of the
> functions of a text is to enable one person to ask another,
> "But what do you mean?" Interpretation is a crisis in the
> community because it makes apparent the diversity of eco-
> nomically divergent interests in the community, a diversity
> which is concealed when the canonical text is merely sung.
> As soon as interpretation is permitted, the community be-
> comes aware of the monadic character of its constituent ele-
> ments, its persons. But the community can be healed when
> the members turn away from the text and toward one an-
> other. The bad diversity of meanings is a diversity unme-
> diated by sociability. This occurs when the text is regarded
> as the only sanctioned answerer, when the text is ontologized
> in such a way that its legitimacy is regarded as prior to the
> legitimacy of the person. When readers turn away from the
> text and toward one another, when the text therefore re-
> cedes and can scarcely be seen, then there arises a new sen-
> timent of textuality, which draws in the souls which have
> been scattered. This is the beginning of *hermeneutic friend-
> ship* in which the dialogic structure of the text, the structure
> characterized by communicable diversity, binds the commu-
> nity back together not through the repetition of meaning
> (the hermeneutic of repetition, which is the continuation
> into the community of the monologic conception of the
> text, and betrays the inherent diversity of interest on which
> the culture of persons is established) but through the dialec-
> tic interplay of meaning which comes to be seen as the pro-
> gressive disclosure of being of which the text that was the
> starting point is then seen as a preliminary indication.

30.5   One version of "an array of loving gestures" is teaching.

30.6   Participation in the poem as a medium and occasion of the communicability of the self (reading) pitches the participant toward the others and those others toward the poem in an unending sunny round.

> *Scholium on the pragmatic assessment of poetic function.* We are close to the "meaning" of the poem when we note what the poem has brought us to. For example, if we are reading together then a function of the poem has been to place us in *this* relationship. If we are reading together and not looking at one another, or not touching one another, then the outcome of the poem's being-among-us has been a diversion of the eyes. Discourse about this poem places us in concrete relationship to one another of a certain sort and administers our powers in concrete ways, and this is what the poem does. We know this because this is *what the poem is doing.* The function and meaning of the poem is what I am doing now with the poem in mind. Not to recognize this as a *meaning* of the poem's existence is not to care what I am doing now. When we discourse about the poem or discourse about discourse about the poem then the poem has brought me to you and you to me about this.
>
> As a consequence, we must inquire whether the relationship among us devised by the poem (our relationship created by the poem) is singular, or like other relationships, or both. The relationship among us devised by the poem is a *topical* relationship, that is to say, it is a relationship of the kind that takes place in *topical or common space.* Its model is triadic, or rather it models the *triadic relationship.* We have narrowed the ground of the concern of each of us in order to approach one another across the abyss of the immiscibility of minds. As the ground of our concern narrows we become increasingly *of use* to one another; we enter, as we enter topical space, the possibility of hermeneutic friendship (Scholium at

44), but we cannot do this if we look beyond, in our preemp-
tive restlessness, the immediate outcome of there being a
poem among us.

30.7 The speaking person in the poem is one version of the self about
whom questions are asked. The teaching person, of whom the
speaking person in the poem is the author, is another.

30.8 There is an irreducible profundity about the self of whom questions are asked.

Scholium.

The Lecture

Place a man in the center, and he becomes
The man who has prepared for a lifetime
To answer, and now is ready.

                                    Sometimes,
There are trees at the edge of the clearing,
More often a sea. He talks on and on,
And his voice is carried up by the thermals
At the sea's edge, or down among the dark
Anfractuous trees, and the textile moss.
The lesson is staggering, and the examples
Come to hand like sheaves in a great harvest.

But, in fact, there are no trees, there is no sea,
And the center is some eccentric region
Of a bed or a room, and the question
Is the half-demented glance of a child,
Or a blurred silence on the telephone,
For which the man who has prepared a lifetime
Is ready.

        But the harvest is a great harvest.

After a long time, the voice of the man
Stops. It was good to talk on and on.

> He rises. And the sea or forest becomes
> A level way reaching to night and the thunder.
>
> But, in fact, there is no night, there is
> No thunder.

30.9   That self is the triumph and the beneficiary of civility (36).

B. *Scholium on hospitium.* In classical and secular civilization the poem or text is a type of the privileged and defiled stranger about whom questions are asked. The privilege of centrality (the poem is centered) conferred on the self by the other when the other or host asks questions about the self, and the splendid remission, the reply of the self, which ensues, is the inner scenario of the poetics of civilization. As Odysseus wanders, fenced around by the privilege and defilement of the stranger, civility unfolds in the conventions of *hospitium.* To the host who asks, the wanderer tells his tale. In the tale there is something of the true nature of things in the eidetic sense, the nature of things constructed as the history of a self. To the immortal host who asks, the half-divine stranger, the poem, discloses the secret names of man.

The staging of the acts which constitute the drama of civility is important (the drama of civility is *hospitium,* and the drama of *hospitium* is a version of the hermeneutic drama, the drama of interpretation): first the stranger (the poem, language) must be known as strange. Known to be unknown (disclosed now as undisclosed). He is the beneficiary of restorative care. He is the bridegroom of the virgin's dream, the husband, the father, the heir, the assassin. Unknown, he is infinitely knowable. The crisis of the ceremony (the *anagnorisis*) is the asking of the name. Then dreaming comes to an end. The poem is the heroic and defiled wanderer through time, whose strangeness is his mark, the *magister* whose privilege is the question toward which his being is prepared.

In Judaeo-Christian civilization, the text is host and the direction of the hermeneutic process is reversed. Humanity comes to the text which is divine and centered, the divine but incarnate word which greets the mortal journeyer and provides a model for his understanding of his true nature. The canonical text interprets the mortal person by showing that person his or her name as part of the description of the central nature of things. In pagan culture, the text is the stranger. In Judaeo-Christian civilization, the stranger is the reader. In pagan culture, humanity chooses to acknowledge the text. In Judaeo-Christian religious culture, the text chooses to acknowledge humanity, setting persons the problem of self-acknowledgment. Herbert's "Love III" is an example of the ceremony of *hospitium* in the form of the greeting of the reader by the text, and the slow consequent discovery by the reader that he is a part of the intelligible order of things.

Love III

Love bade me welcome: yet my soul drew back,
    Guiltie of dust and sinne.
But quick-ey'd Love, observing me grow slack
    From my first entrance in,
Drew nearer to me, sweetly questioning,
    If I lack'd any thing.

A guest, I answer'd, worthy to be here:
    Love said, You shall be he.
I the unkinde, ungratefull? Ah my deare,
    I cannot look on thee.
Love took my hand, and smiling did reply,
    Who made the eyes but I?

Truth Lord, but I have marr'd them: let my shame
    Go where it doth deserve.
And know you not, sayes Love, who bore the blame?
    My deare, then I will serve.
You must sit down, sayes Love, and taste my meat:
    So I did sit and eat.

Inscription

31.   Inscription is the fact which finds something of one sort in-
       scribed (written in) something of another sort.

31.1   The stone, always older than the words inscribed in it, is the
       principle of continuity of the words inscribed which are its oc-
       casion as an object of attention.

31.2   Poems in manifold ways are things (designs in the forms of state-
       ments) inscribed upon other things (more fundamental designs
       and statements).

> *Scholium on figure and ground in poetic structure.* The figure-
> ground relationship is repeated over again at each level of
> construction in the poem. Stress, for example, should be re-
> garded as a figuration of the ground of the word-string of the
> line. The word-string of the line itself should be regarded as
> a figuration of the ground of silence, or the white morpheme
> of the unwritten page. And that white morpheme is un-
> doubtedly a figuration on some more fundamental blank,
> more fundamental and older, which sustains and also contra-
> dicts (the normal relationship of figure and ground) the
> white morpheme of the page. Metaphor is a figure (all re-
> peated verbal strategies in poems are called figures) of differ-
> ence, in effect the inscription of difference on that ground of
> similarity which binds together the two terms which differ-
> ence disjoins. Rhyme, too, is a figure of difference mounted
> upon a ground of phonic similarity. Every feature of a poem
> is one term in a figure-ground ratio which may be more or
> less severe. Some poems, by means of strong marks such as
> capitalization and emphatic stressing, are raised up very high
> from the ground or background of the page. Other poems,
> especially some modern poems, through the reduction of the
> figuring marks, are laid very close to the ground and interact
> with it in intimate ways. The paradox of the figure-ground
> relationship is that ground and figure always contradict each
> other, and always serve each other through contradiction.

The function of the interaction of figure and ground is to create an edge across which transcendence is effected.

31.3   To begin with, poems are finite languages inscribed upon infinite languages.

31.4   The infinite, or first, language is the nontemporal foundation of experience itself, the creative word.

And God said, Let there be light.

Scholium on poetry as language of one sort discoursing about language of another sort. Poetry, and lyric poetry in particular, takes as its subject the relationship between finite or social language (31.5) and the nonfinite founding language, the language of another sort. As the world is created by differentiation from its source in difference, so also poetry is created by differentiation from its source in the nonfinite reality of the global world. In this sense poetry is, as Heidegger says, "being's house." The scenarios of the lyric enact the "bespeaking" of the archetype of speech, the primordial language (the Beloved), and show one way to stay in relation with the archetype. Lyric is, in this sense, an axis upon which it is possible to move from consciousness to its source (which is not conscious) and back again. (This is the drama of Keats' "Ode to a Nightingale.") Poetry is not archetypal language. It is, however, a version of social language which is *in touch.* Note the following from Max Picard, *The World of Silence,* p. 29:

> We have said that language comes from silence and returns to silence. It is as though behind silence were the absolute word to which, through silence, human language moves. It is as though the human words were sustained by the absolute word. Because it [absolute word] is there, the human word is not scattered as the dust. Man would have to be constantly regaining the realm of language if it were not secured from attack in the absolute word. All human words seem to move around that word.

Silence is like a remembrance of that word. The different
languages are like different attempts to find the absolute
word. It is as though words had agreed to divide themselves up into various languages, in order to attempt the
discovery of the absolute word from different directions.
Languages seem to be like so many expeditions to find the
absolute word.

An instance of poetry as "language of one sort discoursing
about language of another sort" is Yeats' "After Long Silence"
(another instance is Wallace Stevens' "Notes toward a Supreme Fiction"):

After Long Silence

Speech after long silence; it is right,
All other lovers being estranged or dead,
Unfriendly lamplight hid under its shade,
The curtains drawn upon unfriendly night,
That we descant and yet again descant
Upon the supreme theme of Art and Song:
Bodily decrepitude is wisdom; young
We loved each other and were ignorant.

31.5 The finite language is social statement mapped upon syntax
which entrains through time. When we speak and understand
we remember and anticipate (4.1).

31.6 In poetry this finite language is inscribed on the language of
another kind.

Scholium on Word Infinite: the stream of speech. "It was reck-
oned one of the offenses of Julian the Apostate that he tried
to revive the oracle at Delphi. He sent there a famous doctor,
named Oribasius, who was acting as imperial questor. But
the attempt failed, for Oribasius only brought back the answer:

'Tell the king, the fair wrought hall has fallen to the
ground. No longer has Phoebus a hut, nor a prophetic

laurel, nor a stream that speaks. The water of speech even is quenched' " (H. W. Parke and D. E. W. Wormell, *The Delphic Oracle*, vol. 1, pp. 289, 290).

We can correlate the death of the speaking stream in cult with the birth of the *loquaces lymphae* in poetry. From the fourth century A.D., the spring of Castalia was thought to echo when Apollo spoke. "Speaking water" (*pegen laleousan, lalon hudor*) is found at the end of Horace's *Odes* III, xiii:

> Fies; nobilium tu quoque fontium,
> me dicente cavis impositam ilicem
> saxis, unde loquaces
> lymphae desiliunt tuae.

The *fons Bandusiae* (outside of Horace's poem unknown to history) is exhibited in the poem among the *nobilium fontium*. Water from the earth is a secular version of the infinite or first language, the mother tongue (43). As the human poet arises from the earth speaking of what he did not choose (the birth-accident), the spring rises speaking from the behovely earth.

The *lalon hudor* is not segmented like grammatical speech. Compare:

> The old man still stood talking by my side:
> But now his voice to me was like a stream
> Scarce heard; nor word from word could I divide;
> And the whole body of the man did seem
> Like one whom I had met with in a dream;
> Or like a man from some far region sent,
> To give me human strength by apt admonishment.
>> (Wordsworth, "The Leech Gatherer")

The Delphic stream of speech exhibits a primitive unity associated with the divine nature and the first creation of things (Coleridge's primary imagination).

It is in this way, then, that you mean us to understand your Word, who is God with you, God with God, your Word uttered eternally, for your Word is not speech in which each part comes to an end when it has been spoken, giving place to the next, so that finally the whole may be uttered. In your Word all is uttered at one and the same time, yet eternally. If it were not so, your Word would be subject to time and change, and therefore would be neither truly eternal nor truly immortal (Augustine, *Confessions*, 11, 6; Pine-Coffin).

The patristic commonplace that only the numerical unitary is immortal applies. The Word Infinite is the ground of the poetic inscription which bears it across time, the stone. Note Revelation 1:15:

12   And I turned to see the voice that spake with me. And being turned I saw seven golden candlesticks;

13   And in the midst of the seven candlesticks one like unto the Son of Man, clothed with a garment down to the foot, and girt about the paps with a golden girdle.

14   His head and his hairs were like wool, as white as snow; and his eyes were as a flame of fire;

15   And his feet were like unto fine brass, as if they burned in a furnace; and his voice as the sound of many waters.
(Gk., *phone hudaton pollon*; Vulg., *vox aquarum multarum*; Heb., *mayim rabim*)

This account incorporates Ezekiel 43:2:

43:1   Afterward he brought me to the gate, even the gate that looketh toward the east;

43:2   And behold, the glory of the God of Israel came from the way of the east; and his voice was like a noise of many waters: and the earth shined with his glory.

Compare also Ezekiel 1:24:

> As they went I heard the noise of their wings, like the noise of great waters, as the voice of the Almighty, the voice of speech, as the noise of an host: when they stood they let down their wings.

The voice of the Bible God is the same stuff as the primordial waters upon which He moved when He uttered the real (the truth). The gastropod shell (symbol of poetry, Orphic machine [44:3]) gives access to the sound of the waters of the first creation. The poem is written upon the waters of the first creation ("Here lies one whose name was writ in water"). The voice of the god is characterized by multiplicity (see Yeats' "The Emotion of Multitude") and by temporal indifferentiation ("nor word from word could I divide"). This voice (prior to art) is the primary imagination. In Whitman ("the hum of the valved voice") it is the Answerer.

Note that in Horace III, xiii, we find the eternalization (*me dicente*) not of the man alone but of the oak (*ilex*) from the roots of which the stream issues. The tree and the spring are the double symbol (see the last stanza of Yeats' "Among School Children"). The rooted and the flowing are constituents of the cultural self, time-bound and time-less, one and many. *The double symbol:* tree and spring, male and female, individual and collective, speech and meter.

The last word, the final symbol of poems, is always a double symbol, presenting the coexistence, not of contingent irreconcilables, but of absolute irreconcilables, body and soul, human and divine, rooted and wandering.

31.7   The primary language which establishes existence is of another kind than poetry. Upon language conceived as coterminous with reality poets inscribe poems.

31.8   Among the versions of infinite language upon which poets inscribe poems is the language of prosodic expectation (meter). It is a blank—endless, abstract, arbitrary, timeless, sustaining. Who spoke it? The same person who spoke the stone.

31.9 The infinite language is also the language of the child before the child has language. Clearly the stone is of more kinds than the inscription.

> *Scholium on the allegories of meter as ground.* Divinity, primary imagination, word infinite, stone, meter are all versions of the ground on which the figure is displayed by differentiation. From a Freudian point of view the ground and all its allegories may be regarded as a reference to the unconscious life, or alternatively to life and experience prior to infantile amnesia. The infinity (and immortality) of the ground has the characteristics of the unconscious system in that it knows no time and is not troubled by contradiction. The ground is the ocean and its sentiment "the oceanic feeling," with, however, the fundamental difference that upon this water a name is written, and in this element and ocean the person is not carried down but carried up and sustained. In the poem consciousness is allowed access to the lost mother and allowed also return. The poem is one "way" upon which we move to redress losses which time has compelled. This is discussed in Schachtel, *Metamorphosis,* pp. 181, 182. In deformed poetic civilizations the way of art is one along which the journeyer cannot return, the ground swallows up the figure, the *seriousness* of basic criminality (28) has become absolute. Note the following of Hart Crane:
>
> > *The Return*
> >
> > The sea raised up a campanile . . . The wind I heard
> > Of brine partaking, whirling spout in shower
> > Of column kiss—that breakers spouted, sheared
> > Back into bosom,—me—her, into natal power . . .
>
> Another language for this ground, of which the most patent version in poetic construction is meter, is the language of transcendental reference. Human Value Studies are distinguished from studies of other kinds insofar as they concern

themselves with access to transcendental reference. In modernism the pathogenic version of the transcendental reference or ground is the most common. Its theory is to be found in Rudolph Otto, *The Idea of the Holy.*

31.10 Lyric, especially in its pathogenic versions, incorporates as subject the aspiration of language as an infinite system.

> It is the unbetrayable reply
> Whose accent no farewell can know.
> (Crane, "Voyages VI")

But, insofar as the subject in poetry is always definable in social terms, that desire cannot be consummated without passing beyond the limits of art. When the message devours the stone, death ensues. When the stone usurps the message, death also. Think of this as the inscribing of rain.

31.11 In cultures grown weary of inscription, the archaic power of the ground becomes an object of reverence in itself.

> Fond Lovers, cruel as their flame,
> Cut in these trees their Mistress name.
> Little, alas, they know or heed,
> How far these beauties hers exceed.
> (Marvell, "The Garden")

Here we see art as a special case of the violence of all thought. When violence becomes the characterizing gesture of a culture (the way in which it keeps its promises) inscription is an intolerable burden on the loving heart.

31.12 Conceived as something inscribed upon something else, the lyric consists of an accident (a nonrecurrent narrative, an anecdote) inscribed upon an archetype. Neither term is annihilable without the loss of the nature of the whole. Historical styles tend to emphasize one term or the other. The style which loses the difference is called apocalyptic.

> *Scholium on accident and archetype.* At poem opening the double symbol constellates itself (inside the "I" which is a

type of the double symbol [24.1]) by the reciprocal assimilation of accident and archetype (20), life and myth, immanence and transcendence, the particular and the general,
the figure and the ground. In "classical" styles the dominant
element is the anecdote, the nonrecurrent feature. In "romantic" styles the anecdote is treated as transparent, and the
dominant element is the ground. The relationship of figure
and ground we call the figure-ground ratio. This ratio can be
understood as time or space or history—the whole of what
intervenes between the beginning and the end, the substance of the difference, as between birth and death, creation
and revelation. In another sense the figure-ground ratio is
the ignorance of the poem, and that ignorance is the opacity
of the countenance of the person, its representability (25.7
and Scholium). For the knowability of the countenance inheres in its unknowability, in its nontransparence. Poetry
like mortality is absence from felicity, the stay of gnosis.
Apocalypse (the final disclosure of secrets) is the death of
the countenance, the collapse of the figure into the ground,
the surrender to natal power. The transparency of the figure
in romantic styles is correlative with the disposition of poetry
in those styles toward apocalyptic resolutions.

31.13   Metaphor (17) is an instance of inscription, an always two-
termed system (A is like B) inscribed upon a more fundamental
two-termed system (Subject perceives Object), which it resembles and imitates. The condition which sustains metaphor,
namely that the two terms are not one, is the same condition
which enables perception. The centrality of metaphor in the
analysis of poetry derives from the universality in the poem of
the dramatic predicament of the man or woman who perceives.

31.14   Metaphor defines elements in mind as nonidentical, thus recovering in a stated relationship what is lost at the moment the
relationship becomes a perceptual possibility. That metaphor is
regarded by the philosopher as a mistake in language calls attention again to the dialectical habit of lyric by which it unfolds

itself just where nature has placed, and the philosopher finds, a knot. (See Scholium at 16.3.)

31.15 Lyric inscribes individual upon collective life, private upon public life, mental upon physical life—imposing by violence a reciprocity from which struggle is never absent (31.2 and Scholium). The poem exhibits what is in it in a form which is the opposite of unity. Meaning and ground are endlessly hostile, and endlessly serviceable, one to the other. The completion of one in the other would be "the linen clothes folded up" (Blake, "Marriage of Heaven and Hell," plate III).

> *Scholium on poetry and unity.* The romantic idealization of poetic unity requires qualification. The very existence of poetry, as of art in general, implies world brokenness. The inherent elegiac character of representation as record of the residue of the postcatastrophic experience of perception also implies the fundamental incompleteness of the world in art. Further, the poem is a partial statement in the sense that its open or *general* "texture" of reference requires completion by a reader (see, for example, Wolfgang Iser, "Indeterminacy and the Reader's Response in Prose Fiction"). In this sense, the poem has the incompleteness of the unborn thing. But even more central, the poem is stationed upon the antinomies of being, placing them as it were in diplomatic relation. The poem has no power to reconcile what is at war in experience. Further, and most important of all, realms that are whole in experience come into poetry as antinomic complementarities. The poetic world is the "broken world" (Crane's "Broken Tower") where hope lives as it were in exile from its kingdom, which is reality. The will in art is precisely that defeated will which has discovered the limits of its power with respect to its own ends, and has exchanged for participation the secondary consolations of narration. Metered language, metaphoric perception, symbolic meaning are less ordered states of language, perception, and meaning than their natural counterparts. The wholeness which poetry *does* mediate is the colloquial and interhuman wholeness of two per-

sons who have met upon the ground which the poem has illuminated but from which it has withdrawn its odd uncanny presence.

31.16 Think of it as a kind of skywriting.

Radical, Aesthetic, and Religious Humanism

32.   A radical humanism would have two components:
        1. The sentiment of participation (radical imagination).
        2. The will to intervention (radical reason).

32.1   A radical humanism is the antithesis of aesthetic humanism.

32.2   In a radical humanism a tragedy becomes an event from which no one goes home.

> *Scholium on Hellenic and Judaic.* Aesthetic culture is founded on the distinction between actor and audience established as theory when Aristotle supposes a different fate for the character (who dies) and the audience (who is purged of pity and terror). The distance implied by the difference in destiny between actor and audience is the "aesthetic distance." This withholding from the spectacle, or suspension of participation, defines also the relationship to experience when experience is taken as fiction. The basis of aesthetic humanism is Hellenic. The Bible, by contrast, has no theory of truth or participation other than the historical processes which it thematizes. The structure of Bible specifies a discipline from which the reader can only exempt himself by making the one interpretive error which repudiates the whole text. The basis of radical humanism in Western civilization is Judaic.

32.3   Aesthetic humanism is based on a hierarchical communalism in which the symbolic order is participated across the barrier of the fictional premise. Value is remitted through a feudal mutuality of obligation, the terms of which require a higher and lower order, the former (the higher) serving as the substantiating image by which the latter knows itself to be in existence.

32.4   Radical humanism desiderates an immanent communalism in which eidetic privilege is universally and equally possessed, being received and remitted in the horizontal plane. The whole must derive its nature from the individual at the same time that it remits to the individual a self-identity undiminished in specificity. But where there are no invisible persons, are there any visible persons?

> *Scholium on image-life and egalitarianism.* At present, it is impossible to conceive, or even to construct as theory, a community in which the whole is the archetype and model of each of the parts, and at the same time its central nature. The persuasion about the self in liberal culture which requires that the person be perceived as a particular, and valued as a general nature, involves paradoxes which are surmounted neither in theory nor in practice. At present, inclusion is obtained by exclusion, the seen thing by reference to the unseen thing, the acknowledged soul by reason of the unacknowledged. The central obstacle to egalitarianism is the fact of the foundation of the culture of visibility and acknowledgment upon the metaphysics, politics, and economics of difference (that is to say, differentiation through hierarchy). Nonhierarchical differentiation is inimical to the nature of personhood itself, since inside the person there is the history of eidetic construction which is itself a process of hierarchical differentiation, a product of displacement from a transcendental reference.
>
> Inside the dialectics of poetic structure there arises at all times a clear recognition of the paradox of human value and the conditions of acknowledgment. This recognition is manifested in poetic practice by experimentation with the relationship of the figure and the ground. As the figure-ground ratio becomes smaller, the terms of general and particular life

converge (as in Whitman). But as the ground rises up inside the figure, the lineaments of the human countenance and the gestures of human love (the greeting by the particular name) fade. In poetry it is possible to register and explore the limiting conditions of the pacification of social life (the paradoxes of sociability [28]) but not to surmount them. As a consequence, all the poetries which we now know seem to lie under the shadow of the general problem, and the envalorization of visibility and particularity in liberal and lyric culture seem to be retrograde to the peace of the world.

32.5   In aesthetic humanism unreality is the repository of the first fruits of instinctual life—gigantic, startling, perhaps insane. From that thesaurus of real human desires men and women have derived, age after age, a life in human scale by a ceremony of sacrifice and remission. The binding of Isaac is the type of this cultural process.

> *Scholium.* In aesthetic humanism the mind of the human community, and the world in which it lives, are experienced as out of human scale and therefore inimical to the construction of a well-formed human image. Mankind's first gesture in aesthetic humanism is the disavowal of its central creativity in the act of surrendering through sacrifice (or feudal subordination) the first fruits of the libido. Having sacrificed its autonomous will and its immanent powers of immortality, mankind receives back its wage from the god and lord—the human image in human scale, the picture of the person consistent with the god's ideology of mortality. All scenarios of poetic construction imply the sacrifice of the present person to the past and future image. This is as clearly true in Jeremiah as it is in the Freudian scenario of sublimation. The impossibility of being whole is similar to the impossibility of being together. The totalization of the human self and the totalization of the human community are equally inconceivable in the poetic model. Aesthetic humanism is a name for the culture of images as it really is. Radical humanism is its contradiction. In aesthetic humanism structure dominates

value to produce art, in the same manner in which structure dominates value in history to produce such social order as we have. There are no instances either of social order or of art in the radical culture in which value dominates structure and the means of human enterprise are reconciled with its ends.

32.6 Religious humanism derives the irreducible value of personhood from the prior perception of the inhuman other. Poetry, being nothing in itself, is the bride and chattel of religious humanism in the aesthetic tradition. In religious humanism the knowability of the human other is authorized and enabled by God, the substantiating image by which the mortal person "knows itself to be in existence."

> Scholium. Religious humanism is the point at which radical and aesthetic humanisms converge. In the idea of God, the master becomes a part of the self, and the inhuman other is incorporated into the human genealogy by the symbolic of source, while at the same time He is differentiated by the "edge" of transcendence and thus placed at that distance necessary for the establishment of the displaced particularity. But the idea of God contravenes the freedom of man's heuristic autonomy and thus proves vulnerable to the forces in history which seek salvation in the elaboration of agency. The realism which seeks the world in itself is the corrosive tendency that defeats the image of humanity, for the image of the person is unreal and the arguments for the existence of man are no better, and of the same order, as the arguments for the existence of God.

32.7 Aesthetic humanism and religious humanism converge in the notion of redemptive sacrifice. In the latter mode the dying God suffers on behalf of the (Christian) soul, whose redemptive labor is on its own behalf. In aesthetic humanism the poet in history, like the protagonist in Aristotle's definition of tragedy, is made desolate on behalf of the other. The Christian god is the type of the cost for another of any being in a world characterized by scarcity. The tragic hero and the damned poet (blind, bereft, laborious) are also versions of this type. This type alludes to the social cost of art.

32.8   Radical humanism desiderates a version of mimetic identity in which the price and the prize are remitted to the same person.

32.9   The motive of radical imagination toward the practice of radical reason (32) is limited by the elite origin of the terms of mimetic identity (26).

> "But speaking more broadly, and coming back to Wells, whom I have not mislaid, Dr. Lal, the problem all along has been the inheritance of a minority civilization, an aristocratic culture, by the whole mass of mankind. This was how Wells himself saw it, and he was hopeful of creating orderly conditions for this transmission. Orderly British-style conditions. Decent, Victorian-Edwardian, nonoutcast, nonlunatic, *grateful* conditions. But this gentle British model could not succeed in such colossal turmoil." (Saul Bellow, *Mr. Sammler's Planet*).

32.10   Revolution becomes a question wherever the means of self-representation-to-the-other remitted by the feudal hierarchy fail to compensate the social creditor at whose expense the hierarchy (divine or human) is sustained. The questions raised by class-conscious scepticism about "universal" symbolic education (universal higher education) contain the limiting terms of the life of aesthetic humanism.

32.11   If the "human form divine" is the hostage or dependency of a defunctive aristocratic civilization, then the overthrow of that civilization, the breaking of the dead hand, is mandated. If the "human form divine" is a pure contingency of that same aristocratic civilization, then the aims and the means of revolution are mutually contradictory, knotted together as mutually exclusive terms of an insoluble historical paradox.

32.12   But there must be an aesthetics of participation, as there is now an aesthetics of distance.

Opening (16) (20)

33.   We awaken in the poem. How did we come there?

33.1   The marriage was aristocratic. But love will follow.

33.2   Indeed, we came there because the straight way was lost (*Divine Comedy*, canto 1).

33.3   The way out is the way of the master of our speech, the winding stair, the straightening of our disposition, the achievement of rule, the encounter with our Lady, the passing beyond humanity, the taking of our place.

33.4   Finally, nothing is changed.

> *Scholium.* Part of the *paideia* (culture of instruction) of the poem is the extinction of the experience of the poem; or, the removal of the experience of the poem from the category of act. Although the lyric sponsors the notion of *sentiment as act*, it does not sponsor the notion of *poetic sentiment as act*. Like Dante the Pilgrim in Dante's poem, the reader returns to the problem of real life with no privileges after the journey. When the experience of poetic reading begins to accumulate privileges for the reader, we find a decadent literary culture in which art is being used as a means of sustaining social hierarchy. Note Wallace Stevens' "Thirteen Ways of Looking at a Blackbird" (IV):
>
> > A man and a woman
> > Are one.
> > A man and a woman and a blackbird
> > Are one.

Person II (6) (13)

34.   In the poem as object, language (the familiar handmaiden of thought) is metamorphosed into a type of the cold and unknowable origin of percept. (See Scholium at 4.)

Scholium on poetry as language gone strange. Poetic language is language gone strange. One feature of *archaism* (4.3) is the status of language in poetry as an object of perception like any other object—remote, imperfectly knowable. The experience is like that of seeing your own body (which you are accustomed to know intuitively) as somebody else's body. The incompletability of the interpretive process is, in part, attributable to this estrangement of language in poetry—this setting of it at *the* distance of an object.

This process should be thought of, not merely as the making strange of the familiar, but as the making most strange of the most familiar. Language is the most intimate environment of the self. The experience of coming upon it as a place never previously known, because never before recognized as an object having its most vital life outside the self, is central to the *paideia* of poetry. The experience of encountering the self as the not-self is the preparation which poetry affords for the terms and conditions of immortality.

34.1   In the poem considered as the speech of a person, language becomes the evidence across time (*vestigium hominis*) of personhood which is, in turn, a type of the self-disclosure of divinity.

Scholium on the countenance. A person (*persona*) is not a mask but a countenance. That is to say, a person is not the fiction of a face but the face known always to be a fiction. Speech, as it comes into poetry, is absorbed in, centrally preoccupied with, its status as a synecdoche of the countenance. In this sense, speech is the countenance which you *can* see that *means* (points toward) the countenance that you cannot see. It is the portrait of the inner and invisible (intuitional) person. This countenance is the one great reference of art acknowledged in these pages. The philosopher of the countenance is Emmanuel Levinas. See *Totality and Infinity,* especially section 3, "Exteriority and the Face." For example:

Inasmuch as the access to beings concerns vision, it dominates those beings, exercises a power over them. A thing is *given,* offers itself to me. In gaining access to it I maintain myself within the same.

The face is present in its refusal to be contained. In this sense, it cannot be comprehended, that is, encompassed. It is neither seen nor touched—for in visual or tactile sensation the identity of the I envelops the alterity of the object, which becomes precisely a content (194).

The face resists possession, resists my powers. In its epiphany, in expression, the sensible, still graspable, turns into total resistance to the grasp. This mutation can occur only by the opening of a new dimension. For the resistance to the grasp is not produced as an insurmountable resistance, like the hardness of the rock against which the effort of the hand comes to naught, like the remoteness of a star in the immensity of space. The expression the face introduces into the world does not defy the feebleness of my powers, but my ability for power. The face, still a thing among things, breaks through the form that nevertheless delimits it. This means concretely: the face speaks to me and thereby invites me to a relation incommensurate with a power exercised, be it enjoyment or knowledge (198).

Hence the countenance is not really visible or knowable but rather the limit of visibility and knowability. It marks the point at which the power of this self (the classical subject) which is inside all it sees and knows comes to an end. This, too, is part of the strangeness of language in the poem, and a truer account of its otherness than the preceding scholium.

34.2   The notion of person which arises in the presence of the speaker in the poem (4.2, 6.1, 6.2, 6.8, 23) is alluded to by Kant:

Now, I say, man, and, in general, every rational being exists as an end in himself and not merely as a means to be arbitrarily used by this or that will. In all his actions, whether they are directed to himself or to other rational beings, he must always be regarded at the same time as an end. All objects of inclinations have only a conditional worth, for if the inclinations and needs founded on them did not exist, their object would be worthless. The inclinations themselves as the sources of needs, however, are so lacking in absolute worth that the universal wish of every rational being must be indeed to free himself completely from them. Therefore the worth of any objects to be obtained by our actions is at all times conditional. Beings whose existence does not depend on our will but on nature, if they are not rational beings, have only a relative worth and are therefore called "things"; on the other hand, rational beings are designated "persons" because their nature indicates that they are ends in themselves, i.e., things which may not be used merely as means. Such a being is thus an object of respect. . . . Such beings are not merely subjective ends whose existence as a result of our action has a worth for us but are objective ends, i.e., beings whose existence in itself is an end. Such an end is one for which no other end can be substituted, to which these beings should serve merely as a means. For, without them, nothing of absolute worth could be found, and if all worth is conditional and thus contingent, no supreme practical principle for reason could be found anywhere (*Foundations of the Metaphysics of Morals*, second section, p. 52).

34.3   The rationality of the poet in the poem consists in all the entailments of speaking—of which the first is the inference of the countenance.

34.4   The place of the poem in education is as the likeness or type of the origin of percept upon which is inscribed (31) the speech act of a person.

Scholium. The status of the work as an object of attention, which invites to the world now seen as a set of objects of

attention created as objects by the work, is alluded to in a
conventional way by Susan Sontag:

> In one of its aspects, art is a technique for focussing atten-
> tion, for teaching skills of attention. (While the whole of
> the human environment might be so described—as a
> pedagogic instrument—this description particularly ap-
> plies to works of art.) The history of the arts is tanta-
> mount to the discovery and formulation of a repertory of
> objects on which to lavish attention.

The limits to this reduction of the work of art as an object of
attention are determined by the criterion "inscribed with the
speech acts of a person."

34.5   Consciousness is in search of (in a restless way) an object as
complex and mysterious as the object of which it is a contingency (the body). The mind has no other object of the same
order of mysteriousness as the body. The poem comes in the
way of this restlessness and is one of its occasions of repose (the
question in the answer, the outcry in the echo).

> *Scholium on the restlessness of the mind and the one Object.*
> The mind is restlessly on pilgrimage in search of an object of
> equivalent value to itself—worthy of its attention. There is
> no such object in existence except the person, of which the
> body is an incompletely knowable version. The function of
> divinity is to provide the mind with an object worthy of at-
> tention which is knowable. The function of art is to provide
> other such objects. In the case both of art objects and of
> divinity as object, the underlying term or value is the person.
> This quest is thematized in art in many forms; and indeed the
> quest-romance and the quest motif is a reasonable (though
> not very satisfactory) formulation of the general subject of
> art. What lies at the end of the quest is the person, and the
> work of art which is its surrogate.

34.6   The ontological affirmation (18) always inherent in the "reading" of a poem is to this effect: Here is a person.

34.7   It should be clear that a poem used experimentally (in view of another truth) is not a poem, as a person used experimentally is not a person.

The Traditional Unity of the Poem (31.15)

35.   Poems as structures are traditionally said to possess a unity which is otherwise without a name.

> *Scholium.* The name of the unity for which the poem stands is the person. Hence, once again, discourse about poetry is displaced discourse about the person. In the person, the "paradox of sociability" (Scholium at 28) is negotiated. The poem as structure is usually treated as an instance of the negotiation of that paradox, and as "good" in proportion as the management of the terms of the paradox is successful. Hence, the inner name of the unity of the poem, and the person, is the name of the community of discourse in which the poem is a mediation. "Poetic unity," therefore, is expressed in terms of the sufficient condition of the continuity of the community. The idea of the poem as an instrument of socialization is a generalization from structure as dominant, and propagating its dominance. The idea of the poem as antinomic in any given present may derive in two ways: (1) it may indicate a preference for models of order not manifest in the present and therefore in conflict with it; (2) it may indicate an identification of the "meaning" of the poem with the ambivalent characteristics which the life of the speaker in the poem thematizes (28). For the poet as a world-historical socializing power, see Horace, *Ars Poetica*, ll. 390ff., as follows:
>
> > Orpheus, a holy man and spokesman for the gods, forced the wild men of the woods to give up human killing and gruesome feasting; he is said, because of these powers, to soothe tigers and the raging of the lion; yes, and Amphion, the builder of the city of Thebes, is said to move

rocks with his lyre and with the softness of song to lead them where he will.

I will tell you what was once the poet's wisdom: to decide what were public and what were private suits at law, to say what was sacred and what was not, to enjoin from sexual license, to provide a code of conduct for marriage, to build up towns, and carve the laws on wooden tablets. This was the way honor and renown came to god-like poet-preachers and their songs (400).

After these, Homer gained renown, and Tyrtaeus with his verses whetted the spirits of males for Mars and war; oracles were given in the form of poems and the way of life was shown; the favor of kings was sought in Pierian strains; and dramatic festivals were invented and thus the end of a long task [of development]—in case the Muse in her lyric artistry and Apollo with his song embarrass you.

35.1   As the defining analogy for the *singularity* of the poem is selfhood (7), or the person (12, 34), so the defining analogy for the *unity* of the poem will be whatever social hypothesis of personal success seems most noble. The poem is the model of the perfected social individual (the self in death [Scholium at 14.4]) in whom the rational (cognitive) and the irrational (sensory) powers have come to rest in a matrix of a third order.

> *Scholium.* Poetry is divided by Horace (*Ars Poetica*, ll. 332ff.) into its character as sensory stimulus (something which delights, *delectare*) and its character as social agent (something which instructs, *prodesse*). The poem as one object is perceived as a division within the faculties of an audience. The division between the instructive and delightful aspects of the poem also corresponds to the traditional distinction between the public and the private realms of being. The aspects of the self invoked by the *delectare* include sense experience, privacy, irrational apprehension, divinity, collective identity. The aspects of experience evoked by the term *prodesse* include intelligible experience, public access

and advocacy, rational apprehension, social humanity, and individuation.

35.2   The poem is a solution to the mind-body problem in the same sense that a self is a solution to that problem. The unity of the poem, like the unity of self, being otherwise without a name, is disintegrated by discourse and restored by experience.

35.3   Any speaker-in-a-poem which fails of unity in this sense (a unity which is not a harmony or a mathematical oneness but a totality [Scholium at 27.3]) fails of the social nature which is the mark without alternative of the lyric speaker-in-the-poem.

> *Scholium on poetry and sanity.* The speaker in the poem is the model of the sane human being. The sane human being is a fiction of which the poem provides an instance. In a similar sense, the speaker in the poem is a model of the successful person. The successful person is the person whose life has "come out," the implication being that what has "come out" is "well." Indeed, the word "success" indicates the coming to completion of a process. In the poem closure exemplifies the coming to completion of a process. And closure is the fiction of success. The socialization of *privacy*, which is the structural enterprise of the lyric, takes up the problem of sanity at its most difficult human "moment," for privacy or the deprivation of public estate is the central nature of insanity, and the consciousness which faces altogether toward the inner abyss is incapable of coming out, has no resources toward totalization. Hence, the closure of lyric as the picture of privacy is that fragile triumph of sanity, a finitude which has taken the abyss inside it.

35.4   The value of the poem lies in its manifestation of rational personhood and inheres in the poem to the extent that rational personhood is manifested. The most noble hypothesis of personal success as exhibited in the lyric poem is the social manifestation of private being. Questions are asked. The triumph of civility. (30.9, cf. 28.1.)

35.5   The existence of the poem suffers no unity less than this unity, but will bear upon its body the inscription of an infinite set of more familiar images. A speech is always the manifestation both of a person and of an ideology (5). The "figure" in the poem, in this sense, is always aspiring toward and failing to achieve the condition of its ground (31). And the ground of the poem broods upon its subject (description) as a sea upon its waves, a mountain upon its shadows, a god upon the mind of which it has perfect knowledge.

Line II (29)

36.   Line is diagnostic (not causal) of poetry.

Scholia.

A. *Line as lineament.* Line is a formalism independent of any specific actualization. As it is the first structure encountered in the poem that is specific to poetic discourse (syllable and stress being elements of natural language), line is the threshold at which the poem is entered. The line may be considered either as a vertex turning upon its center or as a horizontal (linear in the more restricted sense) array moving from opening to close, from beginning to end, from Genesis to Revelation. As a formalism it may be considered as rotating inside the poem. The allegories of line are packed in the verbal root: line (as bond), linen (as textile and text), linnet (a songbird which feeds on flax), lineaments (the characterizing marks of the countenance of a person). The lines of a poem are the characterizing marks of the countenance which is the central reference of the poem as a whole. As a "formalism independent of any specific actualization," line is a transcendental reference, a representation of the ground in which the figure of language is borne up and across time.

B. *Horizontal and vertical coordinates in poetry.* The various themes and systems of poetic analysis should be conceived as sortable along either vertical or horizontal coordinates.

Thus, line-forms and the constituents of line (syllable-count, stress, etc.) are horizontal systems, and line-series and rhyme, as the terminal diacritics of line, are vertical systems. When we do this we observe that horizontal systems tend to be metrical (in the sense of measured-ahead-of-time) and vertical systems tend to be nonmetrical except in the (exceptional) cases of vertically measured stanza-poems such as sonnets, villanelles, sestinas, and some few others. Horizontal *metrical* closure tends to "lie inside" vertical *semantic* closure, metrical systems inside systems which are in the strong sense closed semantically but not metrically.

Blank-verse sequences, for example, are metrical horizontally, but are nonmetrical vertically. Sequences of heroic couplets, as in Pope, have local metrical organization in the vertical coordinate but are not measured ahead of time in the whole structure. Sequences of lines arranged in isometric stanzas, as in Donne's "Songs and Sonnets," have vertical measure internal to the stanza, but are only in a loose sense (by analogy with other poems in the group) measured in the vertical coordinate. We may speak of the horizontal line-form (what we normally call line) and of the *vertical line-form*. The horizontal line is a left-to-right sequence of syllables. The vertical line is the top-to-bottom sequence of positions in which each line is analogous to the syllable in the horizontal line. Hence, we observe that the metrical horizontal line, when understood as a position in the nonmetrical vertical line, stands as a closed structure inside an open structure. The vertical line should be read as diacritically marked (for example, by a center) in the same way as the horizontal line is read.

The activity in the horizontal line is ontological, the will exploring the boundaries of its possessions, discovering its deaths at the limit of contraction and the limit of expansion. (See 29.5.)

The vertical line concerns the exploration of the finitude marked out in the horizontal coordinate. By contrast to the horizontal line which can be understood as an exploration of space and its horizons, the vertical line conducts motion and unfolds action in *time* which is, in the horizontal coordinate, suspended. (See Barbara H. Smith, *Poetic Closure*, p. 72.)

36.1   The line is a picture of a sentence or a part of a sentence, and is the least element of the poem describable in terms of unity.

> *Scholium on line as horizon.* The line is a picture of a sentence in the same sense in which the body is a picture of the human soul. The line as lineament is the countenance of the person. In what sense is the body a picture of the human soul, or a countenance the picture of a person? (Ludwig Wittgenstein, *Philosophical Investigations* 2, 4.) As the principle of its manifestation. Hence, the line is like a horizon, a representation of the sufficient conditions of perception of a specific kind. As a horizon, the line is a piece of the world broken off from the world in the interest of the perception of the world. Hence lineation is a reductive process which binds the stream of speech into visibility through breakage, and the series of lines is a repetition of the breaking which compensates, but imperfectly, the loss of the primordial stream either of speaking or experience. (John Thompson, "Linguistic Structure and the Poetic Line," in *Poetics*.)

36.2   As the poem is language become conscious of itself (the waking and wonder of Eve [16]), the line, which has all the structural features of the poem as a whole, represents the sentence in the form of an image. The line is a frame, which by being everywhere within the thing framed makes that which enters a picture, an entity which finds its concern not in itself but over against itself. The poem is pictured whole in the line. The line is a picture of the world's history from Genesis (opening) to Revelation (terminal closure).

> *Scholium on the topos of great in small.* The *topos* of great in small is central to poetic discourse. Not only great in small but greatest in smallest. As the elements or marks of structure discriminated become less and less, pass toward invisi-

bility, the reference effected becomes greater and greater. In poetic analysis least is most. This may be true in symbolic discourse in general, where each element repeats the mystery of mind itself; the human head in which the whole of the universe finds, somehow, room. The theological analogy is the entrance of Jesus, the master and origin of all things, into the body of his mother. Note the second sonnet of Donne's "La Corona":

2. Annunciation

Salvation to all that will is nigh;
That All, which alwayes is All every where,
Which cannot sinne, and yet all sinnes must beare,
Which cannot die, yet cannot chuse but die,
Loe, faithfull Virgin, yeelds himselfe to lye
In prison, in thy wombe; and though he there
Can take no sinne, nor thou give, yet he'will weare
Taken from thence, flesh, which deaths force may trie.
Ere by the spheares time was created, thou
Wast in his minde, who is thy Sonne, and Brother;
Whom thou conceiv'st, conceiv'd; yea thou art now
Thy Makers maker, and thy Fathers mother;
Thou'hast light in darke; and shutst in little roome,
Immensity cloystered in thy deare wombe.

Reading III (2) (22)

37.   When I read, I gather the meaning of things (Aristotle, *Poetics*).

37.1   When I gather the meaning of things (*florilegium*), I am either Leah or Rachel.

In the hour, I think, when Cytherea, who seems always burning with the fire of love, first shone on the mountain from the east, I seemed to see in a dream a lady young and beautiful going through a meadow gathering flowers and singing: "Know, whoever asks my name, that I am Leah, and I go plying my fair hands here and there to make me a garland; to please me at the glass I here adorn myself, but my sister Rachel never leaves her mirror and sits all day. She is fain to see her own fair eyes as I to adorn me with my hands. She with seeing, and I with doing am satisfied" (Dante, *Purgatorio*, 27).

Scholium on accommodation and assimilation. This is the dream of reading. Note that theories of reading are versions of theories of perception. Leah is the accommodative model. She gathers beauty from the world as Other who speaks, like Jonathan Swift's honeybees (see also Porphyry, "De Antro Nympharum"). In her practice the text is at the distance of the hand from the eye. This is the distance of the man of craft, the classical maker. Leah practices the Hellenic mimesis. Rachel, beautiful in herself, takes the text as mirror. She represents the assimilative model of the text, the romantic reader who sees herself in the world, and as sufficient world. Leah is the active master, and Rachel the contemplative master. In the biblical story both are brides of the patriarch, but relation to Rachel, the preferred woman, is deferred until Leah the elder has been taken in marriage. The implication is that the relation to the different is prior to the relation with the same, that in reading the relation to the other is the first but the relation to the same is the higher stage of one process.

37.2   In either case, something like a person is affirmed to be, wild surmise. (See Keats at 37.6.)

Scholium. The final meaning of reading is the discovery of the person. The question arises, "How do we know a person is present to us?" As there is no one origin of the world and no unitary center to the constituent elements of nature (no atom), so also there is no essence of the person accessible to the human participant in civility. Reading is an exercise in (an occasion of experimentation with) the inference of the presence of the person. The world in the poem is a world such as a human eye might see. The goal of reading is not the world but the world in the eye. The "meaning of things" is the aim of poetic reading insofar as things with meaning are the trace, the spoor, of the person—the debris of an encampment. The sufficient condition of the operation of this process of inference of the person is that the person be both other and same. The marriage is first with Leah and then with Rachel.

37.3   In reading there is an interface of fantasy (the "drama of reading") which intervenes between the eye and the page. While I gather the meaning of things, I am always more or less in a state of dream. The interpretation of the text requires the teasing into consciousness of this interface of dream.

> *Scholium.* The poem is the friend as hermeneut who interprets the dream of the reader. Only the dreamer can be read; only the dreamer can read. To dream is to be awake in the self. To wake is to be asleep in the self. The wakefulness of dream and the wakefulness of the speaker in the poem communicate with one another. The inference of the person leads to the generosity of the person to the self who makes the inference. In a practical sense, the poem is an occasion for the discovery of the themes of the reader's self.

37.4   The distinction between meaning and significance cannot survive the test of lived experience. We had better say (2.8) that the meaning is what we are within it.

37.5   In reading the poem twice the asymmetry of memory (wherein we remember the past but not the future) is destroyed (Scholium at 27.3). In successive readings the future of the poem is exchanged for the future of the self. The poem ceases to revise itself through surmise and correction (Scholium at 29.6), and the self begins to remember its own past in terms of the fixed text (4.4). In representing the fixed text to itself the consciousness of the reader begins to grasp its own processes as accessible

to revision, through successive representations to itself of the
same order of words.

> *Scholium on the text as friend.* The hermeneutic friendship of
> the text toward the reader takes the form of the concession
> of freedom by the text, and perhaps its mediators, in the
> interest of the freedom of the reader. The point at which it
> is "handed in" (Collingwood) and becomes the *vox missa* of
> Horace ("*nescit vox missa reverti,*" *Ars Poetica*, l. 390) is the
> point at which the life of the text becomes accessible to the
> reader. It is the point of transmission, the point of exchange
> of life for death on the part of one of two, and death for life
> on the part of the other. (See James Wright, "Prayer to the
> Good Poet," in *Two Citizens.*) The text as a person who has
> come to the end of its choices (see Scholium at 27.3) has by
> reason of this disavowal, this finishing, become an occasion
> of choices for the reader. The poem is, therefore, the dead
> friend, and a type of the salutary relationship between the
> dead and the living. (Note with care in this respect the bal-
> lad called "The Unquiet Grave.")

37.6   Reading is a repetition of the terms of relationship, a version of
personal meeting. Reading for the first time ("On First Looking
into . . .") is a repetition, paradoxically, of the terms of first
meeting, when we enter into the program of surmise, the complex inferences of personal presence. The meeting has been prepared for, the meaning has been preformed through the reader's
lifetime of expectation of meaning and persons, and the lifelong
readiness toward meeting of persons and poems (Eliot's "How
unpleasant to meet Mr. Eliot"; Pound's "I had overprepared the
event"). The process of meeting is based in the verification of
rumor ("Oft of one wide expanse had I been told"), the testing
of predictions about knowledge, the now extensively discussed
preformation of knowledge. (See, for example, Gombrich,
Kuhn, Gadamer.) The first consequence of the first reading is
the silence of the reader who was a speaker—his privilege as a
speaker has been conceded to the speaker in the poem. The
final consequence of first reading is the silence of acknowledg-

ment of difference, the primordial apprehension, not of the otherness of another in terms of characterizing marks, but of the characterizing marks of another in terms of the inference of something personal which is not the self—the new planet, the unnamed thing which was always there but never till this moment acknowledged. This is the paradox of discovery. Discovery creates nothing, but concedes the existence of a thing not previously known.

> *On First Looking into Chapman's Homer*
> Much have I travelled in the realms of gold,
>   And many goodly states and kingdoms seen;
>   Round many western islands have I been
> Which bards in fealty to Apollo hold.
> Oft of one wide expanse had I been told
>   That deep-browed Homer ruled as his demesne;
>   Yet did I never breathe its pure serene
> Till I heard Chapman speak out loud and bold:
> Then felt I like some watcher of the skies
>   When a new planet swims into his ken;
> Or like stout Cortez when with eagle eyes
>   He stared at the Pacific—and all his men
> Looked at each other with a wild surmise—
>   Silent, upon a peak in Darien.

37.7   The problem for the reader is the return, the bringing out of the poem of *something for* the natural, and ethical, life. (Cf. 33.4.) The answer to this most troubled of all poetic questions depends on the prior question: "What kind of witness with respect to human affairs is the poem?" If the poem is a witness to the common struggle, a completed version of a central enterprise which the reader brings to the poem incomplete, then the poem is paradigmatic in a simple ethical sense. If, however, the poem is witness to a special and limited process (for example, the process of making poems), then the poem is a distraction from the common struggle, another instance of history as the story of the struggle to find space in history—life humbled by the terms of record. A third possibility is that the common struggle is in fact the very special and limited process of finding representation in the space of appearances, and that the concern in the poem for the processes of representation constitutes a thematization of the general human effort to become a subject of justice. Keats' poem begins with reference to immortality considered as a function of changelessness and light (gold, as Marx reminds us, is light from the earth) and ends with the vast surmise of difference conceived as planetary distance and (virtually) astral novelty, on the one hand, and oceanic peace, the consummation of nostalgia for origins, on the other. Light enables acknowledgment, difference and space ratify it, and peace is the end, the success.

Myth

38.   The state of affairs which finds the human image conceivable in human scale only against the background of an image not in human scale (the transcendental or mythic reference) is an instance of inscription (31), the general situation which finds a statement of one sort inscribed upon a more fundamental statement of another sort. The "substantiating image" may be "found" in the poem, or incorporated in the poem, but is not an implication of the artistic fact in itself. In other words, artistic civilization is not describable as autonomous or productive of its own conditions of existence.

> *Scholium on the finding of human scale.* A major program or "plot" in representation is the finding of scale. The finding of scale is prerequisite to the construction of a well-formed human image. In order to "find scale" it is necessary to measure, and the conditions of measure are the same as the location of the self in a congruent world—which for the person is the world of persons. Consequently, the story about finding scale is *the story about relationship,* which as a prototypal plot unfolds as the narrative in which the well-formed image is produced from its contradiction in the other

who constitutes the edge or benchmark from which the dimensions of the self become known by reference. (The process is consummated by marriage in comedy, by death in tragedy, and by recognition of the conditions of the continuity of the self in lyric.) Normally, the hero is first encountered as global in form (and therefore out of form) because total in demand, in effect prior to and incapable of relationship because unmeasured (e.g., Gilgamesh). In lyric this accords with the fact that the lyric person moves from least differentiation to most differentiation as the "I" traverses the course of the poem (24). The well-formed image, the countenance as recognized (Scholium at 34.1), is achieved in struggle with the contradiction of its primordial totality, that is to say, in struggle with the horizon which takes the human form of the beloved companion, the hermeneutic friend, and the divine form of the god-who-sets-limits (e.g., the Delphic god who counsels, "Know that you are a man and not a god"). The well-formed image is constructed by reference to the horizon constituted of the human and divine other (cf. the Miltonic construction which maps the boundaries of the face in the phrase "human face divine"). In other words, the *eidos* is generated from its contradiction. The finding of scale is prerequisite to entrance into civility, the "space of appearance." Since representation in the majority of instances is an account of preparation toward acknowledgment in the space of appearance, the finding of scale is a central motif in representation.

38.1   The substantiating image (mythic or transcendental reference) is derived for the poem from a collectivity not in itself an artifact. That is to say no more than that access to the substantiating image is always a function of membership in a social group. Any attempt, therefore, to found eidetic existence in the artistic fact itself is a mistake about the nature of representation.

38.2   Myth is somebody else's religion.

38.3   "Myth" is a way of referring to the collective imaginal resource prior to the speech act (the individuating superinscription) which issues in self-representation. Myth is the state of the collectivity prior to and exclusive of the conservation of names.

> *Scholium on the fear of myth.* The distinction is made between myth and fiction. For example: "Fictions, notably the fiction of apocalypse, turn easily into myths; people will live by that which was designed only to know by" (Frank Kermode, *The Sense of an Ending,* p. 112). The lyric speaker equivocates the distinction between myth and fiction because, as the speaker in the poem, that self does not *know* the difference. Poems are fictional frames in which surrogate persons experiment toward intimacy with myth, wander as it were in and out of the sacred grove. For Kermode and others the "fictional frame" of the poem protects the natural person from participation in the mythic collectivity, from the seriousness of that sort of commitment (13, 20.8, 28). Since, however, myth is from many points of view necessary for the production of human images, a program is required for obtaining access to myth without loss of self in the lethal complexities of the collectivity (Scholium at 14.4). One instance of such a program is the Jungian proposal that myth be distanced along a way or road of access which is open for the natural person and along which the self can move freely in both directions (Edward F. Edinger). Pathology supervenes when the capacity for moving along the way of access in one or the other direction is foreclosed. The decline of centrality of poetry derives in part from the inaccessibility of myth (38.9) and in part from the withering away of the category of the fictional.

38.4   Hence, poetry and myth are contradictory phenomena. Poetry is the thing with style. Myth is the thing without style (Lévi-Strauss). As poetry is the thing which has found human scale (the inscribed speech act), myth is the thing beyond human scale (the ground).

Scholium on displacement. The mediation between myth (or archetype, or paradigm) and art is generally referred to as displacement. In some theorists (notably Frye and his followers) works of art are constructed by displacing the myths, as prior, more general forms are incorporated or incarnated in the process of "creation" or actualization. This displacement is a form of the breaking of the idea in such a way that it becomes manifest in the one world of perception. Reading is the reverse of this process, a tracking backward or decreation of the work in such a way as to recover the archetype from which it was displaced. Thus creation in the normal sense is a form of decreation of the archetypal whole, and interpretation is a decreation of the concrete manifestation, the work. The *culture of the ground* forms itself around preference for the archetype (31.11). The *culture of the displacement* forms itself around style as central value. The distinction between displacement and archetype is the same as the distinction between inscription and ground. Modernism was a culture of inscription and its fetish was style. Postmodernism tends to solicit a culture of the ground, entailing all the lethal complexities of the idealism of the collective.

38.5 Myth is a perceptual instrument with which the human image can be seen, and without which (or its like) the human image (the person) possesses no access to collective substantiation, and is invisible. In such a world there is no death, as there is also no life.

38.6 The price of myth (what it will cost you to possess one) is self-identification in terms of a human community, which requires the sacrifice of certain features of individuality. Since, in addition, mythic self-identification is amoral (there is no morality of collectivities), the achievement of eidetic status through myth creates a (unwanted, perhaps abhorrent) mystery about the character of the selfhood thus achieved.

Scholium on meaning, collectivities, and the reference of poetic languages. The speaker in poems, because the language of the poetic speaker is the language of a collectivity (4.1), embodies a solution to, or choice within the terms of, the paradox of sociality. The didactic of the speaker in the poem is the didactic of sociality, the propagation of the sacrifice of individuality. Hence, the tendency to describe reading as an immolation of the self, a replacement of the inner world-describing voice of the reader by another which offers one strategy toward the achievement of the reader's self-interest. One description of that strategy is service or affiliation (22.1).

Insofar as the speaker in the poem is a collective person the question of value is equivocated, because corporate persons or collectivities are not normally conceivable in terms of ethical identity. Only the individual can choose. Hence, theories which stress archetypalism tend to disparage the judicial element in reading. (See Northrop Frye, "Polemical Introduction," in *Anatomy of Criticism.*) Hence, also, the tendency to regard the reference of language in poetry as equivocal, the normal conception of intention being founded in the expectation of an individual speaker.

The speaker in the poem is, therefore, uncanny; and, insofar as the collective and the holy are equivalent, that uncanniness resembles defilement—"the iniquity of holiness" (Scholium at 28).

38.7 There is an aspect of lyric individuation (the selfhood of the speaker in the poem) which has no moral identity, that aspect which contributes mythic substantiation. As amoral existence it tends to insist on itself absolutely. It is a serious person (28). At certain times of the world (this present is an instance) mythic self-identification seems too dangerous to solicit because it seems to threaten the extinction of the image of the person in time (the ground swallows the inscription, as after generations of weather); and also seems too dangerous to abandon, because its loss threatens the existence of the individual in eternity (the inscription devours the ground).

Scholium. It is a characteristic of Postmodernism that the terms on which image-life are to be had seem to be corrosive of any humane end which image-life may be conceived as serving. Hence, the idea of *greatness*, which implies the full unfolding of the potentialities for representation (the achievement of central instances in all the major kinds), has ceased to pertain to poetic enterprise. The politics of form are manifested as the choosing either of the culture of the ground or the culture of the figure, whereas the excellence of the art consists in the confronting of the two cultures. The danger of direct relationship to the ground as force is intelligible only when it is seen as abolishing the countenance as figure. Reciprocally, the danger of inscribing the countenance, as it were, in air can be understood only by comparison with the countenance against the ground.

38.8   As mythic selfhood passes toward and into the lyric medium, it tends to become pacified to the extent that it *actually becomes the subject of poems.* The lyric self has no moral identity, but the lyric medium does. In the lyric *medium* the mythic self (the speaker in the poem) acquires positive moral valence (becomes ethical), and is a thing of value of a given sort (5).

> *Scholium on the value of structure and the value of reference* (5.2, 5.3). As experience enters the poetic frame it is broken or contracted in view of the compositional principle and its constituent rules, which are the conditions of the visibility of experience. When we say that the poem resolves or compensates a state of affairs, we are observing that the value of structure has been traded against the losses which are thematized as "subject" in the poem. The poem as text exists in the one world of linear time and perceptual scarcity. The time of the internal realm of the poem is, however, of another sort. The poem as text signifies the breaking or termination of the state of affairs in the poem at the point of manifestation, the completion or handing in of the text. The immortality of the speaker in the poem and the claims upon

totality of the will in the poem are subjected to the ideology of mortality by the constraints of manifestation which require "closure" or "ending" as the price of visibility in the one world. The medium is in effect the real life of the lyric self, and the process of closing is a birth process by which a death is brought into the world. (See Octavio Paz, "The Consecration of the Instant," in *The Bow and the Lyre*.) For this reason the ends of poems are often preoccupied with the concession of the will to that contraction of reality which is generalized as social value in the didactic of what we call the poem as a whole. Another way of stating the matter is that through the medium, the lines or marks of delineation of the countenance in the poem, the ethical character of the work is produced. Here we see the rationality behind the preference, in the tradition, of the culture of the inscription over the culture of the ground. Often we find distinguished poems by dominantly scribal authors thematizing the fear which the concession to manifestational constraints (the rising of the moon) arouses in the heart of the man.

> Queen and huntress, chaste and fair,
> Now the sun is laid to sleep,
> Seated in thy silver chair,
> State in wonted manner keep;
> > Hesperus entreats thy light,
> > Goddess excellently bright.
>
> Earth, let not thy envious shade
> Dare itself to interpose;
> Cynthia's shining orb was made
> Heaven to clear, when day did close;
> > Bless us then with wished sight,
> > Goddess excellently bright.
>
> Lay thy bow of pearl apart,
> And thy crystal-shining quiver;
> Give unto the flying hart
> Space to breathe, how short soever;

> Thou that mak'st a day of night,
> Goddess excellently bright.
>
> (Ben Jonson)

38.9   The crucial factor in the adaptation of myth to poems is the distance (not always measurable in units of time) between the writer and the substantiating myth. The greater the skew between the writer and mythic image, the more dangerous and chancy the evocation of the lyric self. Where the myth and the self are totally disjunct there is no solution except apocalypse, the annihilation of all elements significant of distance (including time) between the myth and the self.

> *Scholium on cultural lateness.* This matter has been expressed with some vigor but with a different emphasis by Harold Bloom in *The Anxiety of Influence* and other works. The matter may be restated as follows. Poetry is not merely the speech of a person of one class practicing the language of a person of another class (8.4) according to the rule of transcendence, it is also the speech of a successor practicing the language of a predecessor. (Cf. Scholium at 31.4). As the linear time-line in which the text must place itself unrolls, the distance between the successor and predecessor becomes greater, and the struggle for self-founding in terms of the great acts of former times (the *illud tempus* in which the covenants with respect to visibility were first won by the heroic founders) becomes more desperate. Since, in addition, manifestation takes place in the finite space of the one world of manifestation, the struggle with the founders becomes less hopeful as their works and tombs encumber more and more of the ground (Empson's "Missing Dates"). This struggle with the fathers may be conceived as an Oedipal struggle (as Bloom does) or it may be conceived as a consequence of the cumulative nature of a culture which remembers, as time goes on, more and more of its past. More fundamentally, however, the problem is a restatement of the antinomies of immanence and transcendence on the one hand and individual and collective on the other. The apocalyptic abolition of "distance,"

however conceived, is an obsessive subject of "late" poetry. (See Yeats' "Valley of the Black Pig.")

38.10 In modern poetry a distinction arises between "paleo-myth" and "neo-myth." The former represents the collective representations of another community which are more or less available as substantiating images to the poetic mind at any historically subsequent moment in time. The terms on which they are available are often hard, obscure, and even fatal. "Neo-myth" signifies poetic fables based in the experience of ontogenetic self-arising. As phylogenetic experience becomes demythologized, ontogenetic experience must reciprocally be mythologized in order to sustain the possibility of poetry at all. The price of the neo-myth is the depersonalization (an indeterminate shadowing by the Collective) of *mémoire*.

Closure and Aperture

39. The *termini* which everyway bound the poem constellate themselves (can be set up) in such a way as to produce an image either by closure or by aperture.

> *Scholium.* That is to say, you can look from outside in or from inside out. *It is important to limit the reference of the term "closure," so that it can be seen to be nonidentical with composition or representation in general.* The term "closure" carries with it by implication a stationing of consciousness with respect to manifestation such as to predicate a predominance of the value of structure over the value of reference. Traditional forms in poetry are closural; but the contradiction of closure is not oblivion. It is the turning around of the observer which places the observer in the picture and the world in the eye. Closure places the reader, as Renaissance perspective places the viewer, on a grid which issues from a vanishing point within the poem or picture. The fictional convergence of the parallel lines of the world's openness is an image of the perceptual conditions of the viewing mind, and there-

fore constitutes a subduing of the world to the conditions of perception. In aperture, the viewer turns round, converts as it were, and views the world not as a subject views an object but as an object might view a subject. In such a posture what is possible becomes actual in its own form (or that is the hope) and the future ceases to be complicated with the past in terms of the deformities of the old monisms of the "I" (*oculus* and *ego*).

Closure is associated with the culture of immortality considered as infinite past and infinite future. Aperture proposes a culture of immortality considered as present. See D. H. Lawrence, "Poetry of the Present" (Introduction to the American edition of *New Poems* [1918]):

> It seems when we hear a skylark singing as if sound were running forward into the future, running so fast and utterly without consideration, straight on into futurity. And when we hear a nightingale, we hear the pause and the rich, piercing rhythm of recollection, the perfected past. The lark may sound sad, but with the lovely lapsing sadness that is almost a swoon of hope. The nightingale's triumph is a paean, but a death-paean. . . . Our birds sing on the horizons. They sing out of the blue beyond us, or out of the quenched night. They sing at dawn or sunset. . . . Our poets sit by the gateways, some by the east, some by the west. As we arrive and as we go out our hearts surge with response. But whilst we are in the midst of life, we do not hear them. . . . The poetry of the beginning and the poetry of the end must have that exquisite finality, perfection which belongs to all that is far off. It is in the realm of all that is imperfect. It is of the nature of all that is complete and consummate. This completeness, this consummateness, the finality and the perfection are conveyed in exquisite forms: the perfect symmetry, the rhythm which returns upon itself like a dance. . . . But there is another kind of poetry.

39.1   *Closure* (the frame) identifies the central practice of English
       poetry, the self-characterization of the speaking person as a fi-
       nite center of dramatic gestures of infinite implication. The
       world in closure derives its structure from the structure of the
       subject-consciousness. In Blake's terms closure is "seeing WITH
       the eye." In terms of the paradox of sociability (Scholium at 28)
       closure represents the dominance of individuation over partici-
       pation. Closure is the enabling structure of aesthetic human-
       ism. In closure, the poem is characterized as an interior, the
       relationship of which to the rest of being, or other being, is as
       an interior to an exterior. Hence, the interior-exterior or
       inside-outside trope is produced. Insofar as metaphor is a fiction
       of relationship, its function in closure is to establish a relation-
       ship with other beings subject to the qualifications inherent in
       statements of similarity (17). Hence, in closure, other being is
       transcendent to the self-who-speaks-in-the-poem, and the
       poem as a structure is an image or allegory of the monadic self
       which produces world-descriptions in accord with its nature. In
       closure, therefore, the world described in the act of producing
       the *eidos* or countenance is the world reduced to the conditions
       of being of the monadic consciousness. For example, Emily
       Dickinson and the "ample nation," where the "Emperor" is the
       exterior totality.

> The Soul selects her own Society—
> Then—shuts the Door—
> To her divine Majority—
> Present no more—
>
> Unmoved—she notes the Chariots—pausing—
> At her low Gate—
> Unmoved—an Emperor be kneeling
> Upon her Mat—
>
> I've known her—from an ample nation—
> Choose One—
> Then—close the Valves of her attention
> Like Stone—

39.2   *Aperture* (the window) identifies the contrary strategy, the (per-
       haps unactual) alternative possibility. In aperture, the self is
       characterized as identical or "flowing with" the world. In Blake's
       terms aperture is "seeing through the eye," where the self derives
       its structure from the nature of the object. The speaker becomes
       the Beloved or divine utterer whose creative resource is not dif-
       ference but participation. As the characteristic trope of closure
       is metaphor, the characteristic trope of aperture is metonymy
       (see Jakobson). The defining grammatical structures of aperture
       seem to be—the central example is Whitman—paratactic (ad-
       ditive, *this* plus *that* plus *that* . . .) by contrast to hypotactic
       grammars which characterize closure.

> *Scholium on aperture, priority, and cultural lateness.* The sen-
> timent of lateness (Bloom's "belatedness") arises in the po-
> etics of closure in part because the separated self obsessively
> thematizes the conditions of its visibility which involve the
> dialectics of difference. In aperture, the poet claims imme-
> diacy or earliness. The poet's singing is not at the horizons
> but from the midst of things. The poet disappears in the
> stream of things and regards himself as the starting-point of
> dynasties rather than the epigone or inheritor from whom
> time is continually alienating the source. Closure predicts
> that death will be the enemy of the heart, whereas aperture
> incorporates death. The closural poet is at war with the Col-
> lective on which the poet depends for the continuity of ut-
> terance against time. The poet in aperture *represents* the
> Collective and lets go of the individuality of which the Col-
> lectivity is the contradiction.
>
> English poetic culture is peculiarly preoccupied by lateness,
> because its sources are outside its nation and language, and
> because its master poet (Shakespeare) is a social master
> whose persons practice the dialectics of difference as a prin-
> ciple of their being. Hence, the poetry of aperture when it
> arises (as in Crashaw, Traherne, Taylor, Whitman, Williams,
> Stevens) normally has a marginal status from a stylistic point
> of view which corresponds to its marginal status in relation

to national cultural process. English poetry is also the poetry of a modern language, which witnesses interior to itself the loss of participatory relationships, since its own history is coterminous with the individuating socio-cultural developments of modernity. The poetry of aperture, therefore, which produces originality not as a reference to another founding culture (as to the mythologies of Greece and Rome, or the poetic forms of Italy and France) but as an assertion of natural privilege, a claim which requires no sponsorship, has a novelty which is revolutionary in an abnormal sense. The strategies toward novelty of aperture are, in fact, antecultural in the sense in which we normally speak of nature as prior to culture or the ground as prior to the inscription. The closural poem thematizes reduction. The poem in aperture thematizes amplification. The strategies for renewal of the closural poet are atavistic, leading to mythologies of distance and its mastery; the strategies for renewal of the poet in aperture are perceptual, leading to mythologies of immediacy.

In contrasting closure and aperture we can see the difference between totality (the consequence of totalization, the finite set which comes *to stand for* the whole as a result of composition, the discovery of the right relationship of its parts) and universality or inclusion, the whole as participated. The poems of Yeats are closural, achieving totalization through finitization and symbol. The poems of Whitman and Stevens are inclusive (poems in aperture), achieving infinite reference through the equivocation of terminal indications, and the minimalization of symbolic discourse which by its nature repeats the totalization process.

39.3   The poetry of closure is *psycho-mimetic*. That is to say that in closure the world takes the form of mind, and in particular the mind as it perceives. From the psycho-mimetic idealism of the poetry of closure is elaborated the poetics of control, the prosody of vexation. The psycho-mimetic poem imitates the conditions of perception of a subject which has realized itself as finite, and generalizes such conditions as an ethical regime characterized by prudence. Enthusiasm and participation threaten the loss of a representation which identifies the *eidos* with the social countenance. In such poetry lines are above all lineaments, and poetic language is distinguished as the characterizing marks of an individual, not dialect but idiolect.

> *Scholium on closure and penitence.* One version of the discipline of prudence is penitence. From a historical point of view it is the penitential poems of Donne and Herbert and their contemporaries which founded for modern times the psycho-mimetic kind. In such poems the self-realization of the speaking subject as bounded (mortal and sinning) is the precondition of the perception of the unbounded or total real. In the dialectic of the penitential poem the speaker is driven to become conscious of himself or herself as a perishing social individual, and is permitted totalization or redemption only when the complete closural apprehension has been effected. Transcendence is obtained by the realization of fragmentary immanence. The paradigm of such a poem is Donne's "Goodfriday, 1613. Riding Westward." In closure, there is an immanent personalism in which the object of the self-realizing will is particular being. The East is sought through westward riding. In closure, therefore, the unsanctioned nature of emotion in the penitential poem reflects the guilt of world-appropriation which flows from boundedness. The subject matter predicted by closure as a structure is the exile from the whole, attendant on becoming a discrete self, a self which can become actual only by a world-appropriation which is identical with world-loss.

39.4 The poetry of aperture is *cosmo-mimetic* (42). It takes its structure not from mind but from world. It is the world's poem in the process of seizing upon mind as the principle of its manifestation. Whether or not the poetry of closure repeats the boundedness of the subject in the process of manifestation, it does not take the boundedness of the subject as its concern. The poetry of aperture is the Edenic kind of poetry which, having put off world-appropriation and therefore the ideologies of boundedness and hierarchy, finds the world rising within it, not as a symbolic totality, but as a whole. The cosmo-mimetic poem is not penitential but doxological. In the presence of the poem of this kind, the audience becomes conscious of the shame aroused by the fulfillment of wishes.

> *Scholium on the comedy of participation and the hatred of good outcomes.* The poetry of closure, the central poetry of the tradition, is determined toward deprivation. It is the poetry of the imagination which is, in this sense, the will pitted against the losses expected by its own practice. The poetry of aperture is the poetry of success. In it the imagination has no place. To put it another way, the success of the poetry of *closure* is the domination of structure over reference, the purely symbolic comedy of the artifact. The success, by contrast, of the poetry of *aperture* is the deep comedy of the reference claiming its place as structure, the comedy not of triumphant domination but of participation.

The comedy of participation is abhorrent to the culture of the West. The central language of poetry is a language of deprivation and its compensation. In the presence of the doxological state of affairs there is a strong sense of the obsolescence of central powers, a waste, as it were, of language in the presence or at the point of the success of language. To put it another way: as the eye grows whole, the self as bounded, ignorant, finite, dramatic (and therefore hostile and warlike ["batter my heart"]), the self grounded in scarcity, falls away leaving space for self-being of another kind. But as the speaker in the poem ceases to recognize itself in ignorance and scarcity, it ceases to recognize itself as human.

> But I
> Forgot the rest, and was all sight, or Ey.
> Unbodied and Devoid of Care,
> Just as in Heavn the Holy Angels are.
>   (Traherne)

The cost of celebration is individuality, for in aperture the Collective has seized upon the individual as the principle of its manifestation. The audience of the doxological poem experiences as shame and embarrassment (cf. Lawrence on Whitman) the guilt which is the life principle of the speaker in the poem of closure. Full presence is experienced as indecorum; and reality, as it were, *in hand* is experienced as obscenity.

In addition, the prosody of vexation (closure) and the prosody of liberation (aperture) are antithetical in implication for the meaning of words. In closure, words and things are separate and the life of words is thus protected. In aperture, words and things tend to lose their distinctness, and persons are faced with the loss of words as, one might say, the heart is faced with the loss of desire at the moment of the fulfillment of desire. Closure is the way of many different words, many different persons, many names, erotic love, guilt, penitence, the imitation of God (the nonachievement of God), separation from the world, self-realization in human scale. Aperture is the way of one word (the infinite word as in Scholium at 31.6), one person (Whitman, Adam Kaedmon), one name (the Collective), agapic love, the sanction of the whole, innocence, identity with God, transgression against human scale, riding eastward (Sylvia Plath's "Ariel").

In effect, the function of most poetry, the poetry of closure, is the postponement of the end of the world. It is, however, in the experiment toward aperture-discourse that poetry shares the vast human speculation with respect to a future different from the past, seeks in effect an immortality which is other than continuity by seeking a form other than lyric. Aperture is a way of speaking of the state of the past and the birth of the man.

39.5   Some poets (Blake, for example) pass, in the course of a lifetime, from closure to aperture. It may be said that the general loosening of junctural rigor in the late work of most poets

(Shakespeare's late blank verse, for example) suggests a development, inherent in any growing knowledge of the poetic medium, from the situation of closure to the situation of aperture. In the rare case, when nature permits the practice of poetry in old age, the death of the poet and the extinction of the logic of the poetic enterprise seem simultaneous. Since, in addition, there is a dissonance between the nature of poetry (identified with closure) and substantial human success, there is a sense in which the early termination of a poetic life keeps the speaker (by putting an end to the evolution of the implication of the medium) inside the poetic enterprise. The very conditions of poetry may in fact exclude the complete implications of aperture as an actual version of the artistic form of words. In other words, a full working out of the implications of aperture would mean the opening of the Seventh Seal (the only one that opens), the dissolution of the difference between world and word. Hence, aperture is the completion of the word and the death of the word. Closure as an artistic form of language functionsin such a way as to keep the word in sight.

> *Scholium on aperture and relationship.* Closure produces measured or civil interaction through the actualizing dialectic of difference. In the hyperbolic language of Whitman, closure is feudal. Stated another way, closure implies patience with mediation, and the epistemologies and codes of indirection. The prosodies of vexation are consistent with the politics and erotics of vexation. By contrast, aperture solicits the politics of immediacy, an electric, dangerous, indeed an inactual politics, which when it becomes mythic (serious) produces catastrophic states of affairs (*Romeo and Juliet*, "The Phoenix and the Turtle"). In the idealism of closure, friendship, and centrally hermeneutic friendship, flourishes again because of the enhancement inherent in difference of which the invariable actualization is hierarchy. In aperture, friendship becomes equivocal.

Here the anthem doth commence;
  Love and constancy is dead;

> Phoenix and the turtle fled
> In a mutual flame from hence.
> So they loved, as love in twain
>   Had the essence but in one;
>   Two distincts, division none;
> Number there in love was slain.
>
> Hearts remote, yet not asunder;
>   Distance and no space was seen
>   'Twixt this turtle and his queen;
> But in them it were a wonder
>
> So between them love did shine,
>   That the turtle saw his right
>   Flaming in the phoenix' sight
> Either was the other's mine.
>
> Property was thus appalled. . . .

The enabling moralities of literary culture are based in property, that is to say, proprietary individuality, and the enabling perceptual scenarios of literary culture are subject-object scenarios mediated by grids of signs. But, inside closure, there is the velleity or presentiment toward aperture, the new third covenant of no-difference, the "wonder" state of relationship. Since hierarchy is merely the practical expression of difference, then relationships of no-difference are egalitarian relationships, and the poetry of aperture is the heuristic of such relationships—as patently in Whitman. In closure the heuristic of egalitarianism is deferred—as in the eschatology of Dante and in general the body-soul reconciliation of deep Judaeo-Christian fantasy—or displaced toward the mediation itself, as in Leavis' notion that the work of art is a third realm or common space in which the proprietary individual stands in an alternative relationship to his fellow citizen. Hence, the text is precious in closure because it both conserves and repeats the structure of proprietary difference and redresses through deferral or displacement the state of affairs which it represents. Practically speaking, aperture proposes the dissolution of the text and the differences for which it stands (body-soul; self-other; mind-world) in the interest of a value of another sort.

In view of this we observe that a true state of literary culture is one which does not value itself. True literary or textual culture is an ironic culture, a culture of postponement, of conscious surrogation. A decadent literary culture is one which values itself, which has forgotten that its central knowledge is that its next evolutionary state is its negation.

39.6 Common to both the cosmo-mimetic and the psycho-mimetic representation is the *socio-mimetic middle term*. The sufficient condition of the presence of representation is the imitation of the contract or system of relationship, the repetition somehow manifested of the ongoing social contract or settlement. The surface of the poem is a social countenance in which the cosmos (what is above) and the psyche (what is below) meet in a civil gesture. (See Scholium on Blank Verse at 29.8.) This we call style or the embedded form of the name by which we acknowledge the person. All poems are socio-mimetic, and political language (the language of governance and social relationship) is always appropriate to describe the settlement at the surface of the poetic text.

The Inferential (or Tacit) Poem

40. The meaning of speaking is dependent on inferences about the speaker. (See Scholium at 6.2 on the eidetic function of language.)

Scholia.

A. *Reading as the completion of inferences.* The poem is a presence which implies absence. This is what it means to say that language in poems is language which has been mingled with the act of a person, or that language in the poem is a picture of speech and not "language" as such, or that language in poetry is intentional. (Cf. Brentano's phrase "intentional inexistence.") The meaning of speaking is always absent, and requires to be constructed. To put the matter another way, the meaning of speaking (of which poems are instances) is secured as a consequence of the will (the *willingness*) of the hearer to construct, and assent to, the nonpresent personhood of the speaker. In speaking we are in one another's hands. Speaking is an ontological puzzle (18) or maze, which is only solved or completed when the absent person is affirmed as *discovered*. It is a maze colored with hope (poems are pleasing)—about the solution of which there are many rumors and theories (37.6)—but it is a maze which cannot be solved in theory. Reading requires an act, the completion of inference, acknowledgment.

B. *Value lies in the absent (unspeaking) person*. Note the following:

> The reconciliation of the human necessity of speaking with the spiritual need for silence was a problem that every member of the Society of Friends had to contend with throughout his life as a Quaker. In one sense, this was the essence of the Quaker religious experience—reconciling man's natural and earthly life with his eternal and essential spiritual existence. The true Quaker directed his behavior toward making his life maximally expressive of spiritual truth, with the understanding that a silence of the outward man was the best possible way of doing so. However, although this was the goal of existence, it was also essential that an earthly component be present in one's life, in order to maintain an element of spiritual struggle, for the doctrine of salvation through suffering was also central to Quakerism. The tension between the natural and the spiritual faculties—between speaking and silence—was a necessary component of the Quaker experience.
>
> For the Quaker minister, however, the tension took on an added dimension, because the role demanded that the

minister depart from absolute silence by speaking in the very conduct of a fundamentally religious exercise. This was a mixing of speaking and silence within a single behavioral frame in which both components, other-wise contradictory, were indispensable (Richard Bauman, "Speaking in the Light," pp. 159, 160).

40.1   A poem derives its beauty from the promise of communicative success. Try, experimentally, the following: Suppose the speaker in the poem is lying. . . . Suppose the speaker in the poem is insane. . . . Suppose the speaker in the poem is guessing, but does not let on, or is wearing a mask, or is reading a script written by somebody else, or is bent on deceiving. Such poems do not occur. (The speaker in the robot-produced poem is not a robot but the fiction of a person produced by a person through an exceptionally displaced process.) But natural speaking al-ways allows the possibility of duplicity, because the speaker is never *in* the speech, as the whole is never *in* the part, or the thing represented *in* the representation. The meaning of speech in poetry by contrast is substantiated by the tacit promise of the countenance, of which the lines are lineaments.

> *Scholium.* The veracity of the speaker in poems is in part secured by the thematization (taking as subject) in lyric of absence, the search for the beloved. So that *the reader's paradox* of taking presence for absence which implies presence, or speech for tacit being which is the meaning of speech, is begun (or repeated) internal to the poem. The reader finds the speaker in the poem complicit with his or her search for the substantiating ground of speech, the value of the person. The finding occurs at the point of loss, at the point of the actualization or precipitation into experience of difference. In the fiction (the poem) such difference can be complete, as it cannot be in natural situations. Hence, "the meaning of speaking is dependent on inferences about the speaker," one of which inferences is, so far as fictions are concerned, the absence of the speaker altogether.

40.2   In social speaking (natural speaking), the meaning of speaking
is subject to qualification by metacommunicative gestures of
face, body, management of dress, odors, etc. In poems, metacommunicative gesture has been run into the speaking. The
speaker in the poem (*filius nullius*) presents only language, language as face, the odors and secrets of the body, the whole
dance in being of the man before you. How, then, has the body
gotten turned into language, how is the body's meaning-
intention turned into language? The answer lies, in part, in the
fact that the body of the speaker in the poem is now the body
of the reader who pursues the task of inference in the form of
bodily response, who steps into the inferential space and becomes the substantiating tacit dimension. (See Michael Polanyi, *The Tacit Dimension.*) The poem does not need the reader's speech, for the poem is speech; the poem needs the reader's
speechlessness. The willingness of another to complete the life
of the poem which is otherwise mere vagrant *animula*, a mere
text, by submitting his or her body to the constraints of that
speaking is the measure of the poem's success, and its moment
of completion. But the availability of the text as an occasion of
the bodily self-discovery by the reader depends on the severity
with which the poet in history has severed him*self* from the
poem, has given away his voice, and passed into fictional explicitness, speaking.

> *Scholium on reading and creation.* When the God of Genesis
> 1 created the world He caused things to be by language (Let
> there be light, heaven and earth, animals, etc.). When the
> mortal creator, the poet, does *his* "creating" he causes lan-
> guage to be made out of things. He trades the object of ref-
> erence for the reference, and among the objects of reference
> is himself. He allows himself to become, as the God of Gen-
> esis did not allow Himself to become, a myth, or (more ex-
> actly stated) a fiction. The reader repeats the act not of the
> mortal creator, the poet, but of the divine creator, the God.
> He or she makes out of language a world, causes things to be
> by language. The world of the poem is his or her world, as

the body which speaks is his or her body. There was no world until he spoke, and insofar as the poem is a thing, it is his thing (2.7). What is inferred then and becomes the substance of the inferential poem is the tacit life of the reader.

40.3   Again, we must ask, "In what sense is the speaker in the poem an owner of histories?" (The God of the Bible, after all, though outside history, is the God of history. The question is the same as Augustine's question about what God was doing before He created the world.) The inferential poem is a whole poem (a cosmological epic, as it were) which has been totalized in the lyric text before us, but which interpretation must unpack as the narrative which is the poem as meaning. In effect, the inferential poem is history. The poem must be rendered historical in the process of its interpretation, and nothing less than the construction of the whole of history as fiction will complete the task. But to begin with we ask: What was the speaker in the poem doing before he or she began speaking? What will he do after he ceases to speak? What is he doing with his hands while speaking? Is the speaker in the poem alone? When was he last alone? Does he resemble his mother? The normal technique for mastering the inferential poem is biography. Fiction demands history as an account of its meaning; as history demands fiction for the same purpose—as an account of its meaning. Speech in the poem is the trace of the whole being of a speaker.

> Scholium on the question how do we know when we know there is a person present. The central human knowledge which can only be tacit is the knowledge of the presence of the person. In order to build this presence the whole world is not enough or is just enough. On what evidences, in response to what indications, do we say that a person is present here? Whatever the evidences and indications, they are in the poem. The basic inferential or tacit poem is the person whom we construct as meaning but who is the meaning of the meanings we construct. Personhood is the fiction which we undertake to affirm when we construct historical narratives to account for the meaning of poems.

To restate the matter once again: to derive a meaning is to assert personal presence. The process by which this is done is "reading" or the construction by the reader of an inferential poem. The inferential poem is without boundaries other than the totality, as (it is perfectly obvious) the process of meaning-derivation from texts is without end. But the possibility of the assertion of the presence of the person is established only if the natural author of the poem, the author in history, has released the poem into fiction. *No merely natural person is perceptible.*

Poetic reading, then, is a case of the inscription of the value of the person, a case of the construction of the countenance, the willing of the presence of a person. The meaning which flows, the meaning of the text (of which the final form is the countenance), has no limit but the immanent whole, to which there are no boundaries but the transcendent. Nothing less than the world is the adequate image of a person. Where there is no full image of the world, where the world has grown imageless, there is no adequate image of the person. Text, world, and countenance are interdependent fictions.

40.4   The tacit nature of the poem must be conserved so that the fiction of the person can arise. In natural reality, the person is knowable *only* by inference. Therefore, as a matter of prudence, the author in history (as he or she is known on other documentary evidences than the poem) is, to begin with, beside the point. There is a bitter conflict (in which the parties both sustain and also mortally endanger one another) between the author in history and the speaker in the poem. The affinities of the speaker in the poem are transcendental, and the affinities of the author in history are immanent. These two realities are antinomic in relation to each other and the difficult idea of the fictional nature of the person troubles the heart of the secular reader, and disposes the reader against the central nature of the reading enterprise. But it is precisely a matter of life and death that neither be taken as evidence of the existence of the other, for neither is in itself a personal existence. And the substitution of the author in history for the speaker in the poem preempts the inference which it is the function of the poem to produce.

> *Scholium on reading as the suspension of disbelief in the unreality of all experience.* The author in history is an hypothesis about the origin of the speaker in the poem which is false. Insofar as it is known to be false, it calls attention to the extreme mysteriousness of existence (being-at-all) in the specific form of being-as-person. The falsity of the hypothesis of a *human being* as the origin of images we note when we speak of "creativity," for creativity is simply that secular state of affairs in which cause and consequence are disjunct. In reading we will a suspension of our disbelief in the unreality of all experience, and at the same time set boundaries to this willed legitimation of the inferential text (the boundaries being the distinction between the fictional and the natural) in such a way as to call attention to the unreality (more precisely, the contingent reality) of ordinary life.
>
> The shock of the discovery of the "unreality of ordinary life" is inherent in the experience of fictions. The basic scenario of the fiction is the theatrical situation in which the audience (the social person) sees but is not seen. If we see William Blake in a vision but he does not see us, that is a fiction. If we see William Blake in a vision and he sees us in return, that is either a natural or an eschatological situation. The meditative realization of the situation in which we see but are not seen is one source of the cognitive increment, the *anagnorisis*, of the experience of fictions. It enforces the realization that personhood and world are the inferences on which we are bent as a redemptive task.
>
> From a practical point of view, we observe that the speaker in the poem has not heard of the author of the poem, and refuses to explore the question.

40.5 Both metaphor (the figure of similarity) and metonymy (the figure of contiguity) are embedded instances of the process of inferential construction. The inference of the similar from the same in metaphor and the inference of the whole from the part in metonymy are both examples of the gathering of a world from elsewhere or the construction of a world across the boundary of impossibility (similar-same and part-whole are transcendental differences).

40.6   In psycho-mimesis (closure) the inferential poem is produced by a struggle from historicity, the singular person, toward speech across the inner-outer and the individual-collective bounding differences. The person is constructed as the absence or trace of internal difference which is left by the transit of consciousness from other to own being as the self diminishes toward extinction in incomparability. The countenance is apprehended at the point of death and is known as the difference or "distance" between death and life.

> There's a certain Slant of light,
> Winter Afternoons—
> That oppresses, like the Heft
> Of Cathedral Tunes—
>
> Heavenly Hurt, it gives us—
> We can find no scar,
> But internal difference,
> Where the Meanings, are—
>
> None may teach it—Any—
> 'Tis the Seal Despair—
> An imperial affliction
> Sent us of the Air—
>
> When it comes, the Landscape listens—
> Shadows—hold their breath—
> When it goes, 'tis like the Distance
> On the look of Death—
>   (Emily Dickinson)

40.7   In cosmo-mimesis (aperture) there seems no inferential poem because speech and being are identical—as in Whitman below:

It is not needed to remind me as of my own dear
    friends,
(For I believe lately I think of little else than of them).

In aperture, language is itself the inferential poem, or all inference has been preempted by an ideology of inclusion, and the
history of the cosmos, of language, and of the person are identical. But we see the cosmo-mimetic poem, the primary poem,
only as an absence, as a function of our difference from the
whole ("I know very well I could not"); we see it through the
language of closure which discourses about language of another
sort and is not wholly unchanged by it (30.4).

I Saw in Louisiana a Live-Oak Growing

I saw in Louisiana a live-oak growing,
All alone stood it and the moss hung down from the
    branches,
Without any companion it grew there uttering joyous
    leaves of dark green,
And its look, rude, unbending, lusty, made me think of
    myself,
But I wonder'd how it could utter joyous leaves standing
    alone there without its friend near, for I knew I
    could not,
And I broke off a twig with a certain number of leaves
    upon it, and twined around it a little moss,
And brought it away, and I have placed it in sight in my
    room,
It is not needed to remind me as of my own dear friends,
(For I believe lately I think of little else than of them,)
Yet it remains to me a curious token, it makes me think
    of manly love;
For all that, and though the live-oak glistens there in
    Louisiana solitary in a wide flat space,
Uttering joyous leaves all its life without a friend a lover
    near,
I know very well I could not.

The Present

41.   What is the difference *for me* between the poetry of my time, and the poetry of the past (other people's time)? More strictly: How does the difference for me of poetry written in my present differ from the difference for me of poetry written in the past? To begin with: the poetry of my present seems to have less *meaning* and more *interest* for me than the poetry of other people's present.

   Scholia.

   A. *Meaning.* The poetry of my present is less "meaningful." Consider that death has not yet put an end to the on-going of poets in my present. Hence, the meaning of the whole work has not been secured, that is to say, the meaning of death in the work has not yet been established. Since death is not the cause of closure in art, but a closural allusion (and involved in a special way in all closural allusion), there is a sense in which the closural allusion in the poetry of the present is a less complete reference to reality than the closural allusion (for example, in "Lycidas") of the poetry of the past. Perhaps one would have thought it the other way around. But death does secure meaning by putting an end to the freedom, that is to say, the indeterminateness, of the meaning-intending mind. Death is inside the fictional process. The stopping of experience is just that sort of reduction which must intervene in the interest of the intelligibility of experience, for what that interest is worth.

   On the other hand, it seems reasonable to say that the poetry of my present is more *legible* since its system of reference (its information, social recognitions, etc.) are native to the time. But note the social problems raised by 8.4 and especially 38.9 which may account in some part for the fact that this has not been the case in the modern period. The poetry of my present may also be less "meaningful" because of the absence of established interpretive mediations which permit the seeing of the thing at a remove (as it were, in another time). This possibility calls attention to the fact that the idea of the present may merely be the idea of the time when meanings are held in common, and that there is since modernism no such time. In a similar vein, the unsettled value-situation of poetry in the present seems a symptom of the problem rather than a cause. But we have to ask, "Why is the value-situation of poetry in our present more unsettled than the value-situation for us of poetry from other people's present?" The answer lies in the direction of the idea of "interest."

B. *Interest.* The poetry of my present is the poetry of greatest interest. It is in the present that the idea of interest as stake becomes actual. Interest is a motive toward choice. Poetry, chronologically in my present, is poetry which is a consequence of choices in the same (historical) situation in which I also must choose. In addition, poetry in the present is an occasion of choice (shall I prefer this poem or that, this style or that? *Is* it in my interest?). Hence interest involves us in the poetry of the present in the same way that our natural situation involves us, as an occasion of judgment. Compare F. R. Leavis, " 'English,' Unrest and Continuity," in *Nor Shall My Sword*, pp. 111, 112:

> What *is* English Literature?
>
> It is a question to which an English School should be constantly working out the answer—not a theoretical, but a concrete answer. This is to formulate again the proposition that I threw out earlier: that an English School should conceive its business as being to perform, or to make a serious attempt at performing, the function of criticism in our time. For English Literature has its life in the present, or not at all. It will be "there," if it is to be a potent living reality, in a public that cares—and cares intelligently—about it; and that it shall be a living reality it is the function of criticism to ensure.

In this sense the present is identical with anxiety about reality construction. Poetry is an example of reality construction enabled by the perception that there is a sense of the past referable to me. Correspondingly, the idea of a present in poetry is merely the discovery of the self as referent, and the idea of judgment is the acknowledgment of a convergence between the interest of the speaking person and the interest of the self. The moment of literary judgment, then, is the moment of coming to consciousness not of my interest in the past but of the interest of the past in me. But the interest of the past in me is a question (it is the case not of seeing the vision but of being seen by the vision), the answering of which is a moment of astonished joy. In this moment the past becomes the present as present and past are figurally (typologically) identified. (Scholium at 20.3.)

> And did those feet in ancient time
>   Walk upon England's mountains green?
> And was the holy Lamb of God
>   On England's pleasant pastures seen?
>
> And did the Countenance Divine
>   Shine forth upon our clouded hills?
> And was Jerusalem builded here
>   Among these dark Satanic Mills?
>
> Bring me my bow of burning gold!
>   Bring me my arrows of desire!
> Bring me my spear! O clouds, unfold!
>   Bring me my chariot of fire!
>
> I will not cease from mental fight,
>   Nor shall my sword sleep in my hand
> Till we have built Jerusalem
>   In England's green and pleasant land.

C. *Presence and absence.* Speaking more strictly, we say that *the present* is the totality of the world as it is presented to me. Hence, the known past and future, being presented, are also present. The contradictory, then, of the present is not the past or the future but the absent, the nonpresent. The chronologically equivalent, insofar as it is unpresented, is therefore as abundantly absent as is the chronologically inequivalent, "past" and "future" in the normal sense. The poetry of the past and the poetry of "the present" are both the presented aspect of my time realm. And the absent is the unpresented aspect of all time realms. To have a present, therefore, is to situate oneself in the realm of presence, to hear oneself announced; and the critical act is the assessment of the literary conditions most propitious to the eidetic advancement (the becoming present as image) of this self. The poetry of the present is, then, the poetry of my presentness in the realm in which the "past" also is found—it is the occasion of my release from absence—unending night. The poetry of the present is where my interest lies. Jerusalem is the city of presence. The poet knows that poetry establishes the difference not between present and past but between presence and absence.

> Think not the words will perish which I, born near far-sounding Aufidus, utter for linking with the lyre, by arts not hitherto revealed! E'en though Maeonian Homer holds the place of honor, yet Pindar's Muse is not unknown, or that of Ceos, of threatening Alcaeus, or of Stesichorus the stately. Nor has time destroyed whate'er Anacreon once sung in sport. Still breathes the love of the Aeolian maid, and lives her passion confided to the lyre.

> Not Spartan Helen only became inflamed with love, marvelling at a paramour's trim locks, his gold-bespangled raiment, his princely pomp and followers; nor was Teucer first to speed the shaft from Cretan bow. Not once alone has Ilium been beset; nor has great Idomeneus or Sthenelus alone fought battles worthy to be sung by the Muses. Nor were doughty Hector and keen Deiphobus the first to encounter heavy blows for chaste wife and children. Many heroes lived before Agamemnon; but all are overwhelmed

in unending night, unwept, unknown, because they lack a sacred bard. In the tomb, hidden worth differs little from cowardice. Not thee, O Lollius, will I leave unsung, unhonored by my verse; nor will I suffer envious forgetfulness to prey undisturbed upon thy many exploits (Horace, *Odes* IV, ix, 1–32).

41.1   The date of my death has not yet occurred in the calendar of past days. How do I know? Perhaps I have forgotten my death. But something would have reminded me.

41.2   Surely the poetry about past times is about my situation in a way different from the way in which poetry of the present is about my situation. Then the poetry of the present (my time) is the poetry of greatest interest in the same way that my situation is the situation of greatest interest to me.

> *Scholium on my situation.* In order for the poetry of the past to be about my situation (for the visionary to be seen by the vision, the reader to be read) there must be a principle of relationship that is not literary. There must be a membership common between the dead and the living. The poetry of my time is of greatest interest insofar as it is the point of intersection between my space and the *topos* of membership. Hence, the poetry in my present is an instance of the part-whole reduction. In this sense, "I" am the separated part offering itself as candidate to the whole in which interest (which is always, insofar as it is merely interest, not yet actual) becomes actual as meaning or immortality. The function of poetry in the present is to construct the past in such a way as to accord with my interest. In order to choose among the poetries of the present it is necessary for me to make a judgment about my interest, a judgment which is prior to criticism, insofar as criticism is a judgment of texts (9.1). The past is therefore a creation, and indeed a secondary creation, which I must invent as my meaning before I have any past at all. The poetry of the temporal present, insofar as it is a function of my historical situation, is prior to the poetry of the past which comes after.

The order of priority as dictated by the processes of judgment is therefore the reverse of the order of time.

41.3   Is this life, then, the life of greatest interest by contrast to my past or future lives? If this life is related to past lives of this self as inscription to ground, then the poetry of this time is related to the poetry of past times in the same way, that is, as inscription to ground. The situation in which the ground becomes of greater interest than the inscription has already been noted as decadent. (31.10, 31.11, Scholium at 31.12, Scholium at 38.7.)

> *Scholium on past and future lives.* Note, however, that the necessity of choosing between past and future lives on the one hand, and the present on the other, reflects a culturally conditioned constraint. Persons in the West cannot remember their past lives intuitively. The immense concern for textual transmission in the West, and therefore the urgency of inscription as writing and its technologies, is a compensation in the realm exterior to mind for the mind's inability to recover its past lives as part of its own (internal) processes. To prefer past to present or present to past may well be to perpetuate an illusion of distinction, a false difference. The present should be thought of as the moment in which the self enters the realm of presence in which the past and future are lost in the light of presentedness, in which they are, as we have said (Scholium C at 41), one.
>
> From this point of view, the textuality of the past is destructive of (at any rate a clearly limiting constraint upon) the interest of the present on its way to presence. The textuality of the past is, of course, the condition of its transmission and, as an irreducible economic fact, a thing which is self-insistent and takes up space, the limit upon the assimilation of it into any given presentness. Inscription and ground are terms which account for a state of affairs in history, but not a state of affairs in mind.

41.4 There is a sense in which the idea of "a time" is metaphoric.
      When we speak of coinhabitants of a "time," we are speaking of
      a collectivity with a common interest (at very least a common
      language, whose tongue is a common mother [42]). Hence a
      "time" is a chronological tribe whose members are coevals
      (poets of the earlier seventeenth century, poets of the 1940s).
      The poetics of experience, then, in a given time, is a system of
      messages about the management of experience which has the
      weightiness which derives from the criticality of all knowledge
      that pertains to tribal continuity.

> *Scholium on ancient time.* Blake's "ancient time" is an ahis-
> torical allusion to the "realm of priority" where founding
> events occur, and meaning is established as a possibility. In
> view of "ancient time," time is measured as distance from
> that time, and the *problem of interest* is to discover a way
> through to the destiny of interest in meaning, that is to say,
> the ancient. "Ancient time" is the time of foundation, the
> time of primary relationship, the time therefore of meaning-
> construction—not this meaning or that meaning but the
> possibility of meaning. The present is known as the absence
> of the ancient, and "ancient" has as its central connotation
> "meaning-bearing," "meaning-establishing." All poem open-
> ings establish a relationship between the present and the an-
> cient, between what never recurs (the present, the anecdote)
> and what always occurs (the ancient) (33). The present is
> the unique and therefore the unrepresentable. The problem
> of the self in the present is the fear of trusting the power of
> the ancient to restore the self after it has been let go in the
> process of obtaining a relationship to the ancient. "And did
> those feet . . . ?" is not merely the astonished surprise of the
> new consciousness of redemption, but also the wonder at
> having been established at the point of self-loss. "Interest,"
> the sense of unique stake, and "meaning," the sense of con-
> tinuity with the other (the contradiction of the unique), ap-
> pear as antinomic. Ancient time is time as atemporal space,
> tribal time, into which the present is resolved at the point of

meaning-disclosure, at the point of the discovery of the track of the predecessor, the footprint of the foregoer and the foreknower, the self which has gone before.

41.5 The distance between minds is not like space, because space can be traversed. It is more like time as it separates consciousness from an event which has already happened or has not yet happened. There is a marginal sense, therefore, in which the poetry of anybody but myself is noncontemporaneous with me. If, then, my (the one I own?) current poem is the poem of greatest interest to me, the question arises which poem is my current poem. The one I write or the one I read? "My poem" is the one I read, because obviously the poem I write is not yet written; and the poem I have written is one of the poems I read. What falls here is the idea of contemporaneity. There is no immediate temporal present in the same way and for the same reason that there is no immediate presence of mind to mind. A present is like a tribe, and what is common is its situation.

41.6 In concrete experience, the distance between all points in time is not of the same magnitude. But the distance between all minds is precisely of the same magnitude, whether they are living or dead. Clearly, there is no poetry of the present, as there is no unmediated presence (no miscibility of minds); but there is poetry of varying degrees of magnitude of pastness. However, in the abstract realm (where the distinction between the fictional and the natural is hard and fast) the status of the speaker in the poem is always of the same relatedness (as *fiction*); and this establishes a constant concern of a neutral character—concern but not critical concern. This is the aesthetic state of affairs, the empty present. The full present is eschatological.

> *Scholium on immortality as the identity of meaning and interest.* Interest is after all existence reconstituted, out of its indifference, as the stake of a person. As we see in the Blake poem, immortality is the result of the perception of the congruence of interest (being in its presentness) and meaning, England and Jerusalem. Where the present as the interest

which identifies a world, and *ancient time* are found inside one another, *there* immortality arises; and immortality is the *telos* of poetry (1).

Ancient time is the fullness of the world from which present-ness as consciousness is always removed. *The present* is that consciousness for which the fullness of the world was created. At the intersection of these two systems we find the justification of the world, immortal life, "life" just so.

41.7   Since meaning in the present is contingent upon acknowledgment of the past, "the past" is a way of referring to the limit of my freedom. I come to care about poems of past times in the same way I come to care about the irrational givenness of my own unchosen body (the generic given, the social given of me). As the limit of my freedom, the poems of past times cannot become the instruments of my will in any continuous way. They are another will without which I have no will; but above all they are not my will. They are the second law.

41.8   Only those who have an act can *practice* freedom. The dead have no act.

Mother Tongue/Father Tongue

42.   You know who is the mother. You do not know who is the father. The father chooses or is chosen. The mother has rights.

Scholium on mother and father. The legitimation of the mother tongue as a poetic language is an ironic process.

In general, the fictional is distinguished from the natural along lines which are not symbolically, or, for that matter, morally neutral. Traditionally, the fictional is male, paternal, sky-born, antitragic, meaning-bearing, name-conferring, voluntary, light-filled; the natural is female, maternal, earth-born, tragically compelled, not meaningful in itself but the ground on which meaning is inscribed, not just in the sense in which justice is a middle way between rationality and fact, but in the severe Eumenidean sense which allows no choice (as natural process allows no choice). Consequently, a "mother" tongue is associated with the nonfictional (not with prose but with the actual, by contrast to the represented) as also with the nonvoluntary and compelled aspects of the natural. Hence, poetry in the mother tongue is a return of the child into the mother, the choosing of necessity and therefore the defeat of choice. The refusal of Orestes to slay his mother, the marriage of Odysseus and Calypso.

Fictionalization, like education, is normally regarded as an exchange of the involuntary for the voluntary, of the earth for the sky, of darkness for light, of the maternal for the paternal, of history for meaning, of the place of natural origins for the place of symbolic origins. When the mother tongue is raised to fictional status either it ceases to be a "mother" tongue (it is then, for example, taught, which a mother tongue by definition need not be) and by reason of the distancing and framing powers of poetic intention becomes its opposite, the Uranian or sky-creature; or it may happen that in it the poetic, the fictional, is drawn back into the realm of the tragic, the unchosen (as in the case of "radical humanism" at 32 above).

Hence, we find the mother slain in the poetic; we see Orestean murder as the normal rite of passage into the cultural estate. Hence, we see that artistic perception is postcatastrophic and that the marks and ceremonies of closure (which function to secure the fictional estate of the natural utterance enclosed) in fact achieve an irrevocable desituation of language. And with the slaying of the mother in the poetic there arises a loss of knowledge; for the choosing or chosen meaning, the "eternal" meaning, is not known and is not meaning in the same sense as the necessary meaning of the mother's voice, the primordially situated knowledge.

Where poetic languages (4) are truly alternative languages to the mother tongue there is a possibility of moving along an

axis across the threshold of difference between transcendence and immanence such that father and mother are both
conserved in the consciousness-producing enterprise of the
child. Where the poetic language is identified with the
mother tongue there arises the complete seriousness (13, 28)
that drives out light.

In romanticism and in the radical epistemologies of modernism (aperture, 39.4) we find an effort not merely to legitimate the mother tongue as a poetic language but to identify
the natural and the fictional. This follows the process of the
legitimation of the mother tongue which began with the adaptation of vulgar languages as poetic languages (for example, in Dante). From the legitimation of the vulgar language as a poetic language to the identification of the
fictional and the natural is a single historical process. We
must look as clearly as we can at the calculus of loss and gain:
in the choice of the fictional, alliance with the sky-father,
we commit ourselves to the realms of mediate relationships,
the realms of the eye. Our art is postcatastrophic and our
"redemption" lies not in our art but in our capacity to move
between art and experience, between the fictional and the
natural in morally productive ways. In the romantic and
postmodernist disposition to identify the natural and the fictional we only survive as symbolic persons by equivocating
the status of what we experience. Subject-object relationships are exchanged for epistemological equivocation. What
is gained is some relationship to that other knowledge from
which mere choosing shuts us out.

Note: If meaning is paternal and chosen, then meaning becomes universal as possibility. But if meaning is maternal and
constrained, as birth is particular and nonvoluntary, then
meaning is local. The literature based on the transit to the
paternal is, ideologically at least, universal, conversional; the
literature based on the return into the maternal is accessible
only by birthright. Hence, the possibility of fictionalizing all
maternity and rendering it voluntary is a liberal ideal.

42.1   Let the tongue be the mother; then, what is the child? The
child is the person as speaker who goes through his growth.
When the tongue tastes, it does not speak. When it speaks, it
does not taste. (Scholium at 29.) The mother tongue of the
speechless infant is tasting, and of the speaking youth is less and
less of tasting. It is part of the ideology of poetry that poetic
languages conserve, for example, through archaism (4.3), immediacy (tasting) within the context of speaking—that in poetry there is a moment of growth without loss. The incorporation of the silence of immediacy inside the moment of speech
gives the possibility of tasting and speaking together. This
would be one sense of poetic "immortality" as the simultaneity
of meaning (as speaking) and being (as tasting). "Poetry heals
the cruel antinomies of being through the resources of fiction."
But fiction itself exists in an antinomic system (fictional-
natural). The ideologies of poetry are not sane or useful if
naïvely taken.

42.2   All the children of the tongue are brothers and sisters. Erotic
relationships within the tribe of the tongue are, therefore, incestuous (28). Consequently, there must be a philosophy of ex-
ogamy (externality, selfhood) in order to render life possible, in
order to free speaking life from intolerable guiltiness. Note the
following from Hans-Georg Gadamer, *Truth and Method*, p. 15:

> To seek one's own in the alien, to become at home in it,
> is the basic movement of spirit, whose being is only return
> to itself from what is other. Hence all theoretical *Bildung*,
> even the acquisition of foreign languages and conceptual
> worlds, is merely the continuation of a process of *Bildung*
> which begins much earlier. Every single individual that
> raises himself out of his natural being to the spiritual finds
> in the language, customs and institutions of his people a
> pre-given body of material which, as in learning to speak,
> he has to make his own. Thus every individual is always
> engaged in the process of *Bildung* and in getting beyond
> his naturalness, inasmuch as the world into which he is
> growing is one that is humanly constituted through lan-

guage and custom. Hegel emphasises that a people gives itself its existence in its world. It works out from itself and thus exteriorises what is in itself.

Thus it is clear that it is not alienation as such, but the return to oneself, which presumes a prior alienation, that constitutes the essence of *Bildung*.

On the other hand, *the idea of spiritual relationship derives from the idea of linguistic relationship—children of the tongue, children of the Word.* The agapic premise within the family of children of the tongue becomes a model of nonproprietary principles of association. Common language places its practitioners inside one another, and at the same time in one another's hand. Here we see the difference between the mother tongue and the father tongue. Within the tongue considered as Word there is freedom from scarcity because there is a reconstitution of the principle of relationship on the basis of that which is only good when it is divided, and which is enhanced by distribution. As there are no private languages, so in fact the more public the language the more valuable, the more of it *for* its possessor. But this is not true of the mother tongue. The law of the mother tongue is the law of exclusivity, of the pitting of immortality against immortality.

42.3   And yet poetic knowledge is knowledge of the mother tongue.

Scholium on nontranslatability. We have observed that the archaic basis of the power of the poem with respect to immortality is its fixed text, or rather the transmissibility of its text. (4.4, Scholium, and citation.) The mother tongue is the tongue which binds us to earth, and it is our earth (our flesh and the occasions on which we acquire and sustain it, our mortal interest) which secures poetic immortality. The fixed text is the sublimation of the mortal body, as the line is the sublimation of the lineaments, those acquired characteristics which constitute personal by contrast to species (genetically transmitted) identity. From the mother comes the body and from the mother tongue comes the immortality of the denumerable individual whose identity is in singularity as the body is singular. It is the mother who hates collectivization and is excluded from the family of the Word. In the family of the Word texts are translatable. In the family of the tongue texts are nontranslatable. In the family of the Word the transmissibility of texts is a function of translatability. Here we encounter, I think, one strong sense in which poetry is antireligious or at any rate anti-Christian in the Johannine sense. The deep imaginative resolution of the tensions between tongue and Word, mother and father, is in the Jewish doctrine of the resurrection of the body. Insofar as poetry escapes (and I do not think it does) from the realm of tongue into the realm of Word the resurrection of the body is its type or symbol.

42.4   The mother tongue is, roughly, the language of the situation into which we are thrown (that is to say, the situation in which we *are* against our will, or whether we will or no, or, at any rate, before we have willed). It is the language of fate, hence the language of the novel—the realm of the impeded will.

42.5   In the study of literature in the vernacular we learn to practice the mother tongue as a willed act, which was before an unwilled fatality. We take the mother as a problem: as Odysseus holds Antiklea at sword's point until he has conferred with Teiresias.

> *Scholium on the past as mother.* The past as father is studied as the "tradition." The past as mother is the earth as tradition, the body as cosmic participant which is the dark companion of every meaning-intending soul. The past as father is the deathless past which threatens the immortality of the son by occupying the whole propriety of time. The past as mother is the death-bound past which threatens the immortality of the son by redeeming the male figure in the female ground of oblivion. Poetry is always in a wrong relation to the mother, like Blake's *Milton*, because it is pitted against the earth from which it derives its authenticity. From the mother comes existence, the weight of being, of which the

meaning is always a betrayal. Since meaning, the figure, never precisely affirms the whole ground, is never identical with it. The right of the mother is, therefore, never fully retrieved, and the residual rage of the mother—the rage of being against the regime of meaning—is everywhere felt in the poetic line as an unresolvable selvage of ambiguity in the relationship of stress as semantic figuration and the morphemic background on which it moves. It is the rage of the mother that defeats the reading of the line and establishes the realm of interest.

42.6   The willing of necessity in the form of the mother tongue is the acknowledgment of the body as tradition. But the body cannot be completely willed, nor can it be complete in its own will.

42.7   Unlike the father tongue which is primarily word, the mother tongue is the source of silence.

42.8   It would be better to say that the mother tongue is necessity produced as utterance, the speech of the unwilled and the unwillable, the speech of the wordless, of presence (31.6).

> *Scholium on rhyme and the mother tongue.* The mother is present wherever in the poem language is specialized toward sound, as in rhyme which arrests the word in the ear, requiring that it delay in the realm of the body, before passing to sensory extinction as mere notation in the brain. Rhyme like all phonic or merely structural repetition (as in grammatical rhyme) summons to common membership at the level of the species, tending to extinguish difference as transcendence and establish difference at the level of substance. The difference/no difference ambiguity in rhyme functions as the repetition of the sufficient conditions of sensing (the rule of texture), and as the substantiation of the parallel ambiguity at the level of meaning. Sound as silence (rhyme as sensation) articulates silence as sound (the meaning of words and sentences).
>
> The abandonment of rhyme in recent times is not, however, a betrayal of the mother but an attempt to recover her full

participation. Rhyme was for Milton a "modern bondage" because it was precisely the assertion of the rights of the mother tongue. From the point of view of the "modern" poet, however, rhyme is understood in terms of its diacritical function and therefore constitutes a semantic component which presupposes unwanted interpretations of experience. The poetry of aperture (39) is characteristically unrhymed because it is based in the fundamental assertion of rhyme, the irrational nexus in which the natural and the fictional are without distinction.

42.9   The immortality of the father and the immortality of the mother are not the same immortality.

> *Scholium on the competition of immortalities.* The body which is the mother's and the name which is the father's do not share the same destiny in history. The medium of poetry is a sort of eschatological realm in which the mother and the father dwell together though in hierarchy—construct the same destiny.
>
> But, in the realm of reference, the immortality of the species and immortality of the individual compete for immortal estate. This competition is thematized in poetry as the immortalization of the mother as beloved object through the means of the language of the father. The woman is betrayed through praise. Upon her irreducibility as object is founded the immortal estate of the paternal name. The father is speech without countenance, and the mother countenance without speech. Speech is the key to the life of the countenance. Speech is, as it were, the eidetic catalyst.
>
> The preference of the immortality of the word (the father's life) over the immortality of the world (the mother's life) is the constant assertion against the background of which "the reconciliation of opposites in the medium of the art," on the one hand, and the rage of the unavenged right of the mother, on the other, should be viewed.

Orphic Machines

43.   The Orphic machine is the poem: a severed head with face
      turned away that sings. (See Ricoeur.)

> *Scholium on iconographies of poem source.* Each poem is a
> reinvention of the speech source, because each poem estab-
> lishes again, and is also identical with, the fictional "I" (the
> severed head) which is the machine that has speech as its
> product.

> The Orphic machine is the source of the fictional presence,
> by contrast to the natural presence. The counternatural sta-
> tus of the fictional presence determines that the fictional
> voice will be postcatastrophic—will repeat the postcatas-
> trophic nature of perception itself—as the "goary visage" of
> Orpheus sings the history of its fictional enablement, the
> "organic" disorder on which the order of song is founded.
> The icons which stand as speech sources and function as
> Orphic machines are fragments of primordial chaos from
> which voice emerged as voice alone (Deut. 4:12). Only if
> voice is voice alone (*kol zoulati*) can the inference of the
> person (the whole man) arise and the countenance be
> formed.

> The visible person is the idol of "man" because it can never
> be perceived whole; but the inferential person (the fictional
> person) is only knowable as a whole. The paradox that the
> person is only knowable by inference because the whole is
> only knowable through the defeat of the natural presented
> thing is of the same sort as the constitutive rules of poetic
> construction in general. Cf. Crane's line:

> Or they may start some white machine that sings.

43.1 Think of it as the shell, the skull, the mummy, the golden bird,
      the garden, the rose, the ark, the bee-box, the labyrinth, the
      whale, the stone, the grail, the bridge, the tower, the pyramid,

the temple, the knot, the breast, the mountain, the sea, the harp, the wind, the countenance.

Scholium on sources of poetry, sources of world. The source of speech, the source of poetry, and the source of world are co-implicated. Symbolic representations of the origination of poetic utterance in Orphic objects and machines indicates that poetry is the speaking of being, and that being comes first. Poetry is the speaking of being in the process of discovering itself as an occasion of the visibility of a person. The Orphic machine is the state of the object at the point of that discovery. Poetry issues from world at the point of the submission of world to countenance, that is to say, at the point of its brokenness as world.

Speech is before and after world. The Orphic song is the speech of the world after it has ceased to be world, and its subject is the speech of the world before it has become world ("the supreme theme") (31.4).

43.2   Take the shell (20). The gastropod, dead, armored, fascinating, a closed book, an interior self (*you* can't see in), utters the oceanic version of the Orphic song. It *is* like a book. When is a book really open? Never. "The stone broken is other stones. The shell broken is fragments" (Valéry).

Scholium. In tradition, the shell is like the mind from which speech issues, but into which nothing can descend (Bachelard). The end of the winding path, which is traceable only in imagination, is the point of origination, the ancestral darkness. The shell of the gastropod manifests interior space as experienced from the outside. When experienced from within (in imagination), it is the winding path of the tower stairs or the labyrinthine descent to Hell, where the transcendental version of one's own death is encountered in the person of the dead ancestor, the Master.

                                Much rejoiced
The dreaming Man that he should have a Guide
To lead him through the Desart; and he thought,
While questioning himself what this strange freight
Which the Newcomer carried through the Waste
Could mean, the Arab told him that the Stone,
To give it in the language of the Dream,
Was Euclid's Elements; "and this," said he,
"This other," pointing to the Shell, "this Book
Is something of more worth." And, at the word,
The Stranger, said my Friend continuing,
Stretch'd forth the Shell towards me, with command
That I should hold it to my ear; I did so,
And heard that instant in an unknown Tongue,
Which yet I understood, articulate sounds,
A loud prophetic blast of harmony,
An Ode, in passion utter'd, which foretold
Destruction to the Children of the Earth,
By deluge now at hand. . . .
                    (Wordsworth, *Prelude* 1805, book 5)

In any case, the journey (which cannot be taken except by
inference) returns us to origins, the ancestral night, the ancestral rose, the ancestral tribe, the ocean which threatens
to recover reality for the Primordial Master by returning it to
its original oceanic brokenness.

When the symbolic journey deteriorates into a psychological
one, the ancestral encounter (the immortality of the collective) converts to a personal encounter (extinction of individuality [14.4]) unless some sacramental version of selfhood is
available to distinguish between the personal and the merely
individual.

Seen from the point of view of the human parallel of the one
and the many the encaverned skull, the shell, the chambered
cairn, represents man alone in the garden.

Two paradises 'twere in one
To live in paradise alone.
(J. B. Leishman cites Aquinas on *vita contemplativa*,
"non proprie humana sed superhumana")

The shell devolves from the body whorl to the spire and apex, becoming a thing centered on the invisible point of its arising (the seed of individual being), and out of that point there arises the solitary reaper:

Behold her, single in the field,
Yon solitary highland lass!
Reaping and singing by herself;
Stop here, or gently pass!
Alone she cuts and binds the grain.

This is the being of the interior life, the *flos florum*, and also the perceiver experienced as perceived (the immortal double). A creature of the threshold she is encountered in the borderland, the marches, where she is "single," "solitary," "alone." Her song is a version of the oceanic voice. "Will no one tell me what she sings?"

43.3   The severed head of Orpheus that sings is text. Text pours reference back toward the world from which it is itself irretrievably separated.

Scholium on text. The text is the matrix of unexchangeable differences among the signs which constitute a particular poem. One place where the text is present is on the page. The definition of the text is one stage of the working through of the question of the ontology of the poem. Other stages are roughly indicated by the lexical compounds into which the "text" element normally enters in ordinary usage—such as "con-text" and "pre-text." It is also possible to speak of "textuality," and to invoke the metaphors "textile" and "texture."

At the level of general definition the "matrix of unexchangeable differences" need not be constituted of linguistic signs. Any state of experience, when regarded as an occasion of interpretation, can be "fixed" and assigned textual status, as when we speak of the "book of nature." What is then *as-signed* is the *hermeneutic possibility*—which regards the complexity of what is always going on in a designated segment of a horizon as the semantic obligation of the reader.

The "textile" metaphor suggests that meaning-intention sees its object as a set of intersections of vertical and horizontal coordinates.

The issue of the boundaries of text affects the question of the ontology of the poem (the answer to the question: where really is it?). The "pre-text" may be regarded as the whole moment of significant intention flowing from now convergent, but originally unknown, sources in history, mind, biology, etc., through the text and then as a moment of semantic force (like an ocean wave) through the reader into a plurality of subsequent histories.

The fixed text is a power (see Ivins, cited at 4.4) over which power is exercised. Text conservation has as its purpose the continuity of the community in its given form and therefore also the continuity of the tenure in power of the ruling group, both political and cosmic. Text and canon are intimately related.

43.4   All Orphic machines are versions of the countenance under the conditions required for poetic utterance. Text as Orphic machine is countenance as speech alone. Reading therefore is the inference of countenance from text, and the conservation of the text is the keeping of the lineaments of the countenance. But why does the countenance, the *eidos*, when we see it, appear mutilated? The gory visage of Orpheus, the countenance *non decus atque decor* of the suffering servant, Christ in passion? The well-formed face and the mutilated face seem the same face. Or we should say the face which gives rise to other faces, the image which is the origin of other images, the form of forms, is deformed as the *eyes* of the singer are blind.

The Orphic machine is, as has been indicated, a thematization in image of the fictional "I" with its defilement and abhorrent deformity upon it (28). The fact that poem-source is represented as Orphic machine implies the assertion that existence is prior to utterance—the source of utterance being representable only as existence. But the existence or world which gives rise to poetic utterance (its origin but not its "source") is always seen as ruined, the devastated mother. When seen, it is ruined. When heard, it is lamentation. . . .

Care

44.   I would like to say that all the scattered terms of a poetic analysis are held together by care.

> *Scholium on hermeneutic friendship as an instance of care.* In hermeneutic friendship we help one another to meaning. Gilgamesh and Enkidu, for example, are hermeneutic friends. Insofar as meaning is an interactive construction, meaning is the house which persons in relationship build; and this dwelling of persons-in-relationship in the house of meaning is hermeneutic friendship, of which dreams are one occasion and poems another. But the helping one another to meaning cannot always be expressed in pacific analogies. Homeric combat is a scenario of hermeneutic friendship— the helping of one another to immortality. Jacob in struggle with his angel acquires a name through hermeneutic friendship. Sexual love is an instance of hermeneutic friendship. In hermeneutic friendship, the plurality of persons (the being of more than one) becomes facilitative of the meaning-bearing life of each. The house built by men and women in relationship in which their dwelling-in-meaning takes place is also called *topical space.*
>
> The central question about hermeneutic friendship, about life in the house of meaning, is whether the relationships which arise accommodate the good destiny of both parties or

whether in hermeneutic friendship (in topical space) there is some background of scarcity, which requires that friend perish on behalf of friend. In this scenario there are first two *virtual* persons, and then one *actual* person. As there are first Gilgamesh and Enkidu, and then Gilgamesh alone. Is human meaning (immortality) an economic good in an economy of diminishing resource?

In hermeneutic friendship we acknowledge the textuality of one another and at the same time seek to undo the *alienation* of the self to its own textuality by pouring the reference of the self back upon the self. We are moved to the other as text by care, and out of care we attempt to compensate the other for being text. At the bottom of care there is a sense of common loss.

Poems are traces of care, *vestigia* as it were of a vast communal enterprise of troubled mutuality which overflows its moment in time (its natural occasion) and becomes as fiction the way of access to one another of unknown others. Poems seem to embody the powers toward relationships of care which detach themselves from specific moments and fly off.

44.1   Care is the social face of the culture of immortality.

44.2   Another way of stating the matter is that care is the principle of otherwise *unaccountable* concern which draws us toward the object—the knowledge of the rightness of knowing that precedes knowledge, or the knowledge of the rightness of loving that precedes loving. First-caring (but is there ever a *first* caring or a *first* reading?) manifests itself as an unaccountable drawnness of the attention toward objects; and care is then practiced (*later* caring) as a sustaining confident resort to objects that has found its reason after finding its object—that has found its reason in its object. But the central fact is that caring is first toward what is not willed, what is unaccountable in terms of the caring self.

44.3   Care seeks to keep the other in being—to keep the other present. Filled with desire for the presence of the other (without

which the self cannot be present to the self), care takes hold of
the poetic means of presence. In the face of the failure of culture to conserve the beloved object care expresses rage:

> Where were ye, nymphs, when the remorseless deep
> Closed o'er the head of your loved Lycidas?
> For neither were ye playing on the steep
> Where your old bards, the famous Druids, lie,
> Nor on the shaggy top of Mona high,
> Nor yet where Deva spreads her wizard stream.
> Ay me, I fondly dream,
> Had ye been there!—for what could that have done?
> What could the Muse herself that Orpheus bore,
> The Muse herself for her enchanting son
> Whom universal nature did lament,
> When by the rout that made the hideous roar
> His goary visage down the stream was sent,
> Down the swift Hebrus to the Lesbian shore?

The failure of care leads to the mutilation of the countenance.
The only significant mutilation of the countenance (the meaning of mutilation) is oblivion. But we see here that the failure
of care (resulting in the death of Lycidas, the death of the mortal singer and therefore the death of the intelligibility of
things—the possibility of song) is preliminary to the establishment of song—for the death of Lycidas repeats the death of the
archetypal singer, Orpheus, whose decapitation is the precondition of his power in history. The functioning of care is therefore founded on a primordial failure of care—or care of one sort
is sacrificed in the interest of care of another sort (particular for
collective). The *topos* of rage at the incompetence of culture to
conserve the image of its members ("Where were ye, nymphs?")
is in fact an inevitable reflection on (has inside of it) the sacrificial conditions of the culture of care itself—insofar as that
culture is symbolic and transhistorical. Care in symbolic culture
is discovered, therefore, mourning for its own more immediate
forms (43).

44.4   One way care has of mingling itself with cultural process is as tradition. Tradition as a human act in a present is the acknowledgment (the establishment as text) of the self that is not willed. Such acknowledgment is a version of interpretation.

> *Scholium on Christ-interpreter.* In Judaeo-Christian (biblical) civilization the Messiah is the interpreter who rectifies the landscape (leveling hills and valleys) and who makes persons whole by acts of interpretation mediated by a version of care which in the Gospels is both psychologized and cosmologized as one sort of love. Christ-interpreter is the master reader who facilitates the wholeness of others by his example of wholeness. He completes the text of the world as an act of hermeneutic friendship on the model of the interpretation which arose the next moment after creation—"and God saw the light that it was good."
>
> The messianic king is the master interpreter and the power of the king is the power of interpretation. He is both god and man—both text and reader; he stands between and goes before, repeating the heroism of the prophet who hears the word of the God in the fire on the mountain and conveys it to the people in the plain.
>
> But as the hermeneutic friend he is not merely the interpreter but also the perfect reader, the reader who accepts the burden of the referentiality of the text, the Quixotic reader for whom the text is true. The final act of the interpreter, the hermeneutic friend, is willed death, a repetition in the structure of life of the structure of the text—an example of mythic seriousness (38) which makes possible the treatment, by all who come after, of text as fiction. Christ takes away death by accepting the text as myth and preempting that relationship for all other readers, thus creating, as it were, the category of fiction—founding metaphor. ("This is my body.")

The interpreter demands meaning. He insists on the eidetic realization of the other. He is the master of recognition and also the manifest instance of the thing known when recognition occurs. His presence exacts the healing of all by making impossible the avoidance of the eidetic basis of human interaction. Those who acknowledge the challenge of their own eidetic nature—of their meaningfulness as text—live forever in the light of meaning; and those who refuse to read the countenance are cast out into darkness for they have refused the light of the interpreter.

44.5 At the level of prosodic order the vehicle of care in the poem is meter, which masters the tendency of speech to disappear, to be swallowed up in the situation in which it arises in the overshadowing teleologies of the persons who speak. Syllable count, and linear order in general, represent the care which keeps world in being. Stress strokes the line into sense; stress is the evidence of the presence of the interpreter internal to the poem. In stress, the person implied by the poem becomes a countenance which can be recognized. Stress then is a version of care as an interpretation of natural existence.

Scholium on stress. Prosodic stress in English poetry is an arrangement of the stress-characteristics of the natural language, in such a way as to explore the possible conformity of the meaning of speakers in natural situations to meaning about meaning and about speakers.

Stress both in the natural language and in the context of the poem points diacritically to the meaning-bearing element in the word. Where there is dispute about stress the reader need only accept as an obligation the semantic consequences of any given stressing. If the reader can affirm the extrapolation of the chosen stressing to an understanding of the entire work in terms of that stressing, then the stressing must be accepted.

The stressing (prosodic) of stressing (natural), or the conformity of natural stress to the laws of the *poem*, establishes meaning about meaning—one such meaning might be that this meaning is not a natural meaning but a fictional meaning.

Stressing is the inscription of the subjective or meaning-intending volition of the speaker (this is for the reader). We may dispute about stress. Syllable count, by contrast, is by its nature at the other extreme of intersubjectivity. It has the character of the "objective" and we do not dispute about it, only correct one another with the understanding that the solution to the counting problem will be univocal. Stress is the point of presence of the hermeneutic issue in the substance of the hermeneutic object itself.

44.6   The self that is not willed (for example, my body, my culture, my natural language) conceived as an experience of the willing self has, to begin with, the character of an accident. In poetry, there is always a residual sense of accident, of stumbling upon order. That is what is meant by felicity, the happy finding of a meaningful order in what could not be willed as order. Care has that necessary openness toward accident which is not possible to the thing that is closed around the fullness of itself.

44.7   We are all tradition to one another, objects of care, selves that are not willed. We are also objects of care to ourselves. When I say "I was born on such and such a day," when I realize (see, for example, Valéry's "My Body") the autonomic systems of which consciousness is a contingency, when I acknowledge the "ownness" of my name (which I have not changed), I find my self in the act of caring. In other words I acknowledge all the nonsense of which I somehow am the sense.

Quies, or Rest

A woman goes from room to room. She extinguishes
One light in each room. Darkness follows her
And in the last room she is overtaken.
Then, she mounts the dark stair confidently
And enters the room she sleeps in, and lies
Down in the dark, where a man in the dark wakes
A little and covers her with his arm.

Works Cited in *Summa Lyrica*
(1–44)

Aquinas, Thomas. *Summa Theologica* (New York: Random House, 1945). Vol. 1, Questiones 50–64.
The questions on angels. Our interest is in how angels know persons. See especially Q. 57, p. 533. (16.7)

Arendt, Hannah. *The Human Condition* (Chicago: University of Chicago Press, 1958).
Note concept of "space of appearance" and great chapter on "Action" in relationship to the founding of stories. Also "Eternity versus Immortality" (1, 3) and "The Social and the Private" (2, 9). (1.2, S; 6.2, S refers to pp. 182, 183.)

Aristotle. *Poetics*, text, translation, and commentary in S. H. Butcher, *Aristotle's Theory of Poetry and Fine Art*, 4th ed. (New York: Dover Publications, 1951). (37)

Auerbach, Erich. *Mimesis*, tr. Willard Trask (Princeton: Princeton University Press, 1953). (26.14, S)

Augustine. *Confessions*, tr. and with an intro. by R. S. Pine-Coffin (Baltimore: Penguin, 1961). (31.6, S)
See 11, 6 and 7. See also Ferguson, Margaret W.

———. *Concerning the Teacher (De Magistro)*, etc., tr. George G. Leckie (New York: Appleton-Century-Crofts, 1938). (2.3, S)
See especially last brief section on the impersonalist, anamnetic notion of learning.

Austin, J. L. *How to Do Things with Words: The William James Lectures*

Delivered at Harvard University in 1955, ed. J. O. Urmson (New York: Oxford University Press, 1965). (6.2, S)

Bachelard, Gaston. *The Poetics of Reverie* (New York: Orion Press, 1969). (43.2, S)
On shells, corners, etc.

Barfield, Owen. *Poetic Diction* (1928) (New York: McGraw-Hill, 1964, pb). (4.3)
See especially "The Poet," "Archaism," and "Strangeness."

Bauman, Richard, and Joel Sherzer, eds. *Explorations in the Ethnography of Speaking* (London and New York: Cambridge University Press, 1974). (3, S; 40, S)
See especially Bauman's "Speaking in the Light: The Role of the Quaker Minister."

Becker, Ernst. *The Denial of Death*, tr. Mary A. Meek (New York: Free Press, 1973). (1.2, S; 28, S)

Bellow, Saul. *Mr. Sammler's Planet* (New York: Viking, 1970). (32.9)

Benveniste, Emile. *Problems in General Linguistics* (Miami: University of Miami Press, 1971). (1.3, S; 14.4, S; 24.1, S)

Black, Max. *The Labyrinth of Language* (New York: Frederick A. Praeger, 1958). (6.2, S)
See especially "The Many Uses of Language."

Bloom, Harold. *The Anxiety of Influence: A Theory of Poetry* (London: Oxford University Press, 1973). (8.4; 38.9, S; 39.2, S)

Cullmann, Oscar. "Immortality of the Soul or Resurrection of the Dead?" In *Immortality and Resurrection*, edited by Krister Stendahl (New York: Macmillan, 1965). (1.2, S)

Curtius, Ernst Robert. *European Literature and the Latin Middle Ages*, tr. Willard Trask (New York: Harper and Row, 1953). (4.3, S)
Note discussion of topic.

Dewey, John. *Philosophy and Civilization* (New York: Minton, Balch and Co., 1931). (14.4, S)

Dodds, E. R. *The Greeks and the Irrational* (1951) (Boston: Beacon Press, 1957). (28.1, S)
See especially p. 151 on the meaning of past lives of the person.

Durkheim, Emile. *The Elementary Forms of Religious Life*, tr. J. W. Swain (Glencoe: Free Press, 1947). (14.4, S)
On collective representations, and immanent and social surrogations for divinity.

Edinger, Edward F. *Ego and Archetype: Individuation and the Religious Function of the Psyche* (Baltimore: Penguin, 1973). (38.3, S)
See, in particular, "Christ as Paradigm of the Individuating Ego."

Eliade, Mircea. *Myth and Reality* (New York: Harper, 1968, Torchbook pb.). (6.2, S)
See "Mythologies of Memory and Forgetting."

Ferguson, Margaret W. "Saint Augustine's Region of Unlikeness: The Crossing of Exile and Language," *Georgia Review* 29, no. 4 (Winter 1975).

Fish, Stanley. *Self-Consuming Artifacts* (Berkeley: University of California Press, 1972). (29.6, S)
See especially "Affective Stylistics."

Fox, G., Stubbs, and Furley. "A Battle-Door for Teachers and Professors to Learn Singular and Plural" (1660). In Bauman and Sherzer, *Explorations in the Ethnography of Speaking* (q.v.). (3, S)

Freud, Sigmund. *Collected Papers* (New York: Basic Books, 1959).
See, in particular, "The Relation of the Poet to Day-Dreaming" (1908), in vol. 4, and "On Transience" (1915), in vol. 5. Freud's views on immortality, etc., are also to be found in the later metapsychological works, such as *Civilization and Its Discontents* (1930) (New York: W. W. Norton, 1962).

Frye, Northrop. *Anatomy of Criticism* (1957) (Princeton: Princeton University Press, 1971). (1.3, S; 38.6, S)
Note, in particular, "Polemical Introduction," "The Rhythm of Association: Lyric," and "Specific Thematic Forms (Lyric and Epos)."

Gadamer, Hans-Georg. *Truth and Method* (New York: Seabury Press, 1975). (6.2, S; 37.6; 42.2)

Gallais, Pierre. "Hexagonal and Spiral Structure in the Medieval Narrative," in *Yale French Studies* 51, pp. 116, 117. (6.5, S)

Goffman, Erving. *Frame Analysis* (Cambridge: Harvard University Press, 1974). (4.5, S)

Gombrich, E. H. *Art and Illusion: A Study in the Psychology of Pictorial Representation* (Princeton: Princeton University Press, Bollingen Series 35.5, 1960). (4.4, S; 26.14, S; 37.6)

Goody, Jack, ed. *Literacy in Traditional Societies* (Cambridge: Cambridge University Press, 1968). (15.1, S)

Guillén, Claudio. *Literature as System: Essays Toward the Theory of Literary History* (Princeton: Princeton University Press, 1971). (1.3, S)

Hart, H. L. A. *The Concept of Law* (Oxford: Clarendon Press, 1961). (5, S)

Hegel, G. W. F. *Early Theological Writings* (New York: Harper, 1961, pb). (14.4, S)

Heidegger, Martin. *Philosophies of Art and Beauty*, ed. Albert Hofstadter (New York: Modern Library, 1964). (4.5, S; 23.3, S)
See especially "The Origin of the Work of Art." A radical impersonalist account. It is also found in:

―――. *Poetry, Language and Thought*, ed. Albert Hofstadter (New York: Harper and Row, 1971).

Hirsch, E. D. "Stylistics and Synonymity," *Critical Inquiry* 1, no. 3 (March 1975). (4.4, S)
See also Nelson Goodman, "The Status of Style," in *Critical Inquiry* 1, no. 4 (June 1975).

Hollander, John. *Vision and Resonance* (New York: Oxford University Press, 1975). (1.3, S; 44.5, S)
See especially "The Poem in the Ear."

Horace. *Odes and Epodes*, Loeb Classical Library ed. (Cambridge: Harvard University Press, 1947). (25.2, S; 35, S; 35.1, S; 37.5, S)

Iser, Wolfgang. "The Reading Process: A Phenomenological Approach," *New Literary History* 6 (1972): 279–99. (31.15, S)

Ivins, William M. *Prints and Visual Communication* (Cambridge: MIT Press, 1953). (4.4, S)

Jakobson, Roman. *Selected Writings II: Word and Language* (The Hague and Paris: Mouton, 1971). (6.2, S; 39.2)
See especially "Language in Relation to Other Communicative Systems," pp. 697–710, and "Two Aspects of Language and Two Types of Aphasic Disturbance," pp. 239–59.

James, William. *The Principles of Psychology*, vol. 1 (1890) (New York: Dover Publications, 1950). (17.2)

Jaspers, Karl. "The Concept of 'Ultimate Situation' in Jaspers' Philosophy." In Latzel, *The Philosophy of Karl Jaspers*. (16.6)
The notion of "situation" derives from Jaspers. The lyric as a mode of the soul's rejoicing in communicability.

Kant, Immanuel. *Foundations of the Metaphysics of Morals*, with critical essays ed. by Robert Wolff, section 2 (Indianapolis: Bobbs-Merrill, 1969). (34.2)

Kantorowicz, Ernst H. *The King's Two Bodies* (Princeton: Princeton University Press, 1957). (14.4, S)

Kermode, Frank. *The Sense of an Ending* (New York: Oxford University Press, 1967). (1.5, S; 31.12, S; 38.3, S; 39.4, S)

Kuhn, Thomas S. *The Structure of Scientific Revolutions* (Chicago: University of Chicago Press, 1970). (37.6)

Laslett, Peter. *The World We Have Lost* (New York: Charles Scribner's Sons, 1965, pb). (25.2, S)

Lawrence, D. H. "Poetry of the Present." In *The Complete Poems of D. H. Lawrence*, collected and edited by Vivian de Sola Pinto and F. Warren Roberts (New York: Viking Press, 1975, pb). (39, S)

———. *Studies in Classic American Literature* (New York: Viking Press, 1975, pb). (39.4, S)

See essay on Whitman, pp. 163–77.

Leibniz, Gottfried W. *Selections*, ed. Philip Weiner (New York: Charles Scribner's Sons, 1951).

See *Monadology*. (4.4, S)

Leiman, Shnayer Z., ed. *The Canon and Masorah of the Hebrew Bible* (New York: Ktav Publishing House, 1974). (28, S)

Leishman, J. B. *Themes and Variations in Shakespeare's Sonnets* (New York: Harper and Row, 1966).

Surely one of the most humane and correct works in modern scholarship. Note his discussion of immortalization and his use of the notion of topic.

Lerner, Daniel, ed. *Parts and Wholes* (New York: Free Press, 1963). (3.4, S)

Levinas, Emmanuel. *Totality and Infinity* (Pittsburgh: Duquesne University Press, 1969). (6.2, S; 34.1, S)

See "Exteriority and the Face," pp. 187–253.

Lifton, Robert Jay. *Revolutionary Immortality* (New York: Vintage, 1968, pb). (1.2, S)

Lukács, Georg. *The Theory of the Novel*, tr. Anna Bostock (1920), (Cambridge: MIT Press, 1971, pb). (4.3, S)

Mill, John Stuart. *Dissertations and Discussions* (1859), vol. 1 (New York: Haskell House, 1973). (16.7, S)

See "Poetry and Its Varieties."

Ong, Walter J., S. J. *The Presence of the Word* (New Haven: Yale University Press, 1967). (6.2, S)

Otto, Rudolph. *The Idea of the Holy*, tr. John W. Harvey (London: Oxford University Press, 1950). (31.9, S)

Parke, H. W. and Wormell, D. E. W. *The Delphic Oracle* (Oxford: Blackwell, 1956). (31.6, S)

Paz, Octavio. *The Bow and the Lyre*, tr. Ruth Simms (Austin: University of Texas Press, 1967). (6.2, S; 38.8, S)
See "The Consecration of the Instant."

Picard, Max. *The World of Silence* (Chicago: Henry Regnery Co., 1964). (31.4, S)

Plato. *The Symposium*. In *The Collected Dialogues*, edited by Edith Hamilton and Huntington Cairns (Princeton: Princeton University Press, Bollingen Series 71, 1969), pp. 526–74. (1.2, S)

Polanyi, Michael. *The Tacit Dimension* (Garden City, N.Y.: Doubleday, 1966). (40.2)

Porphyry. "De Antro Nympharum." In *Thomas Taylor*, edited by Kathleen Raine. (Princeton: Princeton University Press, Bollingen Series 88, 1969). (37.1, S)

Rank, Otto. *Beyond Psychology* (1941) (New York: Dover Publications, 1958). (1.2, S)
Rank is interested in the psychodynamics of immortality. See, in particular, "The Double."

Rasmussen, David. *Mythic-Symbolic Language and Philosophical Anthropology* (The Hague: Martinus Nijhoff, 1971).
See Paul Ricoeur, "What Is a Text?"

Richards, I. A. *The Philosophy of Rhetoric* (New York: Oxford University Press, 1965). (4, S)

Ricoeur, Paul. "What Is a Text? Explanation and Interpretation." In Rasmussen, *Mythic-Symbolic Language*. (2.8, S; 43)

Róheim, Géza. *The Origin and Function of Culture* (New York: Doubleday, Anchor Books, 1971, pb). (1.2, S)

Sapir, Edward. *Language: An Introduction to the Study of Speech* (New York: Harcourt Brace, 1921). (4)

Saussure, Ferdinand de. *Course in General Linguistics*, rev. ed., tr. Wade Baskin, with an introduction by Jonathan Culler (London: Fontana, 1974). (6.2, S)

Schachtel, Ernest G. *Metamorphosis: On the Development of Affect, Perception, Attention, and Memory* (New York: Basic Books, 1959). (31.9, S)

Schachtel's revision of Freud's notion of "infantile amnesia" provides clues to the unstatable features of the life of poems.

Smith, Barbara H. *Poetic Closure* (Chicago: University of Chicago Press, 1968). (1.3, S; 1.5, S; 4.5, S; 36, S)

Snell, Bruno. *The Discovery of Mind: The Greek Origins of European Thought* (1953) (New York: Harper, 1960, Torchbook pb). (20.3)
See, especially, "The Rise of the Individual in Early Greek Lyric."

Sontag, Susan. *Styles of Radical Will* (New York: Farrar, Straus, and Giroux, 1969).
See "Aesthetics of Silence." (34.4, S)

Starobinski, Jean. "The Inside and the Outside," *Hudson Review* 28, no. 3 (Autumn 1975). (4.3, S)

Stirner, Max. *The Ego and His Own: The Case of the Individual against Authority* (New York: Libertarian Book Club, 1963). (14.4, S)

Strawson, P. F. *Individuals: An Essay in Descriptive Metaphysics* (New York: Anchor Books, 1963, pb). (6.2, S; 16.4)

Thompson, John. "Linguistic Structure and the Poetic Line." In *Poetics* (Warsaw, 1961). (36.1, S)

Unger, Roberto. *Knowledge and Politics* (New York: Free Press, 1975). (3.4, S; 4.7, S; 16.3, S; 28, S)

Vico, Giambattista. *The New Science of Giambattista Vico* (Ithaca: Cornell University Press, 1970.) (4.3, S)

Walzer, Michael. *Obligations: Essays on Disobedience, War and Citizenship* (Cambridge: Harvard University Press, 1970). (14.4, S)
See "The Obligation to Die for the State."

Wilden, Anthony. *System and Structure* (London: Tavistock, 1972). (28, S)

Williams, Raymond. *The Country and the City* (New York: Oxford University Press, 1973). (25.2, S)

Wittgenstein, Ludwig. *Philosophical Investigations*, tr. G. E. M. Anscombe (Oxford: Basil Blackwell, 1958). (6.2, S; 36.1, S)

Wordsworth, William. *The Poetical Works of William Wordsworth*, ed. E. de Selincourt and Helen Darbishire (Oxford: Clarendon Press, 1959).
See "Preface to the Lyrical Ballads," in vol. 2, pp. 384–93, and "An Essay upon Epitaphs," in vol. 5, pp. 444–56. (8.4)

Wright, James Arlington. *Two Citizens* (New York: Farrar, Straus, and Giroux, 1973). (37.5, S)

Yeats, William Butler. *Poems*, ed. Richard J. Finneran (New York: Macmillan, 1983). (25.2, S; 31.4, S)

Index to the Two Works

Numbers in italics refer to sections in the "Summa Lyrica." Where such numbers are followed by an S, the reference is to the scholium at that number. Other numbers refer to pages in the "Conversations."

Absence, *40, 41*
Accident and archetype, *16; 31.12S*
Acknowledgment, *9,* 100, 109, 147, 191, 193; *2.1;* paradoxes of value and acknowledgment, *32.4S*
Ambivalence, *20.8S*
Aperture, *39, 42.S*
Appearance. *See* Manifestation
Archetype and accident, *16; 31.12S*
Art, *25.6*
Artifice, *25.1S*
Audience, 81, 122; distinction between actor and, *32.2. See also* Reading
Authority, *42; 8.4;* and lineage, 50; *25.2S*

Baseball, 201
Beloved: philosophical estate of, *4.7S;* preservation of image of, 12
Bildung, 42.2
Blank Verse, *29.8S*
Breath and line, *29S*

Care, *44*
Civility as *hospitium, 30.9S*
Class, 37, 89, 93, 193; *26, 26.7S. See also* Enfranchisement; Representation

Closure, *27.3S, 39;* and aperture, *26.12;* and fiction of success, *35.3S;* and line, *29.3*
Collective, the, *14.4S, 38.6S*
Comedy, *39.4S*
Comic poetics, 162
Common place, 151; *30.6;* line as, 84
Common world, disappearance of, 43
Compositional principle, *5.3*
Continuation, 179, 184; *20*
Countenance, *34.1, 43.4;* acquisition/conferral of, 104; *42.9S;* and lineament and line, 95; *36S(A.);* as severed head, *43S;* shattered, 97. *See also* Person
Criteria: of the ethical, 161; of a good poem, *46;* of representation, *170;* for revision, 145; of value, 196; of wisdom, *170*

Death, 51, 74, 164, 196; *1.1, 14, 41, 42.5*
Decadence, *33.4, 41.3S*
Deficit, representational, 193
Defilement, *20.8S, 28S, 30.9S;* and collectivity, *38.6S. See also* Incest
Demonization, 67, 90. *See also* Aperture; Countenance: shattered; Voice

Desire, 59, 162
Didacticism, 21S; of lyric, 20.8, 21, 28
Difficulty in poetry, 104, 111; 26.12
Discontinuity, 196

Education, 20.8S
Egalitarianism, 193; and image-life, 32.4
Eidetic construction and hierarchy, 32.4S
Eidetic function, 19; 2.3S, 6.2S, 26.13S,
    26.14S; as mutilation, 43.4; as didac-
    tic, 21S; not founded in secondary rep-
    resentations, 38.1
Eidos, 6, 9, 19, 194; 26.14S
Enfranchisement, 89; 26.8S. See also Po-
    etic structures; Representation
Enjambment, 16.2S
Ethical, the, 153, 161; 3.4S, 32.4

Father, 88, 103, 110; 42S
Father tongue, 103; 42S
Figure and ground, 31.2S
Friendship, hermeneutic, 22.6, 30.45,
    30.65, 44S; as care, 44; as Christ inter-
    preter, 44.4

Gender, 22, 90, 94, 193. See also Enfran-
    chisement; Representation
Genealogy, 28.1S
God, 17.5S
Great in small, 36.5S

Hospitium, 30S, 30.9S
Human dignity, 93. See also Countenance;
    Person
Humanism, 32

"I," 6.6, 20.1, 23, 24, 28, 31.12S; lyric
    self and lyric medium, 38.8; as Orphic
    machine, 43, 43.4; as severed head, 43
Ignorance, 25.7S; as representability,
    25.7S, 31.12
Immanence, 34, 37, 40. See also Tran-
    scendence
Immortality, 1, 2.1S, 14; as care, 44.1;
    competition of immortalities, 42.9S; as
    identity of meaning and interest, 41.6S
Impersonality, 109. See also "I"
Incest, 103; 28, 42 (see also Defilement);
    defilement and collectivity, 38.6S

Inferential poem, 40; as person, 43S
Inscription, 31.5; as finite upon infinite
    languages, 31.3; as past upon present,
    38.7S, 41.3
Interiority, 4.3S
Interpretation, 30; as assignment of herme-
    neutic possibility, 44.4; as care, 44 (see
    also Friendship, hermeneutic)

Knowledge, poetic, 8; as incest, 28

Labor, 11, 25.2S; as redemptive, 32.7. See
    also Work
Language, poetic, 86; 4, 6.2S, 31.4S, 34S;
    and collectivity, 38.6; finite and infi-
    nite, 31.4S; as language gone strange,
    8.4, 26.13, 34S
Lateness, 38.9S
Liberation, 26.8
Line, 84; 29, 30.6, 36; analysis of, 29,
    30.6; and breath, 29S; and centering,
    28.3; and closure, 29.3; horizontal and
    vertical, 36.S(B.); as lineament,
    36.S(A.); pentameter, 29.8S
Lineage and authority, 50; 28.1S
Lineament, 36
Love, efficacious, 198; 26
Lyric, 150; 1.3S, 24, 25.2; as defilement
    (see Incest); as inscription, 31.15

Majesty, 21
Manifestation, 4.4S, 20.8S, 21, 23, 27,
    27S, 28
Meaning, 30.4S, 38.6S, 41; as continuity
    with the Other, 41.45
Metaphor, 17, 31.13
Meter, 31S; as care, 44.5
Mimetic enfranchisement, 89. See also Ac-
    knowledgment; Poetic structures; Repre-
    sentation
Modernism, 11, 22, 29, 32, 56
Modern poetry, 28
Mother, 42S; and acknowledgment, 101;
    imagined death of, 116; poetry as com-
    pletion of speech of, 60, 88, 103; and
    teaching, 100
Mother tongue, 103; 42S, 43; as word infi-
    nite, 31.6S
Motive to poetry, 60; 23
Myth, 38

Names, *1.4S. See also* Person
Narration, 178; *6.5, 24.2;* as line, *29.6S;*
  as lyric structure, *24*

Ontological affirmation, 102; *18, 34.6*
Open form as equivocation of death, *29S*
Opening, *20.3S, 23, 33;* as genesis, *24;* as
  line opening, *29.6S;* as poem opening,
  31.12, 41.4S

Pain, *25.2S*
Part and whole, *3.4S*
Past lives, recollection of, *24.6S, 28.1S,*
  41.3S
Pentameter, *29.8S*
Person, *4.2, 6, 7, 23.8, 34, 37.2, 40.3;* as
  distinguished from self, 20, 101; func-
  tion of poetry in preserving image of, 6,
  12; as the one object worthy of atten-
  tion, *34.4;* and religious humanism,
  32.6; as "unity," 23, *35S. See also*
  Countenance
Poet, 23
Poetics, comic, 162
Poetic structures, related to political struc-
  tures, 10, 54. *See also* Line; Representa-
  tion
Poetry as *hospitium*, 5; *30S*
Postmodernism, 11, 22, 102; *38.7S*
Present, *41*
Priority, *4.3S, 39.2S*
Privilege, 26

Reading, 17; *2, 22, 28.1, 37, 40.2S,*
  40.5S; as discovery of person, *37.2;* as
  ontological affirmation, *34.6;* as second
  reading, *37.5*
Recollection of past lives, *24.6S, 28.1S,*
  41.3S
Redistribution, 193; *32.4S*
Representation, *25, 26, 32, 37.7, 39;* crisis
  of, 198; finding an outside to, 185; and
  human dignity, 95; inadequacy of system available, 56; representational deficit, 193; and repression, 170, 192; and
  wisdom, 170
Repression, 155; and representation, 170,
  192; and value, 156
Return, *6.5*

Revision, 141; contextual versus extratex-
  tual, 145. *See also* Criteria
Rhyme and mother tongue, *42.8S*

Satisfaction, critique of, 190
Scale, human, *25.7, 28.4, 38S;* and aes-
  thetic humanism, *32.5;* and blank
  verse, *29.8;* and line, *29.2*
Scarcity, *25.1S;* of meaning, 44
Scripture, *15*
Silence, 3, *19;* and contradiction of speech
  and feeding, *29S*
Social mediation, 81; *40.8. See also* Eidetic
  function; Enfranchisement
Speaker, poetic, *22.6S, 23.1S, 28;* and cri-
  terion of unity, *35.3;* as inferential, *40;*
  and *ius primae noctis, 28.7*
Stress, *42.5, 44.5. See also* Line
Structure, *38.8S*
Subject matter of poetry, 92
Supplement: finding versus supplementing
  the real, 139, 143; poem as, 166; and
  source of worthiness, 198. *See also*
  Transcendence

Teaching, 106, 146; *2.5S, 30.5, 30.7;* and
  acknowledgment, 101; and revision,
  164
Text, *22.6S, 37.5S* as fixed, *42.3S;* as
  matrix of unexchangeable differences,
  43.3S
Totalization, *27.3S*
Transcendence, 17, 32, 35, 40; *24.2, 32.6.*
  See also Supplement
Transgression, *20.8S*

Unity, traditional, *31, 35*

Value, 5, *18, 40S;* criteria of, 164, 197;
  and death, 75; and repression, 156
Voice, 79; *22, 28.8;* demonic-
  mythographic versus eucharistic-mimetic tradition, 83; "immortal," 148;
  31.6S; and social mediation, 81

Whole and part, *3.4S*
Wisdom, criteria of, *170*
Word infinite, *31.6S*
Work, *34.4S. See also* Labor

Allen Grossman was for many years the Paul E. Prosswimmer Professor of Poetry and General Education at Brandeis University. He is at present Professor of English at the Johns Hopkins University. He is a MacArthur Foundation grant recipient and the author of many works of poetry. His poetry is available in one volume as *The Ether Dome and Other Poems New and Selected.*

Mark Halliday is the author of *Stevens and the Impersonal* and *Tasker Street*, which received the Juniper Prize for 1991. He teaches English at Wilmington Friends School in Delaware.